A COMPREHENSIVE GUIDE to

Children's Literature with a Jewish Theme

A COMPREHENSIVE GUIDE to

Children's Literature with a Jewish Theme

ENID DAVIS

Schocken Books • New York

First published by Schocken Books 1981
10 9 8 7 6 5 4 3 2 1   81 82 83 84

Library of Congress Cataloging in Publication Data
Davis, Enid, 1946–
    A comprehensive guide to children's literature
with a Jewish theme.
    Includes indexes.
    1. Jews—Juvenile literature—Bibliography.
2. Judaism—Juvenile literature—Bibliography.
I. Title.
Z6366.D38   [BM107]   016.909'04924   80–54139

Book Design by Marsha Picker
Manufactured in the United States of America

ISBN 0–8052–3760–7

*To my dear parents, Irene and Louis Hellman,
and to all the other Hellmans and Schoenwetters
who made my Jewish childhood so comfortable.*

Make your books your companions.
Let your book shelves be your treasure
grounds and gardens.
                    —Rabbi Judah ibn Tibbon

contents

Abbreviations

adap.	adapter
comp.	compiler
dist.	distributor
div.	division
ed.	editor or edition
illus.	illustrator or illustrated
O.P.	out of print
p.; pp.	page; pages
pb.	paperback
repr.	reprint
rev. ed.	revised edition
trans.	translator or translated
vol.	volume

Note: The names of book publishers have been abbreviated in the book reviews and introductory remarks. Please refer to Appendix B: Directory of Book Publishers and Distributors for their full names and addresses.

preface

More than four hundred and fifty books are reviewed in this guide, which covers books for children from preschool through junior high. Approximately another one hundred titles are mentioned in the reviews. Space limitations do not permit the inclusion of every children's book with a Jewish theme currently available from publishers or libraries, but the materials included constitute the best in their respective fields. A handful of titles that do not meet these criteria have been included because their subject matter, author, or award-winning status prompts automatic interest.

To be included in this bibliography, fiction had to contain good characterizations and an interesting plot; contain a minimum Jewish content (not just a Jewish surname and/or Yiddish expressions); be available for loan or purchase; and be appropriate for the age range of this guide, preschool through junior high. In addition to meeting the last two criteria, nonfiction had to be lucid, well organized, accurate, and relevant, and contain information on Jewish life or history.

Textbooks are included only if they are written in an easily accessible style and discuss aspects of Judaica that are not covered in trade publications. In subject areas where children's materials are scarce or nonexistent, a small number of books published for the adult market are included.

Reference works appear at the ends of chapters or sections. These include adult and juvenile reference books and resources, and critical articles that discuss the state of children's literature with Jewish themes. The last chapter includes a guide to Judaic multimedia resources for children. It lists organizations, newsletters, and companies that review, promote, distribute, and publish films, recordings, toys, and visual aids, as well as a bibliography of Jewish children's periodicals.

It is interesting to note the increase in the number of books that are being published in paperback as well as hardcover editions. The

considerable price difference is causing schools and libraries to recon-
sider the use of paperbacks despite their disadvantages. Parents, of
course, will be more willing to spend $1.75 for a junior novel than
$8.95. Readers will be delighted to discover how many of the finest
picture books, novels, and nonfiction titles in the bibliography are
available in paperback. In the reviews, the paperback publisher of a
title is given if it differs from the publisher of the hardback edition.

The great majority of the works reviewed here are in print. Exceptions are made for recommended books that are still available in
many schools, libraries, and synagogues, or that can be found in Jewish bookstores and on Jewish book distributors' lists. Indeed, most of
the out-of-print titles listed in this guide which are published by Jewish firms are still available from those two sources.

A note about spelling: Hebrew and Yiddish words in the reviews
have been transliterated according to a standard system, so some
spellings are different from those in book titles.

I want to thank the many book publishers who provided me with
review copies, and the Merkaz Bookstore in Los Altos, California, for
allowing me to borrow books for reviewing purposes. And a great big
thank you to my husband, Sanford, and my children, Jennifer and
Bradley, for their patience and good will.

1

introduction

There is a broad spectrum of children's literature with Jewish themes covering such topics as history and biography, literature and the arts, Bible retellings and theology, folklore and fiction. This body of literature mirrors the richness, variety, and vicissitudes of Jewish life throughout the ages—the heroes and "schlemiels" (fools), innocents, and monsters all express one or another aspect of this vast experience.

The heroes in the literature are found of course, in the Bible: Moses, David, Solomon, and Esther. They are joined by contemporary heroes like Albert Einstein, Golda Meir, Marc Chagall—people whose work greatly enriched our century.

It is said that the tools of survival are heroism and humor. The fools of Chelm, an imaginary Polish town, are an embodiment of the tradition of Jewish humor. They have only themselves to blame for the disasters that befall them—as when they set fire to their town in order to rid themselves of a troublesome cat.

If these foolish folk tickle us, the innocents haunt us in memoirs and novels about medieval inquisitions, European pogroms, and Nazi persecution. The fate of children, such as Anne Frank, who perished in Auschwitz Concentration Camp, and even of a fictional character such as the young hero of Hans Peter Richter's *Friedrich*, who dies on the streets of Germany after being refused admission to an air-raid shelter, sensitizes us to the tragedy of prejudice. It is an unhappy fact that innocent Jews have suffered from racial and religious bigotry, and it is difficult and painful to share this history with children. This difficulty makes the choice of suitable introductory texts all the more important.

Tales of monsters accompany stories of innocents and include a variety of legends. Isaac Bashevis Singer's brutes take the form of devils and witches that can be banished only be secret incantations and pure hearts. One of the more sympathetic monsters you.will meet is the golem, a clay figure created out of learning, piety, and desperation. In one of the many versions of this ancient myth, the golem helped the Jews of Prague avoid medieval Christian persecution during the Passover season. It was eventually destroyed by its maker when it ran amok and began to glory in its own power.

If the golem is a mythical hero-monster, his counterpart is not heroic and is only too real. Adolf Hitler figures in countless novels, memoirs, histories, biographies, and poetry titles. The Nazi genocide and the destruction of European Jewry compounded with worldwide apathy are a haunting refrain throughout many of these children's books. In this context, books on the Jewish resistance during World War II and books dealing with the later exploits of the Israeli army have a special significance.

In contrast to these dark subjects, there is an important body of material for children on the joys and pleasures of Jewish life. Many books are available on life in Israel and America, countries where Jews have freely experienced the satisfactions of an authentic Jewish life. An entire chapter is devoted to material on the Jewish holidays, and it is especially in these books that children will find the magic and value of a long tradition.

What is the literary and functional status of such a body of work? Probably no two critics would agree. There are people, such as the noted child psychiatrist and writer Bruno Bettelheim, who do not see the need for a separate body of literature for children at all. Many Jews would similarly agree that the Bible, the Talmud (Jewish law), and the Midrash (scriptural commentaries) say whatever needs to be said better and with more flair than any juvenile book could.

Critics standing on the next few rungs of the literary ladder would be happy to eliminate from fifteen to eighty percent of the available children's books with Jewish themes because they are not Jewish enough. Complaints of this type are voiced against those novels in which the family might have only a Jewish surname and eat a kosher-style meal once in a while. Objections are also raised by Orthodox Jews to books that depict a non-Orthodox way of life.

Arguing as earnestly with those critics who believe that the aim of Jewish literature is to teach Judaica above all else are those people who believe that the first goal of any book is to reach an audience. They applaud books that reach today's child, that include a slice of Jewish life, and that have literary merit. Compare the two awards given to a Jewish children's book in 1978. The Association of Jewish Libraries (AJL) presented its prize to Doris Orgel's *The Devil in Vienna* (Dial, 1978). This engrossing, well-written novel will be read by Jewish and Gentile youngsters alike because of its popular style and best-selling theme: friendship between two girls. Hitler is the devil and not even he can destroy the love that binds a Nazi's daughter and a Jewish girl. In contrast, the Charles and Bertie C. Schwartz Juvenile Award was given to Irena Narell's *Joshua: Fighter for Bar Kochba* (Akiba Press, 1978). This carefully researched historical novel about the Jewish revolt against Roman forces in 132 C.E. has very little child appeal. It makes no attempt to address the interests of contemporary children. Its dull packaging and small print make it difficult to promote.

The body of Jewish children's literature is unique in many respects though flawed in some. The flaws are largely in the area of content. Those books which most emphasize religious teachings and principles are the least read because they tend to preach, sentimentalize, and bore the child. There are happy exceptions, of course. Yuri Suhl, Shulamith Ish-Kishor, Marilyn Hirsh, Barbara Cohen, Molly Cone, and Charlotte Herman have all written solid books of this kind that are also readable.

A second major shortcoming is the lack of books about African Jewry (including the Falashas, the black Ethiopian Jews), South American Jews, and the plight of Soviet Jewry. Only two books in this guide touch upon the last subject.

A third area in which material is lacking is easy-to-read titles for first- and second-graders. There are no Jewish titles equivalent to the beginning-to-read books by such authors as Dr. Seuss, Patty Wolcott, and Else Minarik. This is a source of frustration to children and to day-school and temple librarians.

In recent years much literary criticism has been directed at the use of stereotypes as in sexism and racism. Anti-Semitism is rare in modern children's books. One example is the 1975 Viking Press reprint of Arthur Rackham's *Mother Goose,* which speaks of a swindler as a "rogue of a Jew." Marian Hostetler's novel *Journey to Jerusalem* shows religious intolerance by saying that Israelis "will have to believe in Jesus to be saved just like everybody else." Zionists are stereotyped as cunning and conniving in Neil Grant's *The Partition of Palestine 1947: Jewish Triumph, British Failure, Arab Disaster* (Watts, 1973). Some books by Israeli authors describe Arabs in stereotypical terms. For instance, Joseph Trigoboff's *Abu* (Lothrop, 1975) tells the story of a tough but benevolent Israeli soldier who befriends a young Arab street urchin. The Council for Interracial Books for Children criticized the author's description of the Arab boy.

Flawed as it might be, the body of juvenile literature has many strengths. The resurgence of interest in Judaism that I detect among public library patrons, parents, and friends is nourished by the new and exciting materials available for children. Feminists such as the creators behind Kar-Ben Copies, an alternative publishing house with a series of homey and well-written books for Jewish children, are making certain that female characters exchange hair ribbons and frilly dresses for active participation in holiday services and celebrations.

The chapters of this bibliography are replete with outstanding titles that show variety and talent. They include books that are cherished by many readers. Among them are titles that have won the Caldecott Medal, the Newbery Medal (Honor Book), the National Book Award, the New York Times Choice of Best Illustrated Book of the Year, the Children's Show Bookcase, and the Jane Addams Book Award.

Careful attention has been given to books that have a universal appeal, as well as titles that speak more specifically to Jewish children. This guide will assist librarians developing and maintaining a collection, teachers selecting supplementary materials, parents buying books for their children, and adults purchasing gifts or choosing library books for a youngster's pleasure.

2

the Hebrew Alphabet

Jews have always been the people of the book. From the time the Ten Commandments were set down on stone tablets to the creation of the Torah (the first five books of the Bible) and the Talmud (commentaries on the Bible) and other rabbinical writings, instructions on how to live a good, happy, pious life were written down and studied.

The Hebrew alphabet is the key to this knowledge. There are twenty-two letters in this alphabet, and besides its sound, each of the letters has a meaning (e.g., *alef,* a bull; *bet,* a house) and a numerical value. There is an entire genre of literature concerned with Hebrew letters, their symbolic and mystical qualities.

Two of these mystical titles are reviewed in this chapter. Ben Shahn's *Alphabet of Creation,* is based on a thirteenth-century work that conceives of each letter as petitioning God to use it to create the world. Laurence Kushner's *Book of Letters: A Mystical Alef-bait* draws upon a variety of lively Jewish tales and magical legends about the members of the alphabet family. After reading these works, the student of Hebrew will never again view an individual letter as merely a lifeless symbol.

The ability to read is the key to becoming a good Jew, since being a good Jew has always involved studying Jewish law. In the first century C.E., the Jewish historian Josephus wrote: "Our principal care is to educate our children well." A Talmudic remark on education states that "The hope of the world lies in its school children. Their instruction must not be interrupted even for the rebuilding of the Temple." The twelfth-century ethical will of Rabbi Judah ibn Tibbon contains this piece of fatherly advice: "My son, make your books your companions. Let your book shelves be your treasure grounds and gardens."

During the long Diaspora, the Hebrew language ceased to be the everyday tongue of Jews, but it remained the language of prayer and scholarship. The education of male children was given top priority even by the poorest of the poor, particularly in Eastern Europe, where Jews lived in villages and shtetls (small towns). It was far better to go hungry than to deprive one's son of the chance to go to school and learn.

From the age of three, four, or five, boys were sent or even carried to heder (religious school) to learn the alef-bet (alphabet). In poorly lit, ill-ventilated class rooms, they spent long hours instructed by an underpaid, underfed, often cantankerous melamed (teacher). Early learning was by rote, memorization, and endless repetition. The workbooks were dingy, ragged prayer books.

There were no pictures to break up the text, as there are in *My First Hebrew Alphabet Book* (Jennifer and Susan Lapine) or the *Hebrew Alphabet Book* (Avi Margalit), no brightly colored drawings to coax the very young to learn their first lessons.

There were no story books to stir the imagination like Deborah Pessin's *Aleph-Bet Story,* tales of Jewish history and legend in which the Hebrew letters star in heroic adventures.

There were no educational games to relieve the tedium of study. A beginning student did not have access to the Alefbet Dart Game, the Alefbet Roulette & Bingo Game, or the Alefbet Snake Puzzle, available from the KTAV Gift Catalog.

Girls were not expected to study as long or as hard as boys; they were needed at home to help their mothers. The girls learned Yiddish, the everyday language of the East European Jew, and mastered domestic skills. Frederica Postman's *Yiddish Alphabet Book* is a loving and beautifully illustrated testimonial to this tongue, which uses Hebrew letters but is based on a combination of German, Hebrew, and other languages.

Several of the books reviewed in this guide touch upon education in the shtetl. *Exit from Home* (Anita Heyman), *A Day of Pleasure* (Isaac Bashevis Singer), *Rifka Grows Up* (Chaya Burstein), *Sarah Somebody* (Florence Slobodkin), *Holiday Tales of Sholom Aleichem,* and *On the Little Hearth* (illustrated by Gabriel Lisowski) all allow us an intimate view of the shtetl schoolroom.

The writing of Hebrew is an art as well as a craft. The Torah has always been, and still is, handwritten by a trained scribe, who must follow strict guidelines concerning the shaping of each letter, the ink, spacing, and decorative flourishes. The writing of a Torah scroll is a holy act for which the scribe must prepare himself both physically and spiritually. The traditional and ancient craft of the scribe has sparked new interest in Hebrew calligraphy among both adults and young people. There are several books to help them, such as *Hebrew Alphabets* by Reuben Leaf, *Hebrew Calligraphy: A Step-by-Step Guide* by Jay Greenspan, and Lawrence Kushner's *Book of Letters.*

Alphabet Books

Greenspan, Jay Seth. Hebrew Calligraphy: A Step-by-Step Guide. Illus. by author. Schocken, 1980. $14.95; $7.95 pb.
This title promises to be an invaluable and unique aid to calligraphers of all ages. Greenspan includes instructions on how to form each letter, develop and illuminate a manuscript, and select a text, script, layout and design. Specific guides for the left-handed calligrapher are provided, as is information on the spiritual aspects of Hebrew lettering. Ages 11+.

Kushner, Lawrence. The Book of Letters: A Mystical Alef-bait. Illus. by author. Har-Row, 1975. $9.95.
Kushner's book draws upon ancient Judaic sources, Talmudic legends, Hasidic folk tales, and Kabbalistic thoughts about the Hebrew letters to weave tales and lend spiritual meaning to each symbol. It is done in fine calligraphy on heavy cream stock. It will interest older children and adults who know some Hebrew. Ages 11+.

Lapine, Jennifer and **Susan Lapine.** My First Hebrew Alphabet Book. Illus. by authors. Bloch, 1977. $4.00; $2.95 pb.
Striking illustrations in black, white, and yellow take the young child through the Hebrew alphabet. There is a good variety of the objects to represent each letter. Transliteration of Hebrew words and letters is given. Recommended as an attractive title to introduce young children to the Hebrew language. Ages 3–7.

Leaf, Reuben, comp. Hebrew Alphabets: 400 B.C.E. to Our Days. Bloch, 1976 (new repr.). $17.50.
This handsome book contains plates of the most prominent styles of Hebrew lettering from ancient to modern times and includes historical and technical data on each plate. There are also samples of old tombstone and manuscript lettering, woodcuts, and decorative initials and monograms. Leaf recommends alphabet styles suitable for work in wood, felt, appliqué, bronze, and stone. A useful title for the calligrapher and a fascinating look at imaginative and striking lettering. Ages 11+.

Margalit, Avi. The Hebrew Alphabet Book. Illus. by author. Bonim, 1968. $2.95.
An attractively illustrated alphabet book that translates and transliterates forty-two common Hebrew words into English. This appealing title is appropriate both for preschoolers and older students who want a basic introduction to the Hebrew language. (Note: For two other inexpensive and useful ABC titles that introduce Hebrew to young

children, see Melvin Alexenberg's *Alef-Bet Zoo* and *Alef-Bet Picture Dictionary,* both from Shulsinger Bros., 1963.) Ages 3+.

Pessin, Deborah. The Aleph-Bet Story Book. Illus. Howard Simon. Jewish Pubn, 1946. $3.95.
Here is a painless way to introduce and teach the Hebrew alphabet and to learn a bit about Jewish history and legend in the process. The author uses mnemonics in these twenty-two stories, each starring a Hebrew letter. The book's large print, pleasant illustrations, and charm give it a storybook flavor. Unfortunately, this 1946 alphabet book features an all-male cast. Ages 7–10; younger for reading aloud.

Postman, Frederica. The Yiddish Alphabet Book. Illus. Bonnie Stone. P'Nye, 1979. $8.95.
This will appeal to a larger audience than does the typical ABC genre. It is a guide to the Yiddish alphabet, which uses Hebrew letters. In addition to an informative introduction concerning pronunciation, the author provides the following for each of the twenty-two letters: a large representation of the letter; the name of the letter transliterated into English; a word or words in Yiddish, and their transliterations and English equivalents. A lovely illustration in black, white, and burnt sienna faces each page of text. Skillful bookmaking ties this neat package together. All ages.

Shahn, Ben, adap. and illus. The Alphabet of Creation: An Ancient Legend from the Zohar. Schocken, 1965. $2.25 pb.
The legend freely adapted by Shahn is from the *Sefer ha-Zohar* or Book of Splendor, a basic work of Jewish mysticism. All twenty-two letters of the Hebrew alphabet petition God to create the world through them. Denied their request, the letters return sadly to their places, but God finally decides to begin Creation with the letter *bet;* as it is said: *"Bereshit*—in the beginning—God created the Heaven and the Earth." Shahn illustrates this brief and striking legend with bold black designs and symbols. Whether it is used as a story or as a language lesson, the book's humor, sacred ideas, and handsome format will entertain young readers. Ages 10+.

Reference Aids

The following articles on Hebrew calligraphy will be helpful to the educator or young teenager: "A Treatise on the Making of Hebrew Letters" by Joel Rosenberg; "A Practical Guide to Hebrew Calligraphy" by Jay Greenspan; and "The Calligraphy of the Classic Scribe" by Stuart Kelman. *The Jewish Catalog.* Jewish Pubn, 1973, pp. 184–209.

3

the Bible

For the most part, the books selected for review in this chapter are linked to the Torah, known to non-Jews as the Old Testament. Many of the books reviewed in the chapters on fiction and the arts make use of biblical themes and protagonists. Authors and artists use the Bible as a foundation upon which to build their own works. The art of faithfully retelling biblical stories, however, making them more accessible to youngsters, is a unique chapter in children's literature.

Imagine an artist asked to re-create the Sistine Chapel for children. "Feel free," the artist is told, "to reproduce the ceiling's design in a simpler and less lofty manner. Use your own technique; do not copy the style or approach of the original." Retelling the Bible for children is as difficult a task. The Good Book is a hard act to follow and almost impossible to surpass. In order to write a successful Bible story, the author must accurately interpret the original, skillfully abridge or fill in the text, and create a timeless and universal whole. The books reviewed in this chapter use various techniques to achieve these goals.

There are several titles that admirably imitate the Bible's spare style and authority. Writers such as Walter De La Mare, Sholem Asch, and Meindert DeJong have produced very good retellings.

The second method for retelling involves the insertion of some of the author's individual perspective—but not enough to turn the work into fiction. Such books as *The Binding of Isaac* by Barbara Cohen and Madeleine L'Engle's *Journey with Jonah* faithfully retell the biblical stories but both add a completely fictionalized element that expands the original and shifts the tale's emphasis.

Other authors have chosen to weave biblical versions and legends together. The legends are often derived from the Midrash, a huge collection of biblical commentaries containing a great deal of folklore. Because the Bible's accounts of events are often very concise, authors enjoy embellishing them with legends. For example, Cecil Golann's *Mission on a Mountain* uses a Midrashic source to tell the young reader why God demanded that Abraham sacrifice his son. Midrashic legends are often explanations of why things happened as they did in the Bible. *Legends of the Bible* by Louis Ginzberg, an authoritative collection, is cited in chapter 9, "Folk Tales," under "Reference Aids."

Illustrating a Bible story adds another dimension. Since there is no original to copy, the artist is afforded a free rein, and illustrations often make two picture-book retellings of the same story distinct. Take for example Peter Spier's *Noah's Ark* and Charles Mee's *Noah,* illustrated by Ken Munowitz. Spier's detailed drawings contrast with Munowitz's large black-and-white loopy lines, making these titles as different as Ruth and Delilah. The story of Noah's Ark probably is retold more often than any other, for small children love animal stories and the tale's simple plot lends itself to picture-book adaptation.

Sibling rivalry, a recurring motif in the Bible, is another theme that captures children's interest. It is not surprising that the tale of Joseph and his coat of many colors is often retold—usually for older children, as in *I Am Joseph* by Barbara Cohen.

A third recurring theme with which youngsters identify is the notion that Right can defeat Might. In Ruth Brin's *David and Goliath,* young David is a wonderful role model for children. He may not wear a Superman-style leotard with a red and yellow *D* on it, but his powerful slingshot is as captivating as any flowing cape. His victory over the original big bully is very satisfying to youngsters.

The number of outstanding books in this chapter should have been greater, but writing good Bible stories is an extremely exacting task. The most memorable books stay close to the original but share with the child the author's own emotional involvement. One such successful title was published in Israel. Unlike L'Engle's *Journey with Jonah* or Cohen's *Binding of Isaac* (both fine works), this particular book does not use a fictional element to enlarge the tale.

Hella Taubes, author of *The Bible Speaks,* succeeds in re-creating the vitality of the Bible by giving children a feeling for its plot and language. Taubes's pride in her heritage is contagious. Peter Spier in *Noah's Ark* also evokes deep feelings through his superb illustrations.

In addition to Bible retellings, this chapter includes reviews of books that explore biblical themes. Here you will find books on archeology, history, linguistics, theology, and personal interpretations. Books that are related to the Bible but whose emphasis is elsewhere will be referred to in this chapter but reviewed in another section.

Bible Stories

Allstrom, Elizabeth. Songs Along the Way. Illus. Mel Silverman. Abingdon, 1961. O.P.
Beautiful woodcuts and a brief informative introduction make this a good introduction to the Psalms for young children. The fourteen selections from the Old Testament: Revised Standard Version are written in modern vernacular and are easy for youngsters to understand. Ages 9–12.

Armstrong, William. Hadassah: Esther, the Orphan Queen. Illus. Barbara Ninde Byfield. Doubleday, 1972. O.P.
A distinguished children's author pays tribute to the miracle of Jewish survival with a brief retelling of Esther's courageous deeds. This book shows the total submission of women in those times, putting Esther's bravery before the king in a clear historic light. Pleasantly illustrated. Ages 8–12.

Asch, Sholem. In the Beginning: Stories from the Bible. Trans. Caroline Cunningham. Illus. Eleanor Klemm. Schocken, 1966. $6.00; $3.95 pb.
Thirty-four stories by the Polish-born novelist Sholem Asch (1880–1957). The succinct stories are written in a straightforward and understated style. Asch incorporates Midrash versions into some of his tales, such as "The Sacrificing of Isaac," in which Satan makes an unwelcome appearance. Stories of Abraham and Isaac dominate the selections and are broken up into several episodes. The brevity and wise simplicity of this book make it a natural for reading aloud. Ages 9–13; younger for reading aloud.

Birnbaum, Philip, ed. and trans. The Concise Jewish Bible. Hebrew Pub, 1976. $8.95; $4.95 pb.
From the Creation to the Chronicles, Birnbaum offers an abridged version of the Bible, including an informative introduction to each chapter. His prose is no match for the original version, and all poetry has been rendered as prose. However, people wanting a less difficult and shorter text written in modern English will find this edition quite satisfactory. Ages 12+.

Bolliger, Max. Noah and the Rainbow. Trans. Clyde Bulla. Illus. Helga Aichinger. T Y Crowell, 1972. $7.95; $2.95 pb.
This simple retelling is poetic enough to entertain youngsters. The eleven full-color paintings can be enjoyed on many levels; simple and graceful, they enhance the drama by their bold blacks, emerald

greens, and gold designs. The text and artwork are perfectly balanced
to create an artistic as well as biblical experience. (Note: Bolliger is
also the author of other biblical retellings which are O.P. but still
available in some libraries.) Ages 4–10.

Brin, Ruth F. David and Goliath. Illus. H. Hechtkopf. "Outstanding
Books from Foreign Lands" Series. Lerner, 1977. $5.95.
Brin's pleasant storytelling unites legendary and biblical accounts of
the story of David. Emphasis is put on the boy's task as sheepherder,
his love for music, and his early successes with the slingshot—before
the big encounter. Brin gracefully weaves some Psalms into the story,
giving it a poetic touch. Hechtkopf's distinctive drawings are colorful
and dramatic, but his own prejudice is evident in the contrast between the grotesquely drawn Philistine soldiers and the sensitive
human faces of the Hebrew men. Ages 6–10.

Brin, Ruth F. The Story of Esther. Illus. H. Hechtkopf. "Outstanding
Books from Foreign Lands" Series. Lerner, 1976. $5.95.
A colorfully illustrated and entertaining retelling of Queen Esther's
story. Because of her great beauty, a young Jewish woman is married
to the King of Persia. Later, the anti-Semitism of Haman, the king's
adviser, puts the lives of all the Jews in great danger. Esther uses her
wit and courage to disgrace Haman before the king. Her success saves
the Jewish people. The grotesque features of the king (and Haman)
leave one with a feeling of pity for this woman who saved the Jews by
marrying this ignoble monarch. Ages 6–10.

Brodsky, Beverly. Jonah: An Old Testament Story. Illus. by author.
Lippincott, 1977. $8.95.
A brief first-person narrative about the reluctant prophet who was
swallowed by a huge sea creature, with striking watercolor paintings
in earth tones and gently rounded lines. God's forgiveness is portrayed here, and the repentant Jonah learns a lesson. A unique retelling by a talented artist. Ages 4+.

Bulla, Clyde. Jonah and the Great Fish. Illus. Helga Aichinger. T Y
Crowell, 1970. $7.95.
A well-written text and lovely paintings retell this biblical story.
Bulla's book is more explanatory and detailed than Brodsky's brief
and more personal retelling. Bulla is a prolific author of books for primary readers, and simple, dramatic storytelling is his outstanding
trait. (Note: See also Bulla's *Joseph the Dreamer* for a longish but competent picture book. TY Crowell, 1971. O.P.) Ages 5–9.

Chaikin, Miriam. The Seventh Day: The Story of the Jewish Sabbath. See chapter 7, The Jewish Holidays.

Cohen, Barbara. The Binding of Isaac. Illus. Charles Mikolaycak. Lothrop, 1978. $7.95.

An old man surrounded by grandchildren is relating a tale from long ago: the painful story of a father who almost kills his son in God's name. The storyteller is Isaac himself, and Jacob's lively offspring (who ask questions typical of their biblical personalities) are the audience. Unlike other Bible retellings for children, this book makes us confront Isaac's pain; we become emotionally involved with his tragedy. The illustrations, rendered in earth tones, are realistic and striking; along with the text, they give the work a sense of immediacy. Indeed, the artist makes a strong comment by portraying Holocaust victims in the sacrificial flames, although Isaac has just assured his breathless brood that God will never ask the Jews to sacrifice their youngsters again. Ages 8+.

Cohen, Barbara. I Am Joseph. Illus. Charles Mikolaycak. Lothrop, 1980. $9.95.

Joseph relates his story of sibling betrayal and rise to power in this lengthy and sensuous Bible retelling. Because Cohen tells the story from the protagonist's viewpoint, his character comes to life and we are emotionally involved in his fate. Although the book is produced in a picture-book format, the text and illustrations are not appropriate for a juvenile audience. In one scene, Potiphar's wife unties Joseph's loincloth and he remarks: "Her eyes grew wide as she beheld my nakedness. . . ." The accompanying illustration depicts a seductive Mrs. Potiphar in a transparent gown and a naked Joseph. Cohen's text is smooth and interesting, and the format and illustrations (in vibrant colored pencil with oil glazes) are unusual and handsome. Ages 12+.

DeJong, Meindert. Mighty Ones: Great Men and Women of Early Bible Days. Illus. Harvey Schmidt. Har-Row, 1959. $9.95.

Using Hebrews 11 as a focal point—"Now faith is the substance of things hoped for, the evidence of things not seen"—a respected children's writer tells the story of men and women whose lives depended on blind faith. To set the stage for each of the eighteen accounts, DeJong quotes a passage from the Bible as an introduction, then tells his tale with lively dialogue and deep emotions. These biblical heroes come to life under this good storyteller's pen. The boldly sketched black-and-white drawings add a dramatic abstract backdrop. Ages 10–14.

De La Mare, Walter. Stories from the Bible. Illus. Edward Ardizzone. Knopf, 1961. $8.99.

Thirty-four stories from the first nine books of the Bible are told by the much celebrated English writer and poet, Walter de la Mare (1873–1956). Beautifully written in a straightforward and dignified manner, they blend a biblical cadence with a highly readable English. The black-and-white line drawings by a well-known picture-book artist add a quiet, soothing touch to the often explosive narrative. Ages 9–12.

Efron, Marshall, and **Alfa-Betty Olsen.** Bible Stories You Can't Forget No Matter How Hard You Try. Illus. Ron Barrett. Dutton, 1976. O.P.; $1.25 pb., Dell.
Eight Bible stories (including two from the Christian Bible) are retold in a contemporary tongue-in-cheek style. An arthritic Noah, for example, is shown picking up discarded soda bottles and singing, "Soon it's gonna rain, I can feel it." Later, Goliath causes the Israeli army great suffering—with his bad jokes: "You think you're so strong? I've seen better mussels in a fish store." To which the Hebrews reply, "Get a writer!" The book is great fun for children who are familiar with these stories. The illustrations alone are worth the price of a ticket to Efron's Pharaohland, "an amusement park that is gonna wow 'em for centuries." Efron and company—unlike the first mazzot—have certainly risen to the occasion. Ages 8–12.

Golann, Cecil P. Mission on a Mountain: The Story of Abraham and Isaac. Illus. H. Hechtkopf. "Outstanding Books from Foreign Lands" Series. Lerner, 1975. $5.95.
Golann adds to the original story by explaining why God asked Abraham to sacrifice his beloved son. It seems that Abraham has grown forgetful about inviting poor people to his celebrations, and at a huge feast honoring Isaac he turns away a hungry beggar. Unfortunately, this pauper is actually Satan, who rejoices at Abraham's sin. He tattles to God about the Hebrew's neglect of the poor and urges God to prove Abraham's devotion to Him. It is interesting to note the similarity between this legend and "Sleeping Beauty." In both stories the patriarch snubs someone who should have been invited to a child's celebration, causing the offspring great suffering. Just as Sleeping Beauty pricks her finger (a minor sacrificial act) and almost meets an early death, Isaac, too, is threatened. Isaac is saved by a benevolent God, while Sleeping Beauty's fate is softened by a kind fairy. Brin's picture book is a bit long, although it tells its story well enough. The colorful illustrations are pleasant and abundant. Ages 5–10.

Graham, Lorenz. David He No Fear. Illus. Ann Grifalconi. T Y Crowell, 1971. $6.89;   God Wash the World and Start Again. Illus. Clare Romano Ross. T Y Crowell, 1971. $6.95;   A Road Down in the Sea. Illus. Gregorio Prestopino. T Y Crowell, 1946. O.P.

Graham's books are distinguished contributions to the field of biblical retellings for children. They are written in a style that reflects the speech patterns of Liberians newly introduced to our language. The result is lovely poetry in a lilting English. The distinctive feature of Graham's work is that you cannot read it silently; just try and you will find the words popping out of your mouth. Ages 5+

Guiladi, Yael. The Story of Noah and the Ark. Illus. Riki Ben-Ari. Koren, 1972. $3.75.
The story of Noah is told with a lively, well-written text and beautiful, vibrantly colored illustrations. Unfortunately, the full-page drawings are not always placed near the text they illustrate. In addition, a line of narrative, which detracts from the flow of the story, appears on each drawing. An adult reading this book with a preschooler can skip the long narrative portions and just read the story as it is briefly told on the illustrated pages. Ages 8–11; younger for reading aloud.

Haiz, Danah. Jonah's Journey. Illus. H. Hechtkopf. "Outstanding Books from Foreign Lands" Series. Lerner, 1973. $5.95.
Although the colorful illustrations carry the story along better than the monotonous writing does, this book should prove valuable for young readers. Closely following the biblical version, it reveals a very human prophet who is not too happy in his profession. The text is not overlong, and the ocean scenes are dramatic and effective. Ages 6–10.

Hollender, Betty R. Bible Stories for Little Children. Illus. William Steinel. UAHC, 1955–1960. 3 vols. $4.00 each.
These volumes are written for the early elementary school child to read by himself. Although the writing has a definite textbook ring to it, the stories are not without appeal. Parents should be able to tolerate reading them aloud to preschoolers. The first two volumes cover Noah's Ark through King Solomon; the third volume includes stories less often retold, such as the Prophets and Job. Hollender's stories convey the love of biblical parents for their children and the love of biblical heroes for God. The illustrations suffer from a 1950s textbook style. Ages 6–10.

Hutton, Warwick. Noah and the Great Flood. Illus. by author. Atheneum, 1979. $7.95.
This retelling is distinguished by its emphasis on wickedness and on the eventual death of all the living creatures who missed the boat. Hutton's watercolor paintings depict animals and people drowning in the flood as well as skulls and carcasses along the desolated shores. The writing could be smoother, and the illustrations are striking but

limited. Scenes of the abandoned landscapes are very effective, and the sun, looking like a lost sunny-side-up egg, is certainly unique. But the interior of the ark is too orderly—are the animals stuffed? And the human faces are expressionless, except for those of the drowning ones. Hutton's unusual emphasis and large watercolor spreads give the book a distinctive flavor. Although there is much life in the artist's death scenes, there is too much stillness among the living. Ages 4–9.

In the Beginning: The Picture Bible. Cook, 1978. Vol. 1. $3.95 pb. each.
Only volume 1, which contains excerpts of biblical tales from Genesis to Samuel, has been examined. The text is lucid and engaging. Cook uses soft colors and lines in his pleasant illustrations, thus avoiding the garishness often associated with comic-strip art. The format, too, is appealing, as the text and artwork are neatly spaced. The stories are romanticized a bit and every character is a beautiful specimen, but these are two essentials for comic books. For a hardcover comic, see the brightly colored *Picture Stories from the Bible* (ed. M. C. Gaines, Scarf, 1979. $9.95). Ages 9–13.

Klagsbrun, Francine. The Story of Moses. "Immortals Biography" Series. Watts, 1968. $5.90.
An absorbing full-length account of the life of Moses based on the traditional Bible story as well as legends and biblical commentaries. The book adheres closely to the original text; the dialogue is taken from the Revised Standard Version (World, 1962). Because the author does not guess at Moses' inner emotions or create her own interpretation of his character, the figure of Moses retains its Bible character. Ages 10–14.

Klink, J. L., comp. The Bible for Children with Plays and Songs. Vol. 1: The Old Testament. Trans. Patricia Crampton. Illus. Piet Klaase. Westminster, 1967. O.P.
An attractive anthology of poems, short plays, and songs (with musical directions), as well as narrative retellings of biblical stories. This volume is recommended for collections needing some dramatized materials. Its medley of literary styles and forms, contributed by a variety of Dutch writers, gives the work a unique flavor. Ages 9–13.

L'Engle, Madeleine. The Journey with Jonah. Illus. Leonard Everett Fisher. FS&G, 1978. $3.95 pb.
This charming play by the author of *A Wrinkle in Time* (FS&G, 1962) retells the story of the petulant prophet, Jonah. Written in a light yet philosophical vein, it is stocked with lively animals who carry the ac-

tion forward. In one scene, Papa Rat is trying to persuade Mama to desert the ship before it leaves Joppa. Bad vibrations make him say, "Mark my words, there's a Jonah on board." Fisher's skillful pen-and-ink drawings bring the drama to life. Ages 11–14; younger for reading aloud.

L'Engle, Madeleine. Ladder of Angels: Scenes from the Bible Illustrated by Children of the World. Seabury, 1979. $17.50; $9.95 pb., Penguin.

From the Creation to the coming of Nehemiah, L'Engle retells the Old Testament in capsule form. L'Engle is a talented and a religious writer, and for this book she draws her inspiration not only from her theology but from her young colleagues as well. Her book is lovingly illustrated by the participants in a contest held in Jerusalem to mark the International Year of the Child. Seabury has done a beautiful job in publishing this work, which begs for a grown-up lap (it is heavy) and an accompanying child. The book is expensive but fulfills a literary and spiritual need. As L'Engle put it: "Ho, everyone that thirsteth, come ye for water." Ages 6+.

Lenski, Lois. Mr. and Mrs. Noah. Illus. by author. T Y Crowell, 1948. $4.95.

Lenski's tiny book is sure to be a favorite with the preschool set. The story of Noah's ark is told without mention of God's anger: "God told Mr. Noah to build an ark." Noah and family are depicted as wooden dolls, and the animals and ark are simply drawn and brightly colored. The good humor in the illustrations and the snappy rhythm in the text make the book fun to read aloud. Lenski's picture books too often overdose on sex-role stereotypes, but here is a happy exception. There is just so much ark work to do that even a boy is shown wielding a broom! Ages 2–6.

Mee, Charles. Moses, Moses. Illus. Ken Munowitz. Har-Row, 1977. $4.95.

In this tale we watch baby Moses travel in a basket down the Nile, meet the Pharaoh's daughter, and return home with his own mother. The text is simple and graceful. Moses' journey is expanded so that the artist can depict the various sights seen through the eyes of the infant: frightening nighttime with eyes peering out of reeds and amusing daylight scenes of "curious snakes, friendly crocodiles [?], and hippopotami." The artist's unique black-and-white sketches, composed of loopy lines, create amusing, childlike, and dramatic scenes. Some adults might feel that the animal-like protagonists are disrespectful. However, the book conveys a very real feeling for the baby's fright, and the nonrealistic creatures help relieve the tension.

(Note: See also Mee's similarly innocent version of Noah's Ark: *Noah.* Har-Row, 1978. $5.95.) Ages 3–9.

Paamoni, Zev. Aaron the High Priest; Adventures of Jacob; Benjamin, the Littlest Brother; Yitzchak, Son of Abraham. Illus. Alisa Yemini. Shulsinger Bros, 1970. $6.00 each.
These books by an Israeli writer are written in lively dialogue and are attractively illustrated. Ages 8–12.

Reed, Gwendolyn. Adam and Eve. Illus. Helen Siegl. Lothrop, 1968. $7.92.
A sensuous and poetic text creates a distinguished version of the Creation. In this Eden, "Oranges shone like tiny suns. Melons glowed like moons in the grasses." Appealing woodcuts in oranges and golds enhance this timeless retelling. Although the book is too long for group storytelling, it is perfect for a one-to-one reading. Ages 6–10.

Reeves, James. The Angel and the Donkey. Illus. Edward Ardizzone. McGraw, 1969. O.P.
From the Book of Numbers comes this story of the magician Balaam who was bribed by the Moabite king to curse the Hebrew people. When God sends an angel to thwart Balaam's journey to the king, the donkey stops dead in its tracks and refuses to move. The magician beats it until it calls out to him: "What have I done to make you do this?" The greedy magician suddenly sees the angel himself and repents his evil ways. The book combines fine glowing illustrations by a well-loved children's artist with a brief, nicely told story. Perfect for group storytelling. Ages 5–10.

Rose, Anne K. Samson and Delilah. Illus. Richard Powers. Lothrop, 1968. $6.75.
The bold illustrations in black and red beautifully express the volcanic strength and anger churning inside the mighty Samson. Drawn in red—as is the sun, the lion, the grinning stone idol and the fire streaming from the foxes' tails—Samson plays his stormy drama against a black, forbidding sky. The story is succinctly retold, but too sketchy in parts to really explain Samson's growing anger with the Philistines. Nonetheless, the artistic interpretation compensates for any textual weakness, and the book is recommended both for storytelling and for individual enjoyment. Ages 5–9.

Saporta, Raphael. A Basket in the Reeds. Illus. H. Hechtkopf. "Outstanding Books from Foreign Lands" Series. Lerner, 1964. $5.95.
Originally published in Israel, this attractively illustrated picture book tells about Moses' infancy: how his family hid him from the

Egyptians and finally sent him down the Nile. This lengthy and detailed version includes the dreams of the Pharaoh and Miriam, Moses' sister. (These night visions are Midrash legends.) The writing is adequate, with occasional lapses into sentimentality. The very colorful illustrations are profuse and appealing. Ages 5–10.

Singer, Isaac Bashevis. The Wicked City. Illus. Leonard Everett Fisher. FS&G, 1972. $6.95.
Abraham's nephew, Lot, journeys to Sodom to make his fortune as a lawyer who defends murderers and madmen. His spoiled daughters and shrewish spouse have an easy life in the corrupt city until God ends their fun with a volcanic holocaust. Singer's contemporary retelling duplicates the spirit of the Bible's account, and the protagonists come to life in this dramatic, fast-moving picture book. The artist, famous for his books on colonial America, has done a fine job. His drawings in brown (a sort of red with the blood drained) both intensify the text and expressively portray the emotions of the protagonists. Ages 8–13.

Spier, Peter. Noah's Ark. Illus. by author. Doubleday, 1977. $7.95.
The pictures tell the tale in this 1977 Caldecott Award Winner. The pages are crowded with colorful, detailed, amusing scenes of life on the ark. Witness a mouse desperately trying to budge the heavy foot of an elephant that is resting on the tail of her companion. Notice along with Noah that a sly fox is nestling in one of the cubicles designed to hold a hen. The more you look, the more you chuckle; yet Spier's illustrations of life outside the ark are solemn and dramatic. The book begins with a poem by Jacobus Revius (1586–1658), a snappy, fast-moving verse translated from the Dutch by Spier. This is not a slapstick retelling; Noah's expressions change from scene to scene, and we see the tensions and joys experienced by this old man. Ages 3+.

Taubes, Hella. The Bible Speaks. Trans. Lolla Bloch. Illus. Dan Bar-Giora. Bloch, 1974. 3 vols. $4.50 each.
An appealing trio of oversized books printed on heavy stock. The illustrations, mostly in black and white, are bold and well designed. The numerous retellings are succinct and friendly. The author does not hesitate to insert an opinion or two when dealing with a subject dear to her, such as child rearing or friendship. This is one of the very few books that strives for a nonsexist tone in its introduction, selection of stories, and retellings. Ages 9–12.

Van der Meer, Ron, and **Atie van der Meer.** Oh Lord! Illus. by authors. Crown, 1979. $5.95.

This colorfully and humorously illustrated title depicts God and two little angels creating the world with paint and clay. Offbeat and upbeat, the book will either mildly shock or delight its audience. For example, God is drawn naked taking a shower, eating Holy Wheat Bread, and making some bad mistakes in his animal designs—the three-headed dragon just has to go! Some might not approve of the angels' nudity or the idea of Adam growing more and more excited as Eve emerges from the block of stone. Those who permit a freer interpretation of the Creation will be entertained by the mishaps and successes that lead the trio to a well-deserved rest—God is at the seaside sipping soda and eating chocolates—after creating a beautiful world. Youngsters will especially enjoy watching the childlike angels help and provoke the Lord. Ages 4–10.

Wahl, Jan. Runaway Jonah and Other Tales. Illus. Uri Shulevitz. Macmillan, 1968. $3.95.
With a respectful tongue-in-cheek, Wahl has simplified five Bible stories. Both the narrative and the amusing two-tone illustrations are entertaining introductions to Bible tales for young children. Youngsters will chuckle over the comic drawing of a fat, grinning Goliath, and then laugh out loud when they read how he met his end: "Head first, his body made a hole in the ground, and only his boots stuck out of it." A well-designed book. Ages 7–11; younger for reading aloud.

Weil, Lisl. Esther. Illus. by author. Atheneum, 1980. $8.95.
The story of the lovely and courageous Queen Esther is retold with a succinct narrative and appealing blue and black watercolor sketches. Both the prose and the drawings are soft and understated, giving the Bible tale a quiet dignity but an exciting tone. It is notable that Weil calls Esther's people of yesterday and today "Hebrews"; in the story of a Jewish queen, the word "Jew" does not appear. Brin's *Story of Esther* (reviewed in this chapter) has more bite to it, but this book is briefer and easier to use for storytelling with younger children. Ages 5–9.

Weil, Lisl. The Very First Story Ever Told. Illus. by author. Atheneum, 1976. $7.95.
The story of Creation and the Fall is retold for very young children in this appealing picture book. The pretty illustrations are painted in black watercolor against a tan background, and the childlike Adam and Eve romp and play with the animals of Eden. The author's writing does not flow as smoothly as her brush, but her explanation of the couple's eviction—"a promise must be kept"—is appropriate for her audience. Weil assures the young listeners that God did not stay

angry at Adam and Eve for long. Recommended for storytelling hours. Ages 3–6.

Wengrow, Rabbi Charles. Tales of King Saul: Retold for Jewish Youth. Illus. Zalman Kleinman. Shulsinger Bros, 1969. $6.00.
Follows the biblical account of Saul's anointment as king by the prophet Samuel through Saul's death in battle with the Philistines. The story is well paced, not difficult to read, and filled with adventure and drama. Functional illustrations break up the print. (Note: *Tales of Noah and the Ark* and *Tales of the Prophet Samuel* are also available by this author.) Ages 9–12.

Exploration of Biblical Themes

Asimov, Isaac. Animals of the Bible. Illus. Howard Berelson. Doubleday, 1978. $6.95.
Over forty animals mentioned in both Testaments are briefly described and beautifully illustrated. An informative preface relates the difficulty of translating ancient Hebrew words into the animal names we know today. Guesses are made as to whether the leviathan and the behemoth mentioned in Job refer to the whale and the hippopotamus or to the crocodile and the elephant. We are given the Hebrew name of each animal portrayed, where it can be found in the Bible, and a note about its biblical character. Children, however, will be most attracted to the lovely drawings, rendered in soft reds and blacks, of an auroch, an ibex, an oryx, and other, more familiar creatures. An index would have been helpful. Ages 8–12.

Asimov, Isaac. The Story of Ruth. Doubleday, 1972. O.P.
According to Asimov, the anonymous writer of Ruth expresses this point: "A person was to be considered for himself or herself, and not for anything else. . . ." The writer would not have agreed with Ezra the Scribe who ordered Jews to "separate yourselves from the foreign population and from your foreign wives" (Ezra 10:11). Asimov also rejects Ezra's advice. His book traces the ancestry of King David (the non-Jewish Ruth was his great-grandmother) to show that intermarriage was not always considered harmful or sinful. Asimov puts no fictional words in Ruth's mouth. His quotes are from the 1970 edition of the New English Bible. Asimov's lucid introduction to the story includes maps and historical and biblical background information. On the whole, however, the book seems a somewhat bitter defense of intermarriage rather than a plea for brotherhood. Recommended for discussion groups. Ages 13+.

Asimov, Isaac. Words from the Exodus. Illus. William Barss. HM, 1963. $7.95; Words in Genesis. Illus. William Barss. HM, 1962. O.P.

Asimov reveals how the Bible's language and imagery are very much a part of all of us at all times. The books are easily read and contain a gentle sense of humor. The author succeeds in expanding the meaning of the Bible as well as exploring our own language. Youngsters interested in linguistics will enjoy watching the Bible take on added meaning under Asimov's technique. The Exodus volume includes the books of Exodus, Leviticus, and Deuteronomy. The Genesis volume ranges from the story of the Creation to the story of Joseph. Index and appendix in each volume. Ages 12+.

Coen, Rena Neumann. The Old Testament in Art. See chapter 5, Fine Arts and Domestic Arts: Art History Books.

Farb, Peter. The Land, Wildlife, and Peoples of the Bible. Illus. Harry McNaught. Har-Row, 1967. $8.97.
A distinguished naturalist and writer offers a fascinating look at the natural surroundings of the early Jews. Information is given about Noah's animals, Solomon's Temple, how the climate affected history, etc. No small detail escapes the author's eye. Indeed, he takes the apple out of Eve's mouth and tells us it was probably an apricot. The Bible is still our best guide to nature study in the Holy Land, according to Mr. Farb. He tells how forestry experts planted tamarisk trees in Beer-sheba. Why? Because the Bible says that Abraham planted one. The trees are flourishing. Illustrated with clear drawings. Index, bibliography. Ages 12+.

Ferguson, Walter. Living Animals of the Bible. Illus. by author. Scribner, 1974. $3.95.
Fine paintings of biblical animals, detailed and in color, are accompanied by Bible passages and brief information about the species. In addition, the Hebrew, English, and scientific name is given for each of the many mammals, birds, fish, reptiles, amphibians, and insects mentioned. This is an attractive, interesting, and detailed look at the early zoology of Bible country. Ages 12+.

Freund, Miriam. Jewels for a Crown: The Story of the Marc Chagall Windows. See chapter 5, Fine Arts and Domestic Arts: Art History Books.

Goodman, Hannah. The Story of Prophecy. Behrman, 1965. $4.95 pb.
Goodman addresses the reader in a voice committed to God and Judaism. Her book is a fine review of the Bible's prophets and the two heroes who came before them, Abraham and Moses. The book has an appealing format: drawings, maps, and a variety of typefaces are used. The author gives a detailed summary of each prophet's contri-

bution to Judaism and how each in his or her (Deborah's) own manner preserved Israel's relationship with God. Although not for a wide audience, this title will help interested students. The writing tends toward the emotional at times, but on the whole the book reads smoothly and is engrossing. Ages 12+.

Heaton, E. W. Everyday Life in Old Testament Times. Illus. Marjorie Quennell. Scribner, 1977 (rev. ed.) $15.00.
A highly readable look at everyday living in ancient times. This adult title will be of interest to older children, especially since the juvenile books on this subject are O.P. (for example, Marie Neurath, *They Lived Like This in Ancient Palestine.* Watts, 1965). Ages 12+.

Lapson, Dvora. The Bible in Dance. See chapter 10, Music and Dance.

Lathrop, Dorothy. Illus. Animals of the Bible: A Picture Book. Lippincott, 1937. $8.95.
Lathrop does a fine artistic rendition of the animals described in a wide variety of Bible (and some New Testament) passages and Psalms selected from the King James Bible. The full-page black-and-white drawings show the animals in their natural habitats. They are drawn with dignity and in a realistic style. The book allows the child to focus on creatures that usually do not get much attention: the ram, caught in the bush and watching the knife at Isaac's throat; the lordly camels who are not surprised at Rebekah's kindness at the well; the ravens who bring bread and flesh to a hungry Elijah; and more. Ages 8–12.

Matek, Ord. The Bible Through Stamps. See chapter 5, Fine Arts and Domestic Arts: Art History Books.

Mazar, Benjamin, and **Michael Avi-Yonah.** Illustrated World of the Bible. Davey, 1961. 5 vols. $20.00 each.
This huge undertaking is a richly visual interpretation of the Bible. It strives to elucidate the biblical text by placing particular verses next to relevant photographs of archeological, artistic, sociological, geographical, and physical subjects. This is a scholarly work which takes a modern scientific approach. In addition, there are commentaries on the scenes and objects depicted that inform us of the history and mores of ancient times: The set is recommended for reference and browsing. (Vol. 1: *Law;* vol. 2: *Former Prophets;* vol. 3: *Later Prophets;* vol. 4: *Writings;* vol. 5: *New Testament.*) Ages 11+.

Noble, Iris. Treasure of the Caves: The Story of the Dead Sea Scrolls. Macmillan, 1971. $5.95.
A solid introduction to this subject, combining a smooth blend of facts with imaginative touches and a lively writing style. Noble em-

phasizes the political climate of the discoveries (in 1947) and its effect on the archeological events. She also informs us of the scientific aspects of preparing and preserving the scrolls in order to examine their contents. In addition, there are many good photographs and maps. (Note: Both Uriel Rappaport and Alan Honours also wrote competent titles on this subject, but they are O.P.) Ages 11–15.

Schwartzman, Sylvan. The Living Bible: a Topical Approach to the Jewish Scriptures. UAHC, 1962. $5.00.
Although this title is classified as a textbook, there is no trade equivalent appropriate for youngsters. The author selects nine difficult and often-asked questions: e.g., Who is God? Why is there evil in the world? Is death the end? Who wrote the Bible? Answers to these questions are sought in the Torah and other biblical writings. Any serious Bible student would appreciate this book, which also contains bibliographies, charts and maps, an excellent introduction concerning the Bible's influence, and an index. The writing is lucid and the book has a pleasant format. It has been created to fill the need of educators in the Reform program of education. Ages 12–16.

Terrien, Samuel. The Golden Bible Atlas. Illus. William Bolin. Golden Pr, 1957. $7.95.
Provides a clearly written and visually attractive background to the Old and New Testaments. Using maps, charts, photographs, and illustrations, Professor Terrien achieves his stated goals: "To show the land that shaped the people; and to depict the people's story against the backdrop of their land." Covering the span of the Jewish and Christian Bibles, we learn about the economy, myths, religions, and geography of those early times. The book is colorful and printed in large type. A good choice for gift-giving to readers of all faiths. Ages 8–12.

Reference Aid

Comay, Joan. Who's Who in the Old Testament; Together with the Apocrypha. HR&W, 1971. $18.95; $2.45 pb. Abingdon.
With an introduction to the Old Testament and a chronology of events, Comay presents over 3,000 entries devoted to the people whose stories are told in the Bible and the Apocrypha—the collection of works that bridges the gap between the Old and the New Testaments. The entries vary in length. Moses earns twenty pages; Nahum, two lines. The book is profusely illustrated with prints, color plates, and maps. The biographical entries in the Apocrypha are kept separate from those in the Old Testament. This is an adult title that older children can use. Ages 11+.

4

Biographies

From Sir David Salomons to Mark Spitz, from Ernestine Rose to Bella Abzug, from Louis Brandeis to Barbra Streisand, the Jewish subjects of children's biographies are wide and varied. Rabbis, statespeople, pioneers, military heroes, writers, musicians, artists, scientists, philosophers, philanthropists, doctors, entertainers, and athletes are spotlighted. Sharing these biographies with youngsters, however, is not an easy task. Much of the material available is of poor quality and either the writing is flat, the subject is unfamiliar, or the protagonist's field of accomplishments is of little interest to children. A rabbi, for example, is on the whole less interesting to young readers than a magician. This in part explains why there are four children's biographies of Harry Houdini in print, while a book about Rabbi Kook of Jerusalem has yet to be checked out of my temple library.

Because there are so many biographies about Jewish people, I have selected only those which will most appeal to children. Many of these recommended books make for great recreational reading. Their facts are accurate and compelling. One such book is Margaret Davidson's *Golda Meir Story.*

Although the aim has been to include only the best biographies, some of the books that merely inform but do not inspire have been included in this chapter because they are often useful for school reports. In this category are several works in the "Covenant Books" series of the Jewish Publication Society of America. Not reviewed from this series are titles on Rabbi Isaac Aboab, Louis Brandeis, Solomon Carvalho, Louis Fleischner, Daniel Mendoza, Haym Solomon, and Lillian Wald. Other publishers of juvenile biography have produced books that are often sentimental and idealized. An example of this tendency is Miriam Biskin's *Pattern for a Heroine: The Life Story of Rebecca Gratz* (UAHC, 1967).

Several of the reviewed works are out of print but have been included because they are excellent and/or unique in subject matter and can still be found in libraries and on Jewish distributors' lists. A great many adequate biographies are not in print. Stories of such musicians and composers as Jerome Kern, George Gershwin, Irving Berlin, Felix Mendelssohn, and Leonard Bernstein are no longer available for purchase.

A quick perusal of all these biographies will reveal the great variety of contributions. Such figures as Chaim Weizmann, statesman without a state; Marc Chagall, artist extraordinary; and Micky Marcus, soldier, affected, changed, and enriched the Jewish world. Others achieved greatness in fields not directly related to Judaism; for example, Ernestine Rose was a leading feminist and David Sarnoff was a giant in the world of communications. Books about celebrities are also available for beginning readers: Mark Spitz, Sandy Koufax, and Barbra Streisand are some of the familiar names in sports and entertainment whose biographies fall into this category.

This chapter also includes personal accounts and memoirs that have important experiences to share. Not quite autobiographical, many of these books focus on a particular period in the author's life; often they deal with Jewish persecution during World War II. The most famous of these, of course, is *Anne Frank: The Diary of a Young Girl.*

Collective Biographies

Fink, Greta. Great Jewish Women: Profiles of Courageous Women from the Maccabean Period to the Present. Bloch, 1978. $8.95.
The deeds and times of twenty-two Jewish women are described in this adult title, which is suitable for junior and senior high school readers. The early Jewish scholar Beruriah, the nineteenth-century feminist Ernestine Rose, and the contemporary sculptor Louise Nevelson are among the subjects. The writing is succinct and adequate. Photographs, bibliography, and index. Ages 12+.

Henry, Sondra, and **Emily Taitz.** Written Out of History: A Hidden Legacy of Jewish Women Revealed Through Their Writings. Bloch, 1978. $7.95 pb.
An adult book that teenagers might find useful for reports and pleasure reading is this unique feminist discussion of 3,000 years of Jewish womanhood. The original writings of over thirty thinkers and doers—poets, businesswomen, scholars, social workers, etc.—reveal the answer to the old question "A woman of valor, who can find?" Bibliography, index. Ages 13+.

Karp, Deborah. Heroes of American Jewish History. See chapter 6, History Books: American History Books.

Levitan, Tina. Jews in American Life. Hebrew Pub, 1969. $5.95.
Ninety outstanding Jews, including seven women, who have contributed either to American society or to Jewish life are discussed in this adequate collective biography. Less sentimental and more informative than most juvenile Jewish works of this kind, Levitan's work draws upon people from all professions and offers the young reader from one to four pages of facts about each subject (and usually a drawing or photograph). Ages 10–14.

Smith, Betsy Covington. Breakthrough: Women in Religion. Walker & Co., 1978. $7.95.
Smith discusses the struggles of five women who entered the male-dominated clergy in churches and synagogues. Rabbi Sandy Sasso, the first woman Reconstructionist rabbi, is one of the women described. The book is nicely written and will appeal to teenagers interested in a religious profession or in profiles of courageous women. Photographs, glossary, no index. Ages 12+.

Individual Biographies

Abrahams, Robert D. Sound of Bow Bells: The Story of Sir David Salomons. Illus. Dan Dickas. "Covenant Book" Series. Jewish Pubn, 1962. $3.50.
This nicely written story of a Jewish Englishman who fought for Jewish civil rights and eventually became the Lord Mayor of London presents a rare glimpse into nineteenth-century Jewish life in England. The book's poetic touches add an attractive fairy-tale quality to a life filled with nobility of the best kind. No index. Ages 10–14.

Alexander, Lloyd. Border Hawk: August Bondi. Illus. Bernard Krigstein. "Covenant Book" Series. Jewish Pubn, 1958. $3.50.
Written by a noted children's author, *Border Hawk* is a fast-paced and exciting account of a nineteenth-century Vienna-born Jew. One of John Brown's supporters in Kansas and a soldier in the Civil War, Bondi was actively opposed to American slavery. No index. Ages 10–14.

Berkman, Ted. Cast a Giant Shadow: The Story of Micky Marcus, a Soldier for All Humanity. "Covenant Book" Series. Jewish Pubn, 1967. $3.50.
Micky Marcus, a colonel in the U.S. Army, died in battle for Jerusalem during Israel's War of Independence. The personality and dedication of this intelligent, athletic, and very lovable man comes through in Berkman's exciting story. Photographs; no index. Ages 12–15.

Block, Irwin. Neighbor to the World: The Story of Lillian Wald. "Women of America" Series. T Y Crowell, 1969. O.P.
Although no longer in print, Block's work is preferable to Sally Rogow's *Lillian Wald: The Nurse in Blue* (Jewish Pubn, 1966), the only juvenile biography about Wald in print. Faster moving and better written, Block's work includes good photographs, a bibliography, and an index. This story of one of America's greatest social workers is only one biography in an excellent series available in many libraries. Ages 11–14.

Comay, Joan. Ben-Gurion and the Birth of Israel. "World Landmark Books" Series. Random, 1967. $5.95.
This readable account is smoothly written and informative. It includes many photographs, a chronology, and an index. (Note: See also Gertrude Samuel's hefty biography, *B-G, Fighter of Goliaths: The Story of David Ben-Gurion*, T Y Crowell, 1974, O.P. Ages 12–15.) Ages 10–15.

Cone, Molly. Hurry Henrietta. HM, 1966. O.P.
This popular fictionalized biography of the founder of Hadassah, the Zionist women's organization, emphasizes her girlhood and early adulthood on Lombard Street in Baltimore. Written with much dialogue and a lively narrative, the book is entertaining, even if it does not provide an insightful or memorable account of Henrietta Szold. No index. Ages 9–12.

Cone, Molly. Leonard Bernstein. Illus. Robert Galster. "A Crowell Biography" Series. T Y Crowell, 1970. $1.45 pb.
An easy-to-read survey of Bernstein's boyhood and career. The nicely written text is accompanied by pleasant illustrations. This excellent series offers many quality biographies for the beginning reader. Although it is no longer published in hardcover, many libraries carry this story of one of America's most beloved composers and conductors. Ages 6–9.

Davidson, Margaret. The Golda Meir Story. Scribner, 1979. $9.95.
Davidson emphasizes the girlhood of Golda Meir in this lively and entertaining biography filled with anecdotes and personal details. Golda is portrayed as a strong-willed and intellectually curious child, and her daring political escapades at age ten will keep readers amused and amazed. The author's narrative reads like a novel, and her remarkable protagonist becomes very dear to us. This is biography for children at its best! Bibliography, index. Ages 9–13.

Ernst, John. Escape King: The Story of Harry Houdini. Illus. Ray Abel. P-H, 1975. $5.95; $1.50 pb.

This brief and easy-to-read biography describes the daredevil tricks and amazing feats of this master magician, who was the son of a rabbi. Brightly illustrated and fast-moving. (Note: Two other recommended biographies on Houdini are Lace Kendall's *Houdini*, Macrae, 1960, $6.50, Ages 11+, and Florence White's *Escape: The Life of Harry Houdini*, Messner, 1979, $7.79, Ages 8–11.) Ages 8–11.

Fabe, Maxine. Helena Rubinstein: Beauty Millionaire. "Women of America" Series. T Y Crowell, 1972. O.P.
This Polish-born businesswoman began her career in Australia and later established a cosmetic empire in America and Europe. Girls just beginning to take an interest in makeup will find this a most fascinating peek into the secrets of the beauty business. Did you know, for example, that the ingredient used to frost lipstick is fish scales? Fabe's book makes for entertaining reading. Index. Ages 10–14.

Faber, Doris. Bella Abzug. Lothrop, 1976. $8.25.
A lively and upbeat biography about an assertive civil rights lawyer and former New York congresswoman. Best known for her efforts in the women's rights movement, Bella discusses the effect of segregated synagogue seats: "I have a funny feeling that being sent up to that balcony [as a child] had something to do with my being involved the way I turned out to be." Unfortunately, Faber turns away from the spirit of feminism by spending too much time on Abzug's physical appearance. The biography will entertain youngsters and inform them about recent political movements and personalities. Index, photographs. Ages 10–15.

Falstein, Louis. The Man Who Loved Laughter: The Story of Sholem Aleichem. Illus. Adrienne O. Dudden. "Covenant Book" Series. Jewish Pubn, 1968. $3.50.
Sholom Aleichem (Yiddish for "Greetings!") is the pen name of Shalom Rabinovich (1859–1916), who was born in Russia. One of a dozen children, he demonstrated a gift of scholarship and good humor at an early age. His rise to fame as a beloved Yiddish wit and writer came as no surprise to those who knew him in his youth. Emphasizing his boyhood and early manhood, a rags-to-riches affair, Falstein has created a highly readable account. There are attractive line drawings; no index. Ages 10–14.

Gray, Bettyanne. Manya's Story: The Harrowing Account of a Jewish Family's Ordeal in Revolutionary Russia. Lerner, 1978. $7.95.
Manya Polevoi is a secure young woman in a small Russian community in 1917 when the book begins. At its close, four years later, Manya and her young family are escaping to America and from hor-

rendous memories of Jews caught up as helpless victims in the struggle between the Bolshevik Red Army, the anti-Bolshevik White
Army, and the Ukrainian soldiers. The American-born author tells
her mother's story of close encounters with the death and horror of
pogroms. Although this book is not for all children, it is very well
written and very affecting—more so than any history lesson. Photographs, glossary, and chronology. Ages 11+.

Greenfeld, Howard. Marc Chagall: An Introduction. Viking Pr.,
1980. rev. ed. $13.95.
This revised edition of a 1967 Follett publication was published too
late for review. The earlier edition is a well-written account that
blends a critical analysis of Chagall's work and information on his life
and times. In addition, there are color and black-and-white reproductions of Chagall's work and a bibliography for further reading. A
handsome and effective work, the book deserves to be updated. (Note:
See also Greenfeld's *Gertrude Stein: A Biography,* Crown, 1973, O.P.,
Ages 12+, for another excellent title.) Ages 12+.

Hano, Arnold. Sandy Koufax: Strikeout King. Putnam, 1964. O.P.
Sports fans will enjoy this popularly written account of the baseball
career of the former star pitcher of the Los Angeles Dodgers. Photographs; no index. Ages 11–15.

Keenan, Deborah. On Stage: Barbra Streisand. Creative Ed, 1976.
$5.75; $2.95 pb.
Reluctant readers and youngsters who are curious about the career of
this popular singer and actress will appreciate this slim and skin-deep
account of Barbra's style and successes. Photographs; no index. Ages
9–16.

Klagsbrun, Francine. The Story of Moses. See chapter 3, The Bible:
Bible Stories.

Kuhn, Lois Harris. The World of Jo Davidson. Illus. Leonard
Everett Fisher. "Covenant Book" Series. Jewish Pubn, 1958. $3.50.
Raised in poverty on New York's Lower East Side, Jo Davidson grew
up to become a world-renowned sculptor. His great gift for this art,
his ability to relax his subjects and thus capture their inner selves, and
his humane and appealing personality are all brought out in this
lively (although a bit too idealized) biography. The book contains a
fascinating chapter on Jo Davidson and Helen Keller which can be
used to create interest in this title. No index. Ages 10–14.

Mann, Peggy. Golda: The Life of Israel's Prime Minister. Coward,
1971. O.P.; $1.25 pb., WSP.

Recommended for the mature youngster wanting more personal and political details about Golda Meir's life. Mann creates a sympathetic portrait of a unique woman with a good mix of dialogue and a light touch. Bibliography, index. Ages 12+.

Myers, Elizabeth. David Sarnoff: Radio and TV Boy. Illus. Fred M. Irvin. "Childhood of Famous Americans" Series. Bobbs, 1972. $5.95.
A fictionalized, easy-to-read biography emphasizing the childhood of this electronics wizard born in Uzlian, Russia, and raised in poverty in New York City. Both text and drawings are pleasant enough to interest the young reader in this smart little boy who grew up to be called "Mr. RCA." Glossary; no index. (Note: This functional series for beginning readers includes biographies on the following Jewish Americans: Bernard Baruch, Albert Einstein, George Gershwin, Harry Houdini, Joseph Pulitzer, and David Sarnoff.) Ages 7–11.

Neimark, Anne E. Sigmund Freud: The World Within. HBJ, 1976. $6.95.
Freud's life and times are interestingly portrayed in this work, which discusses his theories and his struggles against anti-Semitism and poverty. The author also describes this radical thinker's relation to the political climate of the times. Using both primary and secondary sources, the author successfully portrays the personality and complexities of the man and his work. Bibliography, index. Ages 11–15.

Noble, Iris. Firebrand for Justice: Louis D. Brandeis. Westminster, 1969. $4.50.
A straightforward and succinct account of the achievements and events in the life of this brilliant and humane legal personage and Zionist. Bibliography, index. Ages 10–14.

Noble, Iris. Sarah Bernhardt: Great Lady of the Theatre. Messner, 1960. O.P.
Bernhardt, the daughter of a Jewish Dutch woman, became an internationally renowned actress; many mothers have declared of their young daughters: "She's a real Sarah Bernhardt!" Noble's title is a lively and absorbing account of this dramatic woman's great successes and rough times. Index. Ages 12+.

Olsen, James T. Mark Spitz: The Shark. Illus. Harold Henriksen. "Superstars" Series. Childrens, 1974. $6.60.
Colorful drawings and a brief text trace the swimming career of "Mark the Shark" Spitz. Told by a Munich passer-by: "Hey, Jew boy, you aren't going to win any gold medals," Spitz left the 1972 Olympics (and Germany) with seven gold awards. No index. Ages 7–10.

Omer, Dvorah. Rebirth: The Story of Eliezer Ben-Yehudah and the Modern Hebrew Language. "Covenant Book" Series. Jewish Pubn, 1972. $3.50.

A highly readable and often moving biography of Ben-Yehuda, a Russian-born scholar and rebel who dedicated his life and that of his family to the cause of modern Hebrew. Told from the viewpoint of his oldest son, the book describes Ben-Yehudah's fanatic determination and strong will to make Hebrew the everyday tongue of Palestine. Readers will wonder at a father who isolates his Jerusalem-born son at birth from all foreign words but Hebrew. Ben-Yehudah was opposed by many in the Jerusalem community who thought that Hebrew, the holy language, would be profaned by common usage. His fanatical attitude and the strong opposition he engendered made life difficult for his son. With the help of an introduction by a teacher or librarian, this book will reach a wide audience. Translated from the Hebrew and originally published in Israel, it contains photographs but no index. This book has not had the attention it deserves. Ages 10–14.

Peare, Catherine Owens. The Louis D. Brandeis Story. T Y Crowell, 1970. O.P.

Using lively dialogue and interesting quotes, Peare blends Brandeis's personal life and professional achievements with great skill. She involves us with Louis the young Kentucky boy. His personality, career, and individual beliefs unfold until the reader can sense the greatness of this American leader. Extensive bibliography; index. Ages 11–16.

Raboff, Ernest. Marc Chagall. See chapter 5, Fine Arts and Domestic Arts: Art History Books.

Rothchild, Sylvia. Keys to a Magic Door: The Life and Times of I. L. Peretz. Illus. Bernard Krigstein. "Covenant Book" Series. Jewish Pubn, 1959. O.P.

Rothchild's lively, sensitive, and easy-to-read biography of this beloved Yiddish writer begins with a marvelous introduction to his youth spent in Zamosh, Poland, as a wild and brilliant lad. No index. Ages 10–12.

Schechter, Betty. The Dreyfus Affair: A National Scandal. See chapter 6, History Books: European History.

Shirer, William. The Rise and Fall of Adolf Hitler. See chapter 6, History Books: European History.

Shulman, Alix. To the Barricades: The Anarchist Life of Emma Goldman. "Women of America" Series. T Y Crowell, 1971. $8.95.

One of the titles in an excellent series, this work brings the often hated, fiery anarchist to life. Emma Goldman (1869–1940), born into Russian poverty and religious persecution, was one of the most influential radicals of her times. Goldman's life and struggle against government oppression are clearly and excitingly portrayed in this biography. Photographs, bibliography, and index. Ages 12+.

Suhl, Yuri. Eloquent Crusader: Ernestine Rose. Messner, 1970. O.P.
Rose, a Polish-born suffragist and abolitionist, lived a radical activist life that spans almost the entire nineteenth century. She left Poland because her rabbi-father selected an unappealing husband for her, and she dedicated the rest of her life to women's rights. This is a respectful and lively account of Susan B. Anthony's Jewish colleague. Bibliography, index. Ages 12–16.

Wise, William. Albert Einstein: Citizen of the World. Illus. Simon Jeruchim. "Covenant Book" Series. Jewish Pubn, 1960. $3.50.
A pleasant, readable biography that touches on Einstein's Jewish values and Zionism as well as his personality and scientific accomplishments. No index. (Note: Other adequate juvenile biographies include Alyesa Forsee's *Albert Einstein,* Macmillan, 1967, $5.95, Ages 10–13; Mae Freeman's *Story of Albert Einstein,* Random, 1958, $5.39, Ages 10–13; and M. Hammontree's *Albert Einstein, Young Thinker,* Bobbs, 1960, $5.95, Ages 7–10.) Ages 10–13.

Wise, William. Silversmith of Old New York: Myer Myers. Illus. Leonard Everett Fisher. "Covenant Book" Series. Jewish Pubn, 1958. $3.50.
A talented Early American silversmith and patriot stars in this pleasant and easy-to-read biography of one of New York's first Jewish families. The illustrations are by an artist renowned for his children's books on young America. Both text and drawings warmly portray a man dedicated to his profession and country. No index. Ages 9–12.

Zagoren, Ruby. Chaim Weizmann: First President of Israel. "A Century Book" Series. Garrard, 1972. $5.49.
The history of political Zionism, modern Israel, and Chaim Weizmann's life come together in this adequate, easily digestible biography. Large print, a generous use of dialogue and quotes, several black-and-white photographs, and a chronological chart on Weizmann's life will enable young readers to enjoy this account. Index. Ages 9–13.

Personal Accounts and Memoirs

Flinker, Moshe. Young Moshe's Diary: The Spiritual Torment of a Jewish Boy in Nazi Europe. Board of Jewish Ed, 1978 (copyright 1958). $4.50.

The diary (1942–1943) of an Orthodox Jewish youth hiding from the Nazis in a Brussels apartment shared with his family of six sisters is a memorable and saddening testimony to the suffering of Jews under the Nazi regime. Moshe talks about his schooling, the people around him, and the political situation. This anguished child's dearest wish is that the Americans and British will become as evil as the Germans and Russians so that Jewish redemption will certainly come soon. The introspective writing is not for all readers, but the diary should be made available for the special youngster. Moshe's very genuine and youthful viewpoint makes this book special. Ages 12+.

Frank, Anne. Anne Frank: The Diary of a Young Girl. Trans. B. M. Mooyaart-Doubleday. Doubleday, 1967 (rev. ed.). $8.95; $1.25 pb. WSP.

This incomparable work, one of the rare classics in children's literature to be written by a youngster, is the now well-known diary of the doomed Jewish girl hiding from the Nazis (along with family and friends) in an office building in Amsterdam. Adolescents find this book extraordinary; for not only are strong feelings of sympathy evoked by her predicament and tragic death, but readers identify with her awakening love for Peter and with her changing attitudes toward her family and her life. Anne's diary, published in over thirty languages and made into plays, films, and TV programs, is a tribute to a tormented yet hopeful soul. At the same time it is a universal portrait of girlhood. Ages 10–16.

Hannam, Charles. A Boy in That Situation: An Autobiography. Har-Row, 1977. $7.95; Sequel: Almost an Englishman. Dutton, 1979. $7.50.

In great detail, Hannam re-creates his boyhood as an assimilated well-to-do Jew in pre-Nazi Germany and his subsequent escape to England after the mass persecutions begin. Karl is not a sympathetic protagonist. Fat, crude, and nasty, his personality is well defined before the reader is asked to feel compassion for this now-hunted child. The slow-moving plot, burdened with meticulous detail to food and daily events, will not grab most youngsters. On the other hand, Hannam provides a fascinating look at the recently vanished culture of the assimilated German Jew. Ages 12+. The sequel is a continuation of Karl's candid comments about life in an English village school and a short stay in the army. More of the same for those who want to stick with Karl's (now Charles's) fate. Ages 13+.

Hautzig, Esther. The Endless Steppe: Growing Up in Siberia. T Y Crowell, 1968. $8.95; $1.50 pb., Schol Bk Serv.
Esther Rudomin's comfortable and happy childhood in the cultured city of Vilna (northeastern Poland) was torn asunder in 1941 when her parents were arrested for crimes of "capitalism" and were exiled with Esther for five years in a Siberian labor camp. This memorable and captivating work, which brings Esther's joys and sorrows to life, reads like a novel. Ages 11–14.

Hoffman, Judy. Joseph and Me: In the Days of the Holocaust. Illus. Lili Cassel-Wronker. KTAV, 1979. $4.00 pb.
Hoffman shares her tragic girlhood as a foster child in a Dutch-Christian household during World War II. The author wrote this unpretentious and affecting story in order to resolve her own anguish and to inform children of the harrowing past that must never again be repeated. Hoffman tells of her separation from her family and her close brushes with death. The book has an introduction to the Nazi era which is accompanied by some disturbing photographs of Nazi victims. Their omission would have made the title less graphic but no less meaningful. Ages 11–14.

Joffo, Joseph. A Bag of Marbles. Trans. Martin Sokolinsky. HM, 1974. $6.95; $1.75 pb., Bantam.
Two Jewish schoolboys escape Nazi capture by traveling incognito through the French Alps. Simply written, yet very dramatic, this stranger-than-fiction account of two children on the run is very popular with young readers. Ages 11+.

Koehn, Ilse. Mischling, Second Degree: My Childhood in Nazi Germany. Greenwillow, 1977. $8.50; $1.95 pb., Bantam.
A vivid memoir of a bright, resourceful girl, who does not know that she is part-Jewish and who witnesses the insanities of Nazi Germany as a reluctant Hitler Youth. The divorce of her parents in order to save her (Grandma was Jewish) is only the beginning of her suffering. This astounding and compelling story offers an unusual viewpoint. Ages 11+.

Reiss, Johanna. The Upstairs Room. T Y Crowell, 1972. $8.95; $1.75 pb., Bantam.   Sequel: The Journey Back. T Y Crowell, 1976. $8.95; $1.75 pb., Bantam.
Young Annie, along with her older sister, found a cramped refuge

from the Nazis for three years with a Gentile family of simple Dutch farmers. Reiss has written a dramatic and well-told story; believable characters draw us into their lives, and the pace never slackens. This book reaches a very wide audience. The sequel describes Annie's postwar reunion with her much-changed family. It is not as fine a literary achievement as the first book but should draw a willing number of Annie's fans. Ages 10–15.

Richter, Hans Peter. I Was There. Trans. Edite Kroll. HR&W, 1972. $5.95; $1.25 pb., Dell.
Hans Richter, author of the memorable children's novel *Friedrich,* describes his membership in the Hitler Youth—a tightly structured military organization for German children during the Nazi regime. Used with Ilse Koehn's *Mischling, Second Degree: My Childhood in Nazi Germany,* this well-written and fast-paced book will give a clear picture of how tyranny controls its own. Chronology. Ages 11–15.

Senesh, Hannah. Hannah Senesh: Her Life and Diary. Trans. Marta Cohn. Schocken, 1972. $4.95 pb.
Called the Joan of Arc of Israel, Senesh was tortured and murdered by the Nazis at the age of twenty-three for her Jewish rescue activities. A poet and a highly spirited Zionist, Hannah had a unique personality that comes through in this fine book. Catherine Senesh has edited her daughter's works (written between ages 13 and 21) and has added her own descriptions of Hannah's early life and tragic death. Teenagers who were moved by Anne Frank's spirit might like meeting another young woman of similar nobility. Photographs. Ages 13+.

Singer, Isaac Bashevis. A Day of Pleasure: Stories of a Boy Growing Up in Warsaw. Photos by Roman Vishniac. FS&G, 1963. $8.95; $5.95 pb.
Nineteen stories about the author's boyhood, five of which have not appeared in a previous publication. The destroyed world of East European Jewry is beautifully described with humor, sympathy, and a good story line. A lovely choice for reading aloud, Singer's reminiscences of life in Warsaw will keep the whole family or classroom amused and interested. Handsome black-and-white photographs of Warsaw's streets and Jewish population enhance the rich flavor of this literary memoir. Ages 10+.

Zemach, Margot. Self-portrait: Margot Zemach. See chapter 5, Fine Arts and Domestic Arts: Art History Books.

Ziemian, Joseph. The Cigarette Sellers of Three Crosses Square. Trans. Janina David. Lerner, 1975. $6.95; $1.50 pb., Avon.

Written by a Jewish Resistance fighter, this is the memorable account of a group of Jewish girls and boys who managed to escape the harrowing Warsaw Ghetto and evade Nazi persecution on the Aryan side of Warsaw by begging, hiding, and employing brilliant survival tactics. Stranger than fiction and just as gripping, Ziemian's detailed and honest narrative will be remembered by the reader for a long time. Ages 12+.

Reference Aids

In addition to the encyclopedias mentioned in chapter 6, History Books: General History, the following titles will help children locate additional information on well-known Jews.

Commire, Anne, ed. Something About the Author: Facts and Pictures About Contemporary Authors and Illustrators of Books for Young People. Gale, 1971–. 17 vols. $34.00 each.

For children and adults wanting to know more about their favorite author or illustrator than the dust jackets tell, this appealing and informative set of reference books provides some personal and professional data as well as lovely photographs of the subjects and their work.

Silverman, Judith. Index to Collective Biographies for Young Readers: Elementary and Junior High School Level. Bowker, 1979 (3rd ed.). $19.95.

Many entries of Jewish subjects discussed in a large variety of collective juvenile biographies can be found in this book's index.

5

Fine Arts and Domestic Arts

Art history is not a subject that is in great demand by youngsters. Perhaps this is why there are so few suitable books on the topic. However, the many lovely picture books available in libraries do meet some of the needs of children. Very few juvenile art histories hold the attention of the average child. Doubleday's "Art for Children" series, written by Ernest Raboff, is the only project I have seen that truly communicates the meaning and relevance of art to the elementary school child. Fortunately, one Jewish artist, Marc Chagall, is represented in this series.

There are very few titles on art that are for or by children. Some deal with children's art as a response to specific political situations, others are collections of paintings by children inspired by the Old Testament, and a few titles are by or about individual artists. There is very little written specifically for children on ancient art, manuscript design, religious and synagogue decoration, skilled folk crafts, and modern and Israeli Jewish art. Some adult titles have been added to this chapter to fill these gaps.

The Bible's stern prohibition against creating images of man or beast has had a great influence on Jewish art through the ages, and until the mid-1800s, Judaism's relationship to art was ambivalent to say the least. It is interesting to note that Marc Chagall's famous stained-glass windows that adorn the synagogue at the Hebrew University Medical Center do not depict the human form in any of the twelve interpretations of the tribes of Israel.

Although there are very few Jewish art history books for children, this bibliography refers the reader to beautifully illustrated picture books that depict Jewish life and culture. Such artists as Uri Shulevitz, Shay Reiger, Margot Zemach, and Ben Shahn will reach children who enjoy fine art but who would not otherwise concern themselves with nonfictional art histories. For a detailed survey of notable Jewish artists, see the *Encyclopedia Judaica.*

As a child, I used to think that the most perfect form of home art in the Jewish family was cleaning. Newspapers and plastic covers were the materials, and endless polishes and rags were the tools. The children's books in this chapter suggest other means of enhancing the Jewish home.

The craft projects in these titles revolve around the Jewish calendar, offering information on the holidays as well as craft ideas. Each Jewish celebration is characterized by its own unique symbols and rituals. For instance, the lighting of the Sabbath candles on Friday evening gives rise to suggestions for making candlestick holders from spools and blocks, empty tuna cans, and baby food jars filled with colored sand. Children make cups to hold the wine needed for Kiddush (Sabbath blessing), menorot (candlestick holders) to hold the eight candles of Hanukkah, and kippot (skullcaps) worn by Jewish males.

Some of the titles reviewed suggest ways to decorate the house for a holiday: for example, how to make a tree streamer for Tu Bi-Shevat (the New Year of the Trees) or placemats adorned with the shield of Judah Maccabee for the Hanukkah party table.

Many craft ideas are not directly related to Judaism but are suggested as extensions of holiday themes; for example, instructions are given on how to make a cardboard horse like the one Mordecai rode in the story of Purim, or a harvest collage made with dried beans and magazine pictures in honor of Sukkot (an autumn holiday).

It is especially clear from these last two examples that exciting craft books which are not specifically Jewish in content should be examined closely for ideas. The clever instructor or parent can adapt projects to fit many purposes. For instance, Shari Lewis and Laura Ross have some excellent guides on how to make puppets and put on puppet plays. Their material can be adapted to fit puppets representing various nationalities.

There are several Jewish craft books for each different age level. Teachers working with preschool through first grade depend heavily on craft projects to entertain and educate children who are too young for academic studies. Ruth Esrig Brinn's *Let's Celebrate: 57 Jewish Holiday Crafts for Young Children* is a practical aid for the adult working with young students. The projects are simple and varied.

Children who are in the second to fourth grades are ready for projects that need adult supervision rather than step-by-step aid. Some recommended titles for this age group are *The Jewish Holiday*

Book (Wendy Lazar), containing recipes, games, and crafts; *The Jewish Holiday Do-Book* (Lois Englander) with its wide variety of activities; and *Crafts for the Jewish Child* (Ruth Ginsberg), which gives the seven- and eight-year-old a chance to follow through directions on his or her own.

By the time a child reaches ten, the school curriculum devotes less time to arts and crafts and the interested child must seek art experience in after-school classes, recreation centers, or home projects. Susan Purdy's attractive titles (reviewed here) will encourage children to maintain their interest in the creative arts. Graduates of the Purdy books might try Joyce Becker's *Jewish Holiday Crafts,* recommended for a junior high school to senior citizen audience.

People responsible for craft programs for children will benefit from Ruth Sharon's two-volume *Arts and Crafts the Year Round,* and teenagers and adults with a talent for fine craftsmanship will relish the titles by Mae Shafter Rockland.

Although many craft books contain a few recipes associated with Jewish holidays, the serious young cook will be offered a greater selection from the cookbooks reviewed here. Chaya Burstein's *A First Jewish Holiday Cookbook* and Susan Purdy's *Jewish Holiday Cookbook* (more advanced) teach international Jewish cooking and introduce youngsters to the rules of kosher cuisine.

In addition to the pleasure these craft and culinary titles provide, they enable children to experience Judaic customs and rituals as creative and informed participants.

Art History Books

Coen, Rena Neumann. The Old Testament in Art. Lerner, 1970. $4.95.

Many great artists have been inspired by the Torah, and Dr. Coen presents fifty varied creations with biblical themes. Each painting, engraving, sculpture, or other work informs us about the artist, the technique, and the biblical event. The art is universal and covers many centuries and media. The writing is clear and easy to understand. Most of the art is reproduced in black and white, with some color plates. Because of the Second Commandment, fewer Jewish artists are represented here than the reader might expect, but Coen does say that there were Jews nonetheless who were inspired to depict their relationship with God and their ethical responsibilities to each other. The young art student will appreciate this book, although the predominance of black-and-white reproductions might make the title less appealing to the average reader. Ages 11–16.

Avi-Yonah, Michael, supervisor. Lerner Archeology Series. Retold for young people by Richard Currier, Ph.D. Lerner Pubn, 1974–1977. 10 vols. $7.95 each.
This series on basic concepts of archeology was written by Israeli archeologists under the supervision of Avi-Yonah, a professor at the Hebrew University. Rewritten for a juvenile audience by an American anthropologist, these easy to understand, slim volumes contain many full-color and black-and-white photographs. Although the contents are not exclusively concerned with Jewish themes, the information on various aspects of ancient Hebrew life will fill in many gaps. The authors and titles are as follows: Michael Avi-Yonah: *Search for the Past; Ancient Scrolls; The Art of Mosaics;* Arthur Segal: *City Planning in Ancient Times;* Ya'akov Meshorer: *Coins of the Ancient World;* Avraham Ronem: *Introducing Prehistory;* Elisher Linder: *Introducing Underwater Archeology;* Renate Rosenthal: *Jewelry of the Ancient World;* Rivka Gonen: *Pottery in Ancient Times; Weapons and Warfare in Ancient Times.* Ages 10+.

Dayan, Ruth, with **Wilburt Feinberg.** Crafts of Israel. Macmillan, 1974. $16.95.
This adult title can be used by older children with an interest in art. Dayan's beautiful book, with over 300 large photographs (many in color), explores a variety of Israeli crafts from ancient to contemporary times. Covering such media as gold and silver, clay and earth, and threads and fibers, the book reveals the diverse talents of a truly international culture. The appealing format makes this a fascinating addition to the home or public/private library collection. Ages 11+.

Freund, Miriam. Jewels for a Crown: The Story of the Marc Chagall Windows. McGraw, 1963. O.P.
Marc Chagall was seventy-two when he was commissioned by Hadassah to create twelve stained-glass windows for the synagogue of the Hebrew University Medical Center. The book describes Chagall's technical process, interprets the meaning of the artist's designs, and provides bright reproductions of the windows. For his theme, Chagall chose the twelve tribes of Israel, making this book useful both for art and Bible studies. Children will especially love the Levi window, "the Golden Rule in golden glass," in which the Sabbath and the Ten Commandments are bathed in a flood of bright yellow glory. Ages 10+.

Greenfeld, Howard. Marc Chagall. See chapter 4, Biographies: Individual Biographies.

L'Engle, Madeleine. Ladder of Angels, Scenes from the Bible Illustrated by Children of the World. See chapter 3, The Bible: Bible Stories.

Matek, Ord. The Bible Through Stamps. KTAV, 1974. $7.50.
Matek leads a chronological tour of the Bible as it is reflected in the world's postage stamps. We learn about the nationality of each stamp (reproduced in black and white), its date of issue, and its commemorative event. If the stamp is a reprint of a famous work of art, information about the artist is also given. In addition, the author provides the biblical passage appropriate to each stamp, as well as some biblical, legendary, or historical background information. Although many of the subjects depicted on the stamps come from Israel, the book is universal in scope. The stamps represented were issued between 1940 and 1971. A lovely gift and a fine addition to any library collection. Bibliography, index. Ages 11+.

Mazar, Benjamin, and **Michael Avi-Yonah.** Illustrated World of the Bible. See chapter 3, The Bible: Exploration of Biblical Themes.

Raboff, Ernest. Marc Chagall. "Art for Children" Series. Doubleday, 1968. $6.95.
"Art for Children" is a unique series written by Ernest Raboff and edited by Bradley Smith. The book on Marc Chagall describes the artist's life, designs, and philosophy in a way young children can understand. The handwritten text in colorful print and the abundant color reproductions create a lively format. Not only will a child gain appreciation for Chagall's work, but she or he will also discover that art need not reproduce the visible (or even the logical) to be deemed worthy. Ages 10+; younger for reading aloud.

Rieger, Shay. Our Family. Lothrop, 1972. $7.75.
Portraying her large family in clay, stone, and bronze, and adding a lovely narrative, the sculptor introduces us to her European-born family and shares their religious and daily experiences with us. Through these graceful works, which will appeal to children because of their simple lines and sense of humor, we learn about the Jewish family and about one artist's technique and approach. Photographs. Ages 7+.

Shechori, Ran. Art in Israel. Photos by Israel Zafrir. Schocken, 1976. $10.00.
An adult title that can be used with children who have an interest in the fine arts. Containing 148 photographs (many in color) of twentieth-century paintings and sculpture, the book also includes an in-

formative introduction and biographical notes. The plates contain a variety of styles and moods. Ages 11+.

Volavkova, Hanna, ed. I Never Saw Another Butterfly: Children's Drawings and Poems from Terezin Concentration Camp, 1942–1944. See chapter 9, Literature: Folk Tales and Anthologies.

Zemach, Margot. Self-Portrait: Margot Zemach. Illus. by author. "Self-Portrait Collection" Series. A-W, 1978. $7.95.
Margot Zemach was born in 1931 and grew up in theatrical circles. Her book reflects on life with her four daughters and late author-husband, Harve Zemach. Ms. Zemach is the illustrator of many Jewish children's stories written by Isaac Bashevis Singer, Yuri Suhl, and herself. In this self-portrait, Zemach's book characters mingle like invited ghosts among the family scenes. Children will enjoy recognizing familiar book characters who are identified on the page or in notes at the back. As in her marvelous picture books and children's story collections, Zemach's illustrations are colorful, lively, humorous, and pleasantly dreamlike and homey. Children's-book lovers will enjoy sharing this title with youngsters. Ages 9+.

Zim, Jacob, ed. My Shalom, My Peace: Paintings and Poems by Jewish and Arab Children. See chapter 9, Literature: Folk Tales and Anthologies.

Domestic Arts Books

Abramson, Lillian. The Jewish Holiday Party Book. Bloch, 1966. $3.50.
Judaism offers numerous occasions for children's parties. Abramson provides the inspiration and information to get the festivities off the ground. For each of the twelve celebrations (including one that honors the new moon, Rosh Hodesh), the author includes appropriate party invitations, decorations, favors, menus, games, and activities. She also provides background information on each holiday and a useful chapter on making party hats. A handy guide that can be used by teachers, parents, and children. Glossary. Ages 8–12.

Beckelman, Florence, and **Lorraine Dreiblatt.** Some Things Special for Shabbat: A Craft Book for Children. Illus. Mary Warren. Ricwalt, 1978. $8.95 pb.
A large selection of craft projects that will enable children to create holiday objects to be used at home for the Sabbath. The text, written on the elementary-school age level and containing intermediate-level projects, is accompanied by attractive illustrations and stencils. Be-

cause the projects often call for the use of messy materials—spray paint is common—the book is most appropriate for school or camp use. Ages 9–14.

Becker, Joyce. Jewish Holiday Crafts. Illus. by author. Bonim, 1977. $9.95; $6.95 pb.
A good collection of Jewish crafts for families in which adults and children work together, especially recommended for the older child who has access to adult encouragement and to a variety of materials (e.g., wood, tile and tub cork, and masonite). There are a brief introduction to thirteen holidays and more than 200 craft ideas to help celebrate them. Recommended for home and general library collections. (Note: See also Becker's *Hanukkah Crafts,* Bonim, 1978, $9.95; $6.95 pb., for another craft title on the same level but centering on Hanukkah. Some craft projects, however, have a very loose connection with the holiday.) Ages 12+.

Brin, Ruth F. The Shabbat Catalogue. Illus. Ruthann Isaacson. KTAV, 1978. $4.00 pb.
Brin's book is the result of the experimental project, "Shabbat Shalom," sponsored by an American Jewish community center in the hope of enhancing the home celebration of the Sabbath. It is a fine resource for this holiday: stories for children, dialogues explaining customs, craft and game ideas, recipes, songs, blessings, and ceremonies that lay a foundation for Sabbath traditions. The book's stories, especially the one in which Isaac is renamed "Chuckles," are uninspired. Ages 9+.

Brinn, Ruth Esrig. Let's Celebrate! 57 Jewish Holiday Crafts for Young Children. Illus. Stephanie Mensh. Kar-Ben, 1977. $3.50 pb.
A well-planned, well-illustrated, and simple craft guide for very young children. Centering on twelve holidays and featuring art associated with the festivities, the book relies on inexpensive notions and scraps found in kitchen and desk drawers. Children over eight will manage nicely on their own; parents will need to supervise the preschool set. Ages 4–10.

Burstein, Chaya. A First Jewish Holiday Cookbook. Illus. by author. Bonim, 1979. $8.95; $5.95 pb.
Ninety recipes for thirteen Jewish holidays. Burstein offers a brief introduction to each festival as well as hints on kitchen safety, skills, and kosher cooking. Her clearly written and well-illustrated recipes have an international flavor: Pescado A La Greca (Sephardic gefilte fish), Yom Tov Roly-Poly from the U.S.A. (meatballs and mazzah balls), Soomsoom Bars from Israel (crunchy candy), and a host of

traditional East European dishes. Burstein's humorous drawings and commentaries are aimed at a young audience learning how to cook and follow directions. Less advanced than the Purdy title reviewed here, this attractive cookbook will appeal to youngsters. Ages 11+; younger with adult help.

Drucker, Malka. Hanukkah: Eight Nights, Eight Lights. See chapter 7, Jewish Holidays.

Englander, Lois, and others. The Jewish Holiday Do-Book. Illus. Gail Kansky. Bloch, 1977 (rev. ed.). $9.95; $6.95 pb.
Cut, draw, paste, sing, dance, and play your way through ten Jewish holidays. Englander and her colleagues have created a large, lucid, and appealing resource for teachers, parents, and children. The uniqueness of this title is its simple original dances and easy-to-play music with accompanying lyrics. The activities are recommended for preschool through elementary school children. This is a treasure chest very much worth discovering. Ages 4–12.

Ginsberg, Ruth. Crafts for the Jewish Child. Illus. Aby Frishman. Shulsinger Bros., 1976. $5.00.
In a slim format geared for children five to ten, this guide suggests seventeen projects for five well-known holidays. Inexpensive materials found around the house and easy-to-understand instructions make this book suitable for children over seven who need little adult supervision. It is a second choice to Ruth Esrig Brinn's title (reviewed here), which is on a similar level and has many more ideas for less money. Ages 4–10.

Lazar, Wendy. The Jewish Holiday Book. Illus. Marion Behr. Doubleday, 1977. $8.95.
Lazar informs the reader about twelve Jewish holidays and includes recipes, games, and craft ideas to help celebrate them. The instructions for these relatively simple projects are clear and call for inexpensive everyday materials. An appealing format and attractive illustrations add to the spirit of creativity. The level of these crafts is somewhere between Ruth E. Brinn's title and Susan Purdy's books (reviewed here). Ages 8–12; younger with adult help.

Purdy, Susan. Festivals for You to Celebrate: Facts, Activities, and Crafts. Illus. by author. Lippincott, 1969. O.P.
This title is international in scope. From "Chad Gaya" (Passover song) mobiles to Welsh love spoons, Purdy includes projects for thirty holidays, five of which are Jewish. She contributes a good introduction to each holiday, craft ideas using a variety of media, and clearly

written instructions. This is one of the very few titles including worldwide holiday crafts. Because of the high creative levels of the crafts, children will be inspired to borrow other holiday ideas for their own celebrations, e.g., the Halloween foil mask would be useful for a Purim costume party. Indexes, bibliography. Ages 9–13; younger with adult help.

Purdy, Susan Gold. Jewish Holidays: Facts, Activities, and Crafts. Illus. by author. Lippincott, 1969. $8.95.
The meaning of each of sixteen holidays is introduced along with one to three craft ideas. Various media are employed—clay, yarn, cardboard—and there are even a few recipes. The projects vary in difficulty, and the format is appealing, with yellow, green, and blue illustrations. There is good detail in the introductions to the holidays. The crafts require more skill than Brinn's *Let's Celebrate* and less than Becker's titles (reviewed here). Index. Ages 10–13.

Purdy, Susan Gold. Jewish Holiday Cookbook. Illus. by author. "A Holiday Cookbook" Series. Watts, 1979. $6.90; $2.95 pb.
Thirty-five recipes for eleven Jewish holidays. Information on holidays and clear instructions for making a great variety of kosher dishes are given—e.g., Grandpa Harry's Eggs and Tsibeles, Aunt Belle's Rugalach, and Anne Sternberger's Mandlebrot. There is also a lesson on basic skills, measurements, and kosher cooking. Parents who want to cook with children will find this an appealing, well-designed guide. Index. Ages 10+.

Rockland, Mae Shafter. The Hanukkah Book. Schocken, 1975. $4.95
Ms. Rockland's books show a creative artistic talent, an orderly, informative, and friendly writing style, and a deep love for Judaism. This title is a fine resource for adults who want to make Hanukkah an artistic (as well as a religious) event for themselves and for children. Included are sections concerning the origin and evolution of Hanukkah, a history of the menorah, and many home activities: music, decorations, menus, games, gifts, and Hebrew alphabet crafts. The art projects are much more ambitious than those found in the other titles reviewed here and require that readers have a definite interest in sewing and art. It is a beautiful book with many photographs and a well-organized text. Index. (Note: Rockland's other craft and folk art titles will also inspire adults who work with children: *The Work of Our Hands: Jewish Needlecraft for Today,* Schocken, 1973, $10; $5.95 pb.; *The Jewish Party Book,* 1978, $14.95; and *The New Jewish Yellow Pages,* SBS, 1980, rev. ed., $8.95 pb.) Ages: See review.

Sharon, Ruth. Arts and Crafts the Year Round. Illus. by author. United Syn Bk, 1965. 2 vols. $29.00 set.

This hefty (800-page) two-volume set of Jewish craft ideas was prepared for the Hebrew school teacher, recreation leader, and industrious parent. The author, who has an extensive arts and crafts background, selected projects to foster both "a meaningful participation in Jewish events, and creativity." The projects are for a wide range of age levels, techniques, and subject matter. Volume 1 is arranged by holiday, and because many of the craft ideas (e.g., puppets) can be adapted for any event, the detailed subject indexes are an important feature. Volume 2 is concerned with the school and camp curriculum: learning Hebrew, books, music, history, etc. Ages 10–15.

Reference Aid

Rockland, Mae Shafter, and **Dona Rosenblatt.** "Crafts and Folk Art." The Second Jewish Catalog. Jewish Pubn, 1976, pp. 320–336. What makes Jewish crafts and folk art Jewish? Recommended techniques, designs, and background information are offered here.

History Books

Books on Jewish history for children reflect the vicissitudes of Jewish life. In fact, one important aim in writing juvenile Jewish history is to create a balanced perspective that does not concentrate exclusively on the tragedies experienced by the Jews.

There are two excellent general works of history that reflect this balance. *The Sand and the Stars* (Meir and Diana Gillon) retells Jewish history from the time of Abraham to the rebirth of Israel; its authors record the glorious years as well as the forced exiles. *The Jewish History Atlas* (Martin Gilbert) illustrates the worldwide migration of the Jews from ancient to modern times. During his research, Gilbert was pained to discover the unceasing and irrational persecution of the Jew. He determined to search for a countering aspect of Jewish history and his cartography reveals this.

The books on ancient history are mostly concerned with biblical and archeological themes. Isaac Asimov has written a lucid account of Canaan before, during, and after Hebrew rule (*The Land of Canaan*). There are good books on Massadah (70 C.E.) and some titles on everyday life in biblical times. The multivolume reference set by Benjamin Mazar and Michael Avi-Yonah, *Illustrated World of the Bible*, contains a great deal of information on life in ancient times.

European Jewish history, which spans nineteen centuries, is discussed briefly in general Jewish history books. There is not much information on medieval through seventeenth-century Jewish history. Sulamith Ish-Kishor offers two fictional works dealing with Jews in old Europe, *The Master of Miracles* and *A Boy of Old Prague*. Ghettoized and persecuted, Ish-Kishor's Jewish characters expose children to a dark period of Jewish history. Although the Jews enjoyed approximately five centuries of what came to be called the Golden Age in Spain, ending with their expulsion in the late fifteenth century, there is no nonfiction work for children on this period.

Two books exist on East European shtetl life. Milton Meltzer, who writes outstanding history books for children, covers the period from the sixteenth through the early twentieth century in Eastern European Jewish history. His book *World of Our Fathers: The Jews of Eastern Europe* includes some firsthand accounts of the period that add a personal touch to the history and thereby lighten the undeniably bleak facts. *The Shtetl Book* by Diane and David Roskies offers detailed information on daily small-town living between 1800 and 1914 for older children.

There are very few children's books in print that trace the history of Jews in individual countries other than the United States and Israel. Soviet Jewry is discussed in some detail in *Soviet Dissent: Intellectuals, Jews, and Détente* by Albert Axelbank, but books about South and Central American Jewry, Asian and African Jewry (including the Falashas, black Jews) are sadly lacking.

The most written-about era in European Jewish history is the Nazi Holocaust. The books reviewed in this chapter that are concerned with this period fall into two categories: The first deals with the general history of Adolf Hitler and the Third Reich, while the second focuses on Nazi crimes against the Jewish people. Books that record the rise of Nazism are usually less harrowing than ones about Jewish genocide. The more general titles can be used with slightly younger children as an introduction to the Holocaust. A good first title for the child of ten to fourteen is William Shirer's *Rise and Fall of Adolf Hitler*. Several additional books on Nazism are available for the sixth-grader and the older child.

Three books provide an overview of Hitler's persecution of European Jews. Of these, Bea Stadtler's *The Holocaust: A History of Courage and Resistance* is the most appropriate introductory work for the younger child (ages eleven to fourteen). The author emphasizes Jewish resistance to Nazi force by focusing on a number of people who retained their dignity, courage, and humanity in the face of dire consequences. The most memorable book is Milton Meltzer's *Never to Forget: The Jews of the Holocaust*. Focusing on the human experience as well as recounting facts and statistics, Meltzer records the heinous crimes and the acts of heroism that existed side by side. His inclusion of firsthand accounts, such as memoirs, poetry, and ballads, personalizes the history and increases its appeal to young readers. This is a book for anyone twelve years old and older who wants a suitable introduction to this subject. Altschuler's *Hitler's War Against the Jews* is based on a powerful adult work by Lucy Davidowicz. Although Altschuler's book contains much detailed information on German anti-Semitism culminating in the Holocaust, the photographs of victims, of anti-Semitic cartoons, posters, and even games, might prove too graphic. It is not a book for the youngster first becoming aware of the torture and murder of six million Jews.

Many works about the Holocaust can also be found in other chapters in this guide. There are fine works of fiction that can expand the child's knowledge and sympathies on a reading and content level he can handle. Several novels are appropriate for readers as young as nine or ten. In addition, most of the autobiographies reviewed in chapter 4 were written by survivors of the Holocaust. These memoirs and diaries are among the most poignant and widely read books on the subject. Lastly, the subject index lists collections of literary and historical essays, poetry, and art work that deal with the Holocaust.

Moving from Europe across the Atlantic, one finds a body of material documenting Jewish life in America. These books are on the whole disappointing. Most begin with Columbus' journey (he traveled with a group of newly exiled Spanish Jews) and end with a roll call of celebrities of the 1960s. (The contributions of Jewish women are limited to a few names, such as Rebecca Gratz, who seems to be the Jewish answer to Betsy Ross). Historian Milton Meltzer has contributed the most thought-provoking books in this section. In addition, the biographies of American Jews in many different professions (reviewed in chapter 4) also serve to shed some light on the history of American Jewry.

Since the creation of the state of Israel in 1948, children's Jewish literature has tended to focus on various aspects of Israeli life. Kibbutz living, animal preservation, technology, politics, military feats, the Arab-Israeli conflict, Israeli social life, and travel in Israel are among the subjects discussed in these books. Unfortunately, none of the books on Israel deals adequately with the Palestinian issue. Only by reading many sources does a less-than-muddy picture finally emerge. Authors tiptoe around the issue, offering sympathy to all and clarity to none.

Travel and general survey books constitute a subsection of the books on Israeli history. These titles, published by major trade houses, are only infrequently revised and thus few are correct enough for students interested in recent developments. Several of the books reviewed are out of date but are included because they have unique qualities that are not duplicated elsewhere. For example, Miroslav Sasek's *This Is Israel* was written in 1962, yet nowhere else can a very young reader find such an attractive introduction to the Jewish and Christian landmarks of the Holy Land. Many of these older titles help create foundations that can be updated by magazine and newspaper articles.

The subject of Zionism is inseparable from the history of the Jewish people and the study of modern Israel. There are several fine children's books that examine the historical, political, and religious aspects of Zionism. Robert Goldston's *Next Year in Jerusalem* traces the Jews' longing for Zion (Israel) from the time of Abraham, through centuries of persecution, to the emergence of the World Zionist Organization and the rebirth of Israel.

Several of the books reviewed in this guide discuss the political conflicts that emerged with Theodor Herzl's determination to rebuild a Jewish homeland. Harry Ellis, author of *Israel: One Land, Two People,* offers an objective history of the Arab-Israeli conflict.

The discussion of Zionism in children's literature can also be found in the biographies of people whose lives were dedicated to the Jewish state. Colonel Micky Marcus, David Ben-Gurion, Golda Meir, Chaim Weizmann, and Louis Brandeis are some of the Zionists whose stories are reviewed in chapter 4.

The theme of the Jews' longing for Israel is not limited to children's history books. Holiday titles, theological discussions, Bible stories, fiction, etc., all touch upon the desire for a safe and free Jewish homeland.

The books in this chapter are arranged as follows: General History, American History, European History, Israeli History. Books about Israel are further divided: Ancient History, General History and Politics, and Social Life, Description, and Travel. Several reference works, such as children's encyclopedias and articles, are listed in the Reference Aids sections at the close of the General, European, and Israeli History sections.

General History Books

Bamberger, David. My People: Abba Eban's History of the Jews. Behrman, 1978–79. 2 vols. $5.95 pb. each.
Textbook history is made as attractive as possible in this appealing, colorful format with watercolor drawings, photographs, and maps. The books are adapted from Abba Eban's large work *My People* (Random, 1968) and present a clear account of Jewish history. Volume 1 covers the beginnings in the ancient world to the period before the American Revolution. Volume 2 focuses on the years from 1789 to the present. Glossary, index. Ages 11+.

Eldad, Dr. Israel, ed. Chronicles: News of the Past. Dist. Ya-El, c. 1954. 3 vols. $6.25 each.
With headlines like "We Quit Egypt Today," Eldad is sure to get the attention of youngsters who will enjoy seeing biblical events and later

history re-created in newspaper form. Although the print is small, the profuse illustrations and dramatic style will make browsing through the Chronicles enjoyable. Vol. 1: In the Days of the Bible; vol. 2: The Second Temple—Rise of Christianity; vol. 3: The Dawn of Redemption—from the Crusades to Herzl. Ages 10+.

Gilbert, Martin. Jewish History Atlas. Cartography by Arthur Banks and T. A. Bicknell. Macmillan, 1977 (rev. ed.). $8.95; $4.95 pb.
One hundred and twenty-one maps record the worldwide and diverse path of Jewish migration from ancient Mesopotamia to modern Israel. The clearly drawn black-and-white maps include enlightening and often fascinating information about the experiences of Jews in many countries. Gilbert had hoped to report a more cheerful journey, but, he says, "As my research into Jewish history progressed, I was surprised, depressed, and to some extent overwhelmed by the perpetual and irrational violence which pursued the Jews in every century and to almost every corner of the globe." He thus searched even harder for the other side of the coin—and found it. An important work for the study of Jewish history. Bibliography. Ages 12+.

Gillon, Meir, and **Diana Gillon.** The Sand and the Stars: The Story of the Jewish People. Lothrop, 1971. $6.96.
A smoothly written and informative survey of Jewish history. The authors do not ignore the excruciating moments in Jewish history, but they also devote ample space to Jewish victories. Stories of how Jews aided great civilizations by their accomplishments in commerce and scholarship, in addition to Judaism's influence on world religions, are related. The birth of Israel is another important achievement. The Gillons emphasize Judaism's repeatedly tragic relationship with non-Jewish powers and the Jews' striving to make a place in the world for their beliefs and talents. Ages 11+.

Goldston, Robert. Next Year in Jerusalem: A Short History of Zionism. Little, 1977. $7.95.
A highly readable and touching survey of Zionism, from Abraham's wanderings to the establishment of modern Israel in 1948. Goldston launches his history with the 1975 United Nations resolution that equated Zionism with racism. He attempts to prove that Zionism is not an isolated nationalistic movement but rather an integral part of Judaism from its very beginnings. His brief and informative chapters, which highlight Jewish history, provide insights into historical events and individuals. Written from a subjective viewpoint, the book nonetheless offers enough facts and details to substantiate the author's claim that the Jews have an absolute need for a safe Jewish homeland. Bibliography, index. Ages 12+.

Lehman, Emil. Israel: Idea and Reality. United Syn Bk, 1965 (rev. ed.). $3.95.

This textbook on the history of Zionism was prepared by a Jewish publisher for use in Jewish schools, but its format and content make it appropriate for a larger audience. Lehman traces the history of the Jews from the time of the Babylonian Exile to the emergence of modern Israel. Emphasis is put on the persons and events that made Zionism an urgent political movement as well as a religious and cultural one. The book differs from Goldston's title (see above) in that Lehman gives more detail of the development of the twentieth-century Zionist movement and modern Israel. Goldston's title is more up to date and is also more of a general history of the Jewish people. Photographs, index. Ages 12+.

Reference Aids

The following reference books can be used by the student needing brief information on a large variety of Jewish topics. The books feature short articles, large print, and many illustrations and photographs. Only up-to-date volumes have been included.

Ben-Asher, Naomi, and **Hayim Leaf.** The Junior Jewish Encyclopedia. Shengold, 1979 (9th ed.). $12.95.

A comprehensive and readable volume that emphasizes contemporary Jewry. Ages 10–16.

Bridger, David, and **Samuel Wolk.** The New Jewish Encyclopedia. Behrman, 1976 (rev. ed.). $12.95.

A one-volume work aimed at reaching the entire family in its survey of Jewish culture and life. Ages 13+.

Posner, Raphel, ed. My Jewish World: The Encyclopedia Judaica for Youth. Dist. KTAV, 1975. 6 vols. $42.50.

A very appealing multivolume adaptation for children of the renowned *Encyclopedia Judaica*. Ages 8–15.

American History Books

Butwin, Frances. The Jews in America. "In America" Series. Lerner. 1969. $5.95.

Butwin traces the history of American Jewry from the colonial settlements to the present. Like other authors of this genre (Karp, Kurtis, Suhl), Butwin describes the early American arrivals, the immigrants from Germany and Russia (1820–1880), the Jews from Eastern Europe (1880–1924), and well-known twentieth-century figures. The book is adequately written, if not thought-provoking or terribly original. The accompanying photographs are a bit dark and give the book a dingy appearance. Index. Ages 10–12.

Karp, Deborah. Heroes of American Jewish History. KTAV, 1972 (rev. ed.). $5.00 pb.
A well-organized and nicely illustrated history of Jewish life in America. Highlighting the masses who struggled here as strangers as well as the extraordinary individuals whose names live on forever, Karp covers 300 years of American Jewry. The book emphasizes the hardships and anti-Semitism experienced by many immigrants. Fictional dialogue mingles with hard facts, and both are illustrated with prints, photos, and drawings. More detailed than the Butwin and Kurtis titles reviewed here, Karp's book is recommended as an aid for reference work and reports. Glossary, index. Ages 10–13.

Kurtis, Arlene Harris. The Jews Helped Build America. "Helped Build America" Series. Messner, 1970. $4.64.
This easy-to-read history of Jewish settlement in America is accompanied by black-and-white photographs. The reader follows the journey of a fictional family which leaves early-twentieth-century Russia for a new life in New York City. Kurtis includes chapters on their ancient heritage, the religion and holidays, and the daily home, school, and working life of the Jewish American. The book ends with the familiar roll call of famous Jewish Americans. Unmemorable but easy to digest. Ages 9–12.

Meltzer, Milton. Remember the Days: A Short History of the Jewish American. Illus. Harvey Dinnerstein. Doubleday, 1974. O.P.; $2.50 pb.
Tracing the history of the Jews in America from 1654 to the present, Meltzer emphasizes their minority status and the disadvantages it often brings. He also touches briefly on world mistreatment of Jews and its effect on American immigration laws, the birth of Israel, and a comparison of the status of Jews with that of other minorities, especially blacks. Brief (110 pages), succinct, and warmly written, Meltzer's book rings out with the voice of the humanist-historian. There are also attractive charcoal drawings and an index. Ages 11–16.

Meltzer, Milton. Taking Root: Jewish Immigrants in America. FS&G, 1976. $7.95; $1.25 pb., Dell.
A highly readable account of Jewish immigration to the United States between the 1880s and the 1920s. Both the old way of life in Europe (why Jews left) and the new life style in America (especially New York City) are described in this compassionate narrative, which

combines a lucid text with original sources, including poetry and song lyrics. Meltzer ends this social history with two warnings: that the survival of each American minority depends on the survival of all minority groups; and that only when American democracy is liberal and progressive will Jews thrive. Photographs, prints, bibliography, and index. Ages 12+.

Suhl, Yuri. An Album of Jews in America. Watts, 1972. $5.90.
Tracing the contributions of Jews in America from 1492 to the present, Suhl stresses the hardships as well as the successes. His smoothly written narrative and the accompanying photographs and prints highlight the landmarks of Jewish religious, economical, political, and cultural life in the United States. Suhl turns an additional spotlight on the achievements of individuals in three centuries of Jewish-American life. The oversized format is packed with eye-opening views into the recent past. Index. Ages 10+.

European History Books

Altschuler, David A. Hitler's War Against the Jews. Behrman, 1978. $8.95; $4.95 pb.
This detailed history of German anti-Semitism culminating with the Holocaust is a young reader's version of Lucy S. Davidowicz's *War Against the Jews* (HR&W, 1975). This is a painful book to look at because of its many startling photographs: anti-Semitic toys, Jewish orphans staring blankly at the camera, piles of confiscated wedding rings, bodies burning in an open fire, and much more. The small print might also discourage some readers. In addition to the facts, Altschuler discusses questions of morality and values concerning Nazi philosophy and crimes. The author also talks about acts of resistance and provides original source material. This is an important book which perhaps presents just too much disturbing material in one volume. Index. Ages 12+; not for every child.

Axelbank, Albert. Soviet Dissent: Intellectuals, Jews, and Détente. Watts, 1975. $5.95.
Using individuals as examples, statistics, quotes, and his own conclusions, Axelbank discusses the suppression of free thinking in the U.S.S.R. He traces the following topics: the story of Solzhenitsyn's political conflict with Soviet authority as well as those of Sakharov (scientist and civil rights champion); the worsening scene for Jews; ballet rebels; and the effect of dissent on détente. Things have grown worse (especially for Jews) since the book was published, but the author provides a readable account of protest in a land that has no use

for second opinions. Bibliography, photographs, and index. Ages 12+.

Forman, James. Code Name Valkyrie: Count von Stauffenberg and the Plot to Kill Hitler. S G Phillips, 1973. $9.95; $1.25 pb., Dell.

Forman, an expert on Nazi Germany, must have been so elated to find a decent German general that he wrote a compelling history of the man's elaborate but unsuccessful attempt to blow up Adolf Hitler. It is a romantic story: a badly deformed (in combat), repentant soldier, and devoted family man decided that a shred of German honor would be saved if he could wipe out the ferocious Fuehrer. This is a fascinating, detailed look at the Count's difficult mission and of the consequences faced by the conspirators when it failed. Recommended for students with a special interest in World War II and for anyone curious about a handful of disgruntled Nazis. Bibliography, index. Ages 13+.

Forman, James D. Nazism. Watts, 1978. $5.90; $1.50 pb., Dell.

This slim and well-organized book discusses the development, power, and demise of the Nazi regime. Describing Martin Luther (1483–1546), an anti-Semite and antihumanist, as the spiritual godfather of Nazism, Forman traces his and other influences which created the Nazi platform. If Luther provided the spiritual influence, Hitler contributed pragmatic skills. Forman discusses Hitler's political life, asserting that without his demonic energies the Nazi philosophy would never have solidified into a major political power. Although a bit oversimplified, the book does provide a good overall description of this unfortunate period. Bibliography, index. (Note: See Arnold Rubin's *The Evil That Men Do: The Story of the Nazis* for an emotional yet factual account of their misdeeds. Messner, 1977. $7.79. Ages 13+). Ages 12+.

Friedlander, Albert H., ed. Out of the Whirlwind: A Reader of Holocaust Literature. See chapter 9, Literature: Folk Tales and Anthologies.

Klüger, Ruth, and **Peggy Mann.** The Secret Ship. Doubleday, 1978. $5.95.

Adapted for children from the authors' *The Last Escape: The Launching of the Largest Secret Rescue of All Time* (Doubleday, 1973), this is the affecting story of the decrepit ship *Hilda* that carried hundreds of illegal Jewish emigrants to Palestine. Ruth Klüger, a member of the Mossad (a secret organization to save Jews in Hitler's Europe), is the young woman in charge of this mission impossible. This is her true story, and she tells it with passion. The book is easy to read and contains plenty of romance, adventure, and suspense; but the authors spare no details of the horrendous deaths that European Jews were meeting and how the world offered but little aid. This title is especially good for reluctant older readers who want a solid read with big print. Ages 11–15.

Meltzer, Milton. Never to Forget: The Jews of the Holocaust. Har-Row, 1976. $8.95; $1.50 pb., Dell.
Meltzer's unique account of the Holocaust focuses on the human experience on its victims and villains. While not shying away from the horrible truths that emerge from diaries, letters, poetry, and other firsthand accounts, Meltzer does not subject us to an unceasing barrage of shocking incidents. Even in this hell, we are offered glimpses of those special people and moments in which love and kindness prevail. Meltzer places the ultimate blame for the Holocaust on world apathy: "Indifference is our greatest sin," he writes. The book is divided into three sections: "History of the Hatred," "Destruction of the Jews," and "Spirit of Resistance." *Never to Forget* is a book for all ages and all peoples. Bibliography, chronology, maps, and index. Ages 12+.

Meltzer, Milton. World of Our Fathers: The Jews of Eastern Europe. FS&G, 1974. $7.95; $1.25 pb. Dell.
Such a chapter heading as "The City of Slaughter" suggests that our fathers' world was not a bed of roses. And Meltzer's histories never minimize the hatred that overwhelmed the Jews or any of the other oppressed peoples. The story of East European Jewry from the sixteenth to the early twentieth century (as covered here) is one of violence and deprivation of rights—except the right to leave. What kept this persecuted people alive? Who were their (religious) heroes? What was their daily life in the shtetl (small town) like? The author answers these questions by weaving firsthand accounts (poetry, music, memoirs, etc.) into his clear and compassionate text. The autobiographical foreword beckons readers to learn about their ancestors, thus getting to know themselves. Photographs, glossary, bibliography, and index. Ages 12+.

Procktor, Richard. Nazi Germany: The Origins and Collapse of the Third Reich. HR&W, 1970. O.P.
Procktor traces the background of Imperial Germany and the humiliation of German nationalism that followed the First World War. Hitler used the problems of a failing economy and the collapsing Weimar Republic to fabricate his own powerful web spun from every extremist thread in German politics and religion. Procktor plots the

Nazi takeover of Germany and Eastern Europe and their war against the Allies. That the Jews suffered the most under Hitler is made clear by the author; he does not, however, put the blame for this tragedy on anyone but the Third Reich. The book is easy to understand and includes black-and-white photographs of both the murderers and the victims. Bibliography, index. Ages 11–14.

Roskies, Diane, and **David Roskies.** The Shtetl Book. KTAV, 1975. $6.95 pb.
Everything you ever wanted to know about great-grandma's shtetl (small town). Although this is not a best-selling children's book, it is useful for the youngster interested in genealogy or reporting on the subject. Using the shtetl of Tishevits in the Lublin Province as an example, the authors examine the history and way of life of East European Jews between 1880 and 1914. Eyewitness reports, a readable narrative, photographs, and maps touch on the geography, work, play, culture, philosophy, and religion of the small-town way of life destroyed by Nazism. Glossary, index. Ages 12+.

Schechter, Betty. The Dreyfus Affair: A National Scandal. HM, 1965. $3.50.
When a high-ranking Jewish French military official was erroneously and maliciously convicted of treason in 1895, sensitive people around the world were aghast, but the anti-Semites danced in the streets. Heroes, such as the fiery writer Emile Zola, and villains too numerous to mention people this detailed and carefully written story of France when justice took a holiday. While not easy to read, the book is dramatic; and with the good characterizations and lively events, the competent reader will be hooked. The Dreyfus affair is an important event in Jewish history, for it was this very crisis that convinced young Theodor Herzl that Jews needed the protection of their own national state. Photographs, bibliography, and index. Ages 12+.

Shirer, William. The Rise and Fall of Adolf Hitler. "Landmark" Series. Random, 1961. $5.99.
One of the most popular nonfiction titles in children's libraries (for some time now) is this history of Hitler and the Nazi regime. Part of the easy-to-read "Landmark" series, this political account was written by a renowned CBS foreign news reporter stationed in Germany during the war. Using quotes, photographs, and a straightforward style, Shirer's book informs youngsters about how a "one-time Vienna tramp" became a worshiped idol in World War II Germany. Index. (Note: For a painstakingly researched and readable account of what made Hitler tick—like a bomb—see Mina and Arthur Klein's *Hitler's*

Hang-Ups: An Adventure in Insight. Dutton, 1976. $8.95. Ages 13+) Ages 10–14.

Stadtler, Bea. The Holocaust: A History of Courage and Resistance. Illus. David Stone Martin. Behrman, 1974. $4.95 pb.
Stadtler addresses this book to youngsters just learning about the Holocaust. She does not veil the horrors that destroyed six million people, but her picture is not one in which meek lambs go passively to their slaughter. The author writes about the Jews and some Gentiles who fought Nazism: valiant doctors and rabbis, ghetto fighters, spies, women resisters, the underground press, Danish heroes, and more. Eyewitness reports, memoirs, and poetry mingle effectively with Stadtler's narrative. Both in size and content, this book will not overwhelm children. Bibliography, no index. Ages 11–14.

Werstein, Irving. The Uprising of the Warsaw Ghetto, November, 1940–May, 1943. Norton, 1968, O.P.
Drawing upon interviews, trial records, and journals, Werstein describes the events leading to the historic Jewish struggle inside the walled ghetto. Only a few chapters record the actual battles between Jewish resisters (the ZOB) and their enemies, the Nazis. Most of the book describes the incredibly horrible conditions inside the ghetto and portrays some of the personages who played a key role in ghetto politics. Werstein hoped that this book would teach a lesson against intolerance and bigotry; it also instructs about the folly of passive resistance and appeasement in the fight against amoral bullies. Photographs, index. Ages 11–14.

Reference Aid

Stadtler, Bea. "Teaching the Holocaust to Children." *The Second Jewish Catalog.* Jewish Pubn. 1976, pp. 216–232.
Stadtler provides a detailed syllabus and a book and media bibliography on this subject.

Israeli History Books

Ancient History

Asimov, Isaac. The Land of Canaan. HM, 1971. $5.95.
The history of Canaan from its earliest ancient times (2500 B.C.E.) through Hebrew rule, Greek victory, Roman power, the Maccabees, and the triumph of Rome (71 C.E.). Consisting of the nations now known as Syria, Lebanon, Israel, and Jordan, Canaan contributed much to the history of civilization: cities, sea trade, pottery, the alphabet, Judaism, and Christianity. Asimov, a prolific and entertain-

ing writer, provides a highly readable narrative detailing the politics and religion of this ancient world. Maps, tables, and index. Ages 13+.

Heaton, E. W. Everyday Life in Old Testament Times. See chapter 2, The Bible: Exploration of Biblical Themes.

Mazar, Benjamin, and **Michael Avi-Yonah.** Illustrated World of the Bible. See chapter 2, The Bible: Exploration of Biblical Themes.

Pearlman, Moshe. The Zealots of Masada: The Story of a Dig. Scribner, 1967. $2.45 pb.
An excellent narrative about life in the immense fortress of Massadah and the technical skill and hard work that went into excavating it. The Zealots were a group of 960 Jews who sought refuge from the Romans in 70 C.E. and chose death rather than slavery. Josephus, a Jewish commander turned traitor, wrote down this story as he heard it from the few survivors. His report, however, was not verified until 1,800 years later on an archeological dig led by Yigael Yadin. Pearlman's book provides more information about the Zealots than Yadin/Gottlieb's *Story of Masada* (reviewed below) but contains fewer photographs. Ages 12+.

Yadin, Yigael. The Story of Masada. Retold by Gerald Gottlieb. Random, 1969. $6.99.
Gottlieb retells Yadin's *Masada* (Random, 1966) for young people. It is the account of an archeological dig in the early 1960s which verified the story of an ancient historian. This concerned Jewish Zealots who barricaded themselves in King Herod's palace in Israel and held the Roman army at bay for seven months. Gottlieb does a nice job in describing the archeological techniques and findings as well as the historical background. Many fine black-and-white photographs, diagrams, and maps provide a thrilling visual effect. Index. Ages 11+.

General History and Politics

Arbit Books.
This publisher distributes a wide selection of maps of Israel: travel, historical, air photo and satellite maps, geological, and city and town cartography. The maps are available in book and loose form.

Cameron, James. The Making of Israel. Taplinger, 1977. $7.95.
This English author has spent a great deal of time in Israel and has deep feelings for its birth, which "exalted many hearts and broke many more." His detailed (but brief—only 100 pages) descriptions of the events leading to the Partition of Palestine and the founding of the new state are easy to comprehend and are accompanied by many

fine black-and-white photographs. Cameron's exciting account of the impending end of the mandate details the frantic activities of the Jews, British, and Arabs down to the last minutes. More sympathetic to the Zionists than Grant's *Partition of Palestine* (reviewed here), Cameron emphasizes the desperation of world Jewry after World War II. He calls Hitler "the Founding Father of the Land of the Jews." Cameron does not minimize the anguish caused by the political maneuvering of the Western powers and the violence of those parties concerned. Index. Ages 12+.

Ellis, Harry. Israel: One Land, Two People. T Y Crowell, 1972. $7.95.
Focuses on the history of the Arab-Israeli conflict through 1972. Not up to date, it nonetheless provides a clear, objective, and detailed foundation for understanding the political situation. The roles of the United States and Russia are included. In addition, Ellis touches briefly on the history of the Jewish claim to the land and the political Zionist movement to reclaim it. He also surveys the government's structure, the diverse population, and Israel's internal concerns. The attractive format includes good photographs, maps, and illustrations. Bibliography, index. Ages 12+.

Essrig, Harry, and **Abraham Segal.** Israel Today. Illus. Robert Sugar. UAHC, 1977 (rev. ed.). $8.50.
This textbook offers lovely photographs, anecdotes, bibliographies, and a balanced look at the old and the new in Israel. Written for the Jewish student and published by a Jewish firm, the book has a flavor different from that of many other trade histories. It takes a less neutral stand on the Arab-Israeli conflicts, but it includes the young reader as an important part of Israeli history and purpose. Recommended for wide library purchase in spite of its specialized viewpoint. Index. Ages 12–15.

Gilbert, Martin. Atlas of the Arab-Israeli Conflict. Macmillan, 1974. O.P.
Gilbert traces the history of the Arab-Israeli conflict from the turn of the century to March 1974. Included are maps of Jewish settlements, Arab terrorism, Israeli conquests, British and United Nations divisions, the Arab-Israeli wars, oil resources, and more. By quoting statespeople, brief news reports, and statistics, Gilbert provides additional information on the effects of war and terrorism on Jew and Arab alike. Historical geography at its best! Ages 10+.

Gilbert, Martin. Jerusalem History Atlas. Macmillan, 1977. $8.95.
Traces the history of Jerusalem from biblical days to the present. In-

cluded are the trials and tribulations of the city as well as the fate of
its citizens through more than 3,000 years. Facing each of the sixty-six
black-and-white maps is an interesting assortment of prints and photographs. Gilbert's emphasis is on Jerusalem's development during
the last 150 years. Subject maps concerning water supply, parks and
gardens, archeological interests, battles, and political concerns are included. There is also an extensive bibliography of the maps, personal
accounts, biographies, histories, and memoirs used by Mr. Gilbert.
The book provides an intriguing and unique perspective on the history of Jerusalem written from a pro-Israel viewpoint. Ages 12+.

Golann, Cecil Paige. Our World: The Taming of Israel's Negev.
Messner, 1970. $4.29.
Introduces the young reader to the recent and often fantastic development of the Negev Desert. Virtually a wasteland before Jewish settlement around 1940, the Negev now contains agricultural and technical industries as well as a population of diverse citizens living in
desert cities and collectives. The Israeli ingenuity detailed here may
well have important implications for desert dwellers in other parts of
the world. Many black-and-white photographs enable the reader to
witness the transformation of the Negev. This 1970 book should be
updated. Index. Ages 10–14.

Grant, Neil. The Partition of Palestine, 1947: Jewish Triumph, British Failure, Arab Disaster. Watts, 1973. $4.47.
The political history of Palestine from the 1917 Balfour Declaration,
which promised Jews a national home, through the 1947 Partition,
which led to the creation of Israel. The book traces the history of British involvement, American influence, and the fruitless attempts at
Arab-Jewish coexistence. Although Grant strives for neutrality, his
portrayal of Zionists is not flattering. They emerge as a skillful and
intelligent group of determined nags and propagandists. Nor does the
author spare the British. Used with Cameron's *Making of Israel* (reviewed here), this book can give students a clearer perspective on the
subject. Ages 12+.

Hoffman, Gail. The Land and People of Israel. "Portraits of the Nation" Series. Lippincott, 1972 (rev. ed.). $8.95.
A highly readable introduction to Israel. Well rounded and detailed,
the book exudes an enthusiasm and respect for Israel's achievements.
The author discusses modern history, the contemporary way of life,
geography, current issues, and a look at Israel's early leaders. With its
use of poetic biblical passages and references to ancient events, the
text links the new nation to its unique genealogy. Unfortunately, the

rather mundane format and unexciting photographs lessen the appeal. Index. Ages 11–15.

Irving, Clifford. The Battle of Jerusalem: The Six-Day War of June, 1967. "Macmillan Battle Books" Series. Macmillan, 1970. $4.50.
Irving reveals the strategies, actions, personalities, history, and issues behind the Israeli victory in Jerusalem in June 1967. In another David-and-Goliath scenario, Irving compares the huge Arab force with the small Israeli army. Out of the 500 Jewish soldiers who stormed the Arab section of the city, 450 had never before been in combat. Many black-and-white photographs take the reader close to the action, and the maps give a clear perspective of the entire war. This brief and easy-to-read title will be enjoyed by youngsters interested in the details of this historic battle. Ages 11+.

Jacobs, Monty. The Birth of the Israeli Air Force: The Story of Israel's Pioneer Airmen. Illus. M. Arye. Shulsinger Bros. 1954. $3.00.
Challenged by Syria, Egypt, and even England, the infant Israeli Air Force conquered the not-so-friendly skies of the Middle East. Jacobs traces the birth of the IAF from its first single-engined Piper Cub mission in early 1948 to January 1949 when the force consisted of many international and highly capable World War II pilots. Fictionalized characters reveal strategy plans and fly us on dangerous errands. Don't look here for a humanist "war is hell" attitude. This is a straightforward, simplified, self-respecting account of an astounding Israeli accomplishment. (P.S. Underneath the dull dust jacket lies a colorful book cover.) No index. Ages 9–12.

Kubie, Nora Benjamin. Israel. "A First Book" Series. Watts, 1978 (3rd ed.). $5.95.
A nicely written general introduction to Israel that covers ancient and modern history, geography, city and country life, government, and the Arab-Israeli conflict. Touching on the four wars since 1948, it is also one of the few titles to include Sadat's visit to Israel. Although the book's format is dull, the attractive full-page black-and-white photographs, the competent writing, and the contemporary flavor (including nonsexist language) make it very readable. Bibliography, index. Ages 10–15.

Kubie, Nora Benjamin. The Jews of Israel: History and Sources. Behrman, 1975 (rev. ed.). $3.95 pb.
A fast-moving and informative introduction to contemporary Israel. It touches briefly on history and geography, but Kubie's main focus is on the political situation leading up to and including the Yom Kip-

pur War in 1973. She also reports on life in Israel today: schooling, culture, work, and holidays (of non-Jews too). Part 2 is composed of a variety of original sources, which are first referred to in the margins of the first section. Samples from the Bible (Jewish and Christian), Muslim writings, official and political documents, and literary works enable the young reader to appreciate the link between ancient and modern history and between the actual event and Kubie's retelling. Index. Ages 12+.

Peck, Ira. Raid at Entebbe. Schol Bk Serv, 1977. $1.25 pb.
A fast-moving and easy-to-read account of "Operation Thunderbolt," the daring rescue of hijacked Israelis at Uganda's airport in 1976. The author briefly discusses the problem of Arab and pro-Arab terrorists in Israel's past. He also emphasizes that this incredible rescue over 2,500 miles of unfriendly geography was a victory for freedom lovers everywhere. Illustrated with maps and photographs, this book should enjoy a wide circulation. (Note: Older children might like William Stevenson's *90 Minutes at Entebbe,* Bantam, 1976.) Ages 10–14.

Rutland, Jonathan. Looking at Israel. "Looking at Other Countries" Series. Lippincott, 1970. $6.95.
Colorful, inviting photographs distinguish this children's easy-to-read survey of Israel's geography, people, and history. Emphasizing the contemporary sights and features of Israel, the book touches upon life in the cities, on the Ammiad kibbutz (Upper Galilee), agriculture, social life and customs, and a briefer look at history, political problems, and religion. The writing is a bit stilted and not well organized, but the text is easy and the pictures are in color. Index. Ages 9–12.

Spector, Shoshannah. The Miraculous Rescue: Entebbe. Illus. Theo Phalieros. Shengold, 1978. $4.95.
A wonderfully heroic tale about the Israeli liberation of Jewish hostages at the Uganda airport on July 4, 1976. The story begins at a fictional summer camp shortly after the rescue. An Israeli counselor is relating the astounding events to a group of fascinated and proud Jewish youngsters. The book's illustrations are of comic-book quality and do not rate all that prominence on bright red paper. This easy-to-understand account of "Operation Thunderbolt" is exciting to read aloud or to enjoy individually. Ages 8–11.

Social Life, Description, and Travel

Ben Shaul, Dvora. Night in the Wadi. Photos by Werner Braun. Sabra, 1970. O.P.
A devoted naturalist offers brief and poetic sketches on the way of life

for a variety of birds, reptiles, insects, and small.mammals who live in an Israeli wadi in the Judean hills. A wadi is a dry water course, a valley, which comes to life at night as these various creatures emerge into the chilly air. Ben Shaul ends her gentle descriptions with a plea against insecticides and careless campers who are endangering the home of the wilderness creatures. Excellent black-and-white photographs and an attractive format accompany the effective text. Ages 9–12; younger for reading aloud.

Breakstone, David, and **Cindy Jochnowitz.** The Israel Experience Book. Illus. Lika Tov. Bloch, 1977. $4.95 pb.
This nontraditional travel guide to Israel is for young people who want to get their meaning's worth as well as their money's worth out of the trip. Helpful addresses, vocabulary lists, and information on cities and kibbutz life are provided along with sections on Judaism: ancient and modern Jewish history, parables, literary and biblical quotes, holidays, songs, etc. There is plenty of white space too: record your feelings; place a snapshot; play a word game; write your own chapter. The book is recommended for youngsters over eleven who are leaving for Israel. It will encourage them to get in touch with the country and themselves. Amusingly and lovingly written. Ages 11–17.

Comay, Joan, and **Moshe Pearlman.** Israel. "Nations Today Books" Series. Macmillan, 1964. $3.95.
A competent basic introduction to Israel. It presents more information on the Israeli people than the other general history books do. Here you are told about the schooling, the army, the diverse population, the work, and the citizens. Though not up to date, this fast-moving contemporary survey has a solid background in history. Bibliography, index. Ages 11+.

Gidal, Tim, and **Sonia Gidal.** My Village in Israel. "My Village" Series. Pantheon, 1959. $5.69.
With considerably more detail than *A Week in Hagar's World* by Goldman and Reit (reviewed below), the Gidals tell about young Shmuel's life in a kibbutz near the Valley of Jezreel. The authors depict this fun-loving boy at school, at chores, with his family, on digs, and at play. The book is profusely illustrated with black-and-white photographs; many are full-page and quite artistic. Although the book is over twenty years old, it has a timeless quality and does not appear to be terribly out of date. Glossary. Ages 10–14.

Goldman, Louis, and **Seymour Reit.** A Week in Hagar's World. Photos by Louis Goldman. "Face to Face Book" Series. Macmillan, 1969. $4.50.

Interesting black-and-white photographs and a brief commentary record the daily life of a first-grade girl from the Na'an Kibbutz. We see Hagar the schoolgirl, the orange picker (everyone helps on the kibbutz), the daughter, and the granddaughter, as this happy, open youngster reveals the differences between her life and ours. It seems strange, however, that although the author includes religious observances, the words "Jewish" and "Judaism" never appear in the book. Did the author take it for granted that even non-Jewish youngsters would identify these customs as Jewish? On the whole, this is a contemporary, well-rounded look at many aspects of kibbutz life. Ages 7–9; younger for reading aloud.

Grand, Samuel, and **Tamar Grand.** The Children of Israel. UAHC, 1972. $5.50.

A large variety of black-and-white photographs and a supportive narrative introduce the family, home, school, games, customs, and daily lives of Israeli children. The authors highlight kibbutz life, the city of Jerusalem, the holidays, and the variety of cultures among Jews and Arabs. This is a lively and attractive title to read to young children or to give to older youngsters as a first introduction to Israel. Ages 8–11; younger for reading aloud.

Sasek, Miroslav. This Is Israel. "This is . . ." Series. Macmillan, 1962. $4.95.

Sasek takes us on a visual tour of Israel in this oversized book with colorful illustrations, a brief and cheerful commentary, and an interesting use of biblical quotes. Published in 1962, it ascribes parts of Jerusalem to Jordan and mentions that there are no Israeli TV stations. Nonetheless, the book is still useful and will entertain a wide audience. Uniquely for books about Israel for children, Sasek gives considerable attention to Christian attractions. This pictorial guide to the sights and sounds of Israel guarantees an uplifting journey. Ages 5+.

Reference Aid

Sirof, Harriet. The Junior Encyclopedia of Israel. Jonathan David, 1979. $14.95.

An appealing one-volume work that covers the entire history and peoples of the Holy Land. Ages 10–15.

7
the Jewish Holidays

There are several types of Jewish celebrations, the most important of which are mentioned in the Torah (the first five books in the Bible). Of these, the only one mentioned in the Ten Commandments is the Sabbath. Rabbi Hayim Donin, author of *To Be a Jew* (a classic guide to Jewish living), writes that the Sabbath "is truly the pivotal point for all Judaism." For observant Jews this day of physical rest and spiritual and mental rejuvenation is central.

Of the remaining holidays, the period beginning with Rosh ha-Shanah, the new year (also known as the Day of Remembrance), and ending with Yom Kippur (Day of Atonement) is the most sacred. During these ten days, the Jew is commanded to examine his past and atone for any wrongdoing. Yom Kippur is the climax of this period of purification, and adults observe a total fast for twenty-four hours.

Four days after Yom Kippur comes Sukkot. This colorful harvest festival commemorates the forty-year period during which the Jews wandered in the desert before reaching the Promised Land after their exodus from Egypt. To give thanks and to remember these forty years families eat in small sukkot (literally, temporary huts) usually decorated with fruit and greenery. The eight-day celebration ends with Shemini Azeret (The Eighth Day of Solemn Assembly) and Simhat Torah (Rejoicing of the Torah), when the annual cycle of the weekly Torah reading is completed and is started anew. Simhat Torah is a joyous celebration where children and adults march through the synagogue in triumphant procession, holding the Torah scrolls and waving flags.

One of the most popular of the festivals whose observance is commanded by the Torah is Pesah (Passover). Pesah falls in the spring and lasts for a week; it begins with a festive ritual meal (seder) during which Jews are instructed to remember that they were once slaves in Egypt. The seder retells and symbolically reenacts the Jewish exodus from Egypt, giving thanks to God for the passage from slavery to freedom.

The last of the holidays mentioned in the Torah is the festival of Shavuot (weeks). Shavuot falls seven full weeks after Passover and commemorates Moses' receiving of the Ten Commandments on Mount Sinai.

Although they do not derive from the Torah, many of the minor celebrations are very popular among American Jews. Hanukkah (Rededication) comes in December and celebrates the victory of Judah Maccabee over a powerful Greek-Syrian king in 165 B.C.E. Hanukkah commemorates the rededication of the Temple in Jerusalem and has become symbolic of religious freedom. Purim, marking the Jewish victory over the Assyrian Haman as recounted in the Bible's Book of Esther, is a merry holiday celebrated in early spring. Both holidays have an enormous appeal to children, perhaps because of the traditions of giving Hanukkah gelt (money) and having Purim costume parties.

Tishah be-Av, which falls during the summer, commemorates the destruction of the first Holy Temple in 586 B.C.E. and the second Temple in 70 C.E. This day of fasting has become a day of general mourning for all the tragedies that have befallen the Jewish people, and since World War II it has become a fitting day to mourn for those killed in the Nazi Holocaust. (A special holiday, Yom ha-Sho'ah, specifically commemorates the Holocaust.)

There are a number of other notable days. Tu bi-Shevat (Jewish Arbor Day), celebrated in late winter or very early spring, is a day for planting and for eating fruit that grows in Israel. Lag ba-Omer, thirty-three days after the second day of Passover, supposedly celebrates the end of a plague killing young scholars and has become known as the Scholars Festival. Schoolchildren sometimes celebrate it by going on a picnic.

Since the creation of the state of Israel, several secular holidays have been recognized. Yom ha-Azma'ut falls in the spring and celebrates the day on which Israel won independence, May 14, 1948. Yom Yerushalayim, another secular holiday, marks the reunification of Jerusalem under Israeli sovereignty after the Arab-Israeli war of 1967. There are also several minor fast days, as well as the monthly celebration of the new moon, Rosh Hodesh.

The books reviewed in this chapter cover all of the Jewish holidays. There are several good nonfiction titles for children ten years and older, but books for younger children tend to be disappointing. They are usually fictionalized accounts of the holidays and are often marked by poor writing, poor art work, and stereotypical role casting. In these books every Jewish family has one son and one daughter; you won't find a single-parent family, a mixed marriage, a mother without an apron, or even a momentarily unhappy face.

The books reviewed here are more concerned with a holiday's historical background and current customs than with storytelling, Bible stories, or recreational ideas. But descriptions of holidays will also be found in chapter 8, Literature: Fiction, while chapter 3, the Bible: Bible Stories, contains some books that deal with the biblical accounts of holidays. Because so many craft books and cookbooks center on celebrations, chapter 5, Fine Arts and Domestic Arts, also offers information on the Jewish holidays. The subject index will help the reader locate these titles.

Since there are so few good nonfiction books on the holidays for young children, a bibliography of supplementary picture books appears at the end of this chapter. Although these titles are not specifically Jewish, they can be used to communicate the spirit behind some of these holidays.

Jewish Holiday Books

Bearman, Jane. The Eight Nights: A Chanukah Counting Book. UAHC, 1978. $4.50 pb.
This pleasant picture book tells about Hanukkah customs as each night an additional candle is lit. The brief rhymes on each page are not memorable, but the illustrations are pretty and colorful. Also included are holiday prayers and songs and a glossary. The book has a clever way of folding so that the blessings can be read opposite each new Hanukkah picture. A soft cover, however, promises a short library life. Ages 3–8.

Brin, Ruth F. The Shabbat Catalogue. See chapter 5, Fine Arts and Domestic Arts.

Cashman, Greer Fay. Jewish Days and Holidays. Illus. Alona Frankel. SBS, 1976. $8.95.
This attractive book was written and published in Israel. Eleven Jewish holidays are described for a general audience in a lucid, succinct manner. The art work is delightful. Each page is in vibrant color. The stylized collage and line drawings are bright, humorous, and dramatic. Next to each festival is a column of symbols representing the holiday, e.g., a menorah for Hanukkah. The symbols are brought together at the book's closing for a memory matching game. Few titles in this chapter can match the artistic quality of this lively work. Ages 9–12; younger for reading aloud.

Cedarbaum, Sophia. "A Basic Library on Jewish Holiday Observance for the Young" Series. Illus. Clare and John Ross. UAHC, 1961. $2.00 each.

Young Danny and Debbie are the hosts on this functional trip through eight of the year's Jewish holidays. Each volume in the series is well rounded, presenting the reader with the festival's meaning, prayers and songs, foods, and traditional home customs. The series' major drawback is its garish illustrations of shifty-eyed people wearing outdated clothes. Also obsolete is the strict adherence to traditional sex-role models. The weak binding means that the series will need constant replacement or repair, but the books are inexpensive. The following holidays are covered in separate volumes: Hanukkah, Passover, Sukkot and Simhat Torah, Purim, Rosh ha-Shanah and Yom Kippur, the Sabbath, Shavuot, and Tu bi-Shevat. Ages 7–9; younger for reading aloud.

Chaikin, Miriam. The Seventh Day: The Story of the Jewish Sabbath. Illus. David Frampton. Doubleday, 1980. $6.95.
This brief summary of the Torah (the first five books of the Bible) is written with a biblical cadence and leads us to God's commandment to observe the holy Sabbath, that "foretaste of paradise" for the children of Israel. The slim volume also contains some information on the prayers and traditions associated with the Jewish day of rest. Not the choice for those wanting a fact-filled account of this holiday, Chaikin's title is more of a mood piece, enhanced by many dramatic black-and-white woodcuts. When read aloud at family gatherings, the book will enrich the celebration by reminding Jews and Gentiles alike of the Sabbath's hard-won birth and survival. Ages 8+.

Chanover, Hyman, and **Alice Chanover.** Pesah Is Coming. Illus. Leonard Kessler. United Syn Bk, 1956. $3.95.
Here is a twenty-four-year-old title about a family preparing for the holiday of Passover. At the most, it is a reflection of what is happening in many Jewish homes worldwide. It provides role models and comradeship between reader and book. However, the narrative and art work are undistinguished. Hair ribbons and aprons are stuck on every female in sight and euphoria abounds. The book falls short of really meaningful literary, artistic, and even Judaic experience. Holiday books of this genre (information inside a fictional framework) can be found in the backlists of many Jewish publishing houses. Three similar titles still in print are as follows: Chanover, Hyman, *Pesah Is Here,* United Syn Bk, 1956; Edelman, Lily, *The Sukkah and the Big Wind,* United Syn Bk, 1956—a bit better; Salop, Byrd, *The Kiddush Cup Who Hated Wine,* Jonathan David, 1957. All titles ages 4–8.

This book highlights the thirteen holidays "of the annual cycle of Jewish days of joy." Serving as a brief introduction to religious celebrations, the book also has a section entitled "The Geography of Israel" and a survey of Judaism's principal beliefs. Each page of text is encased in a decorative picture frame; each holiday is accompanied by a lovely full-page color painting in soft tones. This book makes a lovely gift for interested older children and adults; Gentiles will benefit from its brief but informative text. Ages 12+.

Chiel, Kinnert. The Complete Book of Hanukkah. Illus. Arnold Lobel. KTAV, 1959. $4.00 pb.
Chiel offers an interesting anthology of Hanukkah stories, legends, history, poetry, songs, recipes, and prayers. Included are pieces by Sholom Aleichem, I. L. Peretz, and Henry Wadsworth Longfellow. The poetry section is especially welcome as there are not many poems for children about Hanukkah. This unpretentious volume has enough engrossing facts and fancies to amuse the read-aloud family looking for Hanukkah material. Ages 9–12.

Cone, Molly. The Jewish New Year. Illus. Jerome Snyder. "A Crowell Holiday Book" Series. T Y Crowell, 1966. $6.89.
This is a pleasant and easy-to-read description of Yom Kippur and Rosh ha-Shanah for a wide audience. Included are customs, legends, historic events, and background information as well as some now little-observed customs such as giving a hen or a rooster away on the day before Yom Kippur. Before killing it however, the bestower would get rid of his bad luck by swinging the hen around his head. Snyder's mostly amusing and attractive red-and-black pencil drawings will appeal to children. Ages 7–12.

Cone, Molly. Purim. Illus. Helen Borten. "A Crowell Holiday Book" Series. T Y Crowell, 1967. $6.89.
Cone's emphasis is on the biblical story of Queen Esther and how its happy ending provided Judaism with its most playful celebration. She also deals with current customs, including foods, gift giving, and merrymaking. The illustrations, which combine woodcuts, collage, and watercolors, are varied and attractive. Ages 8–12.

Cuyler, Margery. Jewish Holidays. Illus. Lisa C. Wesson. HR&W, 1978. $5.95.
A satisfactory introduction for a wide audience to nine Jewish celebrations. Each holiday is accompanied by a small project idea, such as building a sukkah (temporary hut) model from a shoe box. The writing is lucid and the information easy to digest. The heavy car-

toonlike drawings are not very appealing. Still, for an overall survey of Jewish holidays, the text should be applauded. Ages 8–11.

Drucker, Malka. Hanukkah: Eight Nights, Eight Lights. Illus. Brom Hoban. Holiday, 1980. $8.95.
A comprehensive discussion of Hanukkah for a wide audience. Drucker provides information on Hanukkah's customs, rituals, and historic events. In addition, chapters include recipes, games, and craft ideas. The author successfully blends fact with legend, creating an easily understood and slightly philosophical text. (For example, Drucker comments that the spinning dreidl and the spinning earth both bring a change of fortune to us all.) A variety of black-and-white photographs, prints, and line drawings enhance this modestly packaged but useful, inspiring work. This is the first title in a series of books about the Jewish holidays for children. Glossary, bibliography, index. Ages 9–12.

Epstein, Morris. All About Jewish Holidays and Customs. Illus. Arnold Lobel. KTAV, 1970 (rev. ed). $4.50 pb.
In a direct manner and a well-organized format, Epstein surveys twelve traditional holidays, the minor fasts, and two modern commemorations (Israeli Independence and Holocaust Remembrance). His detailed coverage extends to the bar mitzvah, the Jewish home, famous Jewish books, the synagogue, and an explanation of the Jewish calendar. Not a leisurely read, but acceptable as a text or reference tool. Index and (dated) bibliography. (Note: Epstein has also written a similar title profusely illustrated with somewhat dated but still interesting black-and-white photographs: *A Pictorial Treasury of Jewish Holidays and Customs.* KTAV, 1959. $10.00. Ages 11+). Ages 10–15.

Gaer, Joseph. Holidays Around the World. Little, 1953. $5.95.
Divided into sections that describe the various holidays of the Chinese, Hindus, Jews, Christians, and Muslims, and a sprinkling of miscellaneous celebrations, Gaer's book is unique in giving children a worldwide view of festivals. Well written and respectful, the book has gone through twenty-one printings. Attractive red-and-white illustrations add a bright touch. Index. Ages 10+.

Garvey, Robert. Holidays Are Nice. Illus. Ezekiel Schloss and Arnold Lobel. KTAV, 1960. $5.00.
This attractively designed picture book packs a lot of information in its fifty-two pages. Young Judy and Dave—and some subtly talking menorot (Hanukkah candelabra), shofrot (rams' horns)—describe historic events and contemporary customs to young readers. The siblings offer no relief from sex-role stereotyping. (Note: Garvey's *First*

Book of Jewish Holidays, KTAV, 1954, with its unattractive drawings and brief, flavorless text, is not recommended.) Ages 4–10.

Golomb, Morris. Know Your Festivals and Enjoy Them. Shengold, 1973 (rev. ed.). $5.95.
This is an excellent source for both adults and students wanting background information on the Jewish holidays. For each celebration Golomb provides the "How" and "Why" we observe the event; "Terms" relating to each festival; relevant "Numbers to Remember," a quiz, and lovely photographs. Well organized, informative, and interestingly written, the book evokes enthusiasm and respect for these special times. Bibliography and index. Ages 11+.

Goodman, Philip. "Jewish Holidays" Series. Jewish Pubn, 1949–1976. $5–$8.95.
Goodman has gathered an admirable variety of writings together under his holiday umbrellas: biblical and historic narratives, prayers, essays, poetry, and short stories concerning various Jewish holidays. Not only can this series be useful as a resource for educating and inspiring adults working with children, but each volume contains a section on children's poetry and stories. These books make an ideal gift for the book-sharing family. Photographs, glossary, and an extensive bibliography are included. No index. Each of the following holidays has its own anthology: Hanukkah, Passover, Purim, Rosh ha-Shanah, Shavuot, Sukkot and Simhat Torah, and Yom Kippur. Ages: 16+; younger for reading aloud.

Greenfeld, Howard. Passover. Illus. Elaine Grove. HR&W, 1978. $5.95.
A handsome and well-written description of the 3,000-year-old Jewish holiday and an explanation of the seder at which it is celebrated. Printed on cream-colored quality paper and decorated with unique black woodcuts, the aesthetic format and book cover (embossed copper lettering) strike a reverent tone. It is interesting to note that in Greenfeld's retelling the first-born Egyptian sons are not killed by God. Rather, the Pharaoh frees the Hebrew slaves before the threat is carried out, changing his mind soon after Moses departs with his people. The meaning of Passover is thus expressed: "God passed over the homes of the Israelites while forcing the Pharaoh to liberate the enslaved people." (Note: Greenfeld has two other Jewish holiday titles that combine fine bookmaking with an interesting, detailed narrative: *Chanukah,* HR&W, 1976, $5.95; *Rosh Hashanah and Yom Kippur,* HR&W, 1979, $5.95. All three titles make nice gifts for the whole family.) Ages 10+.

Hirsh, Marilyn. The Hanukkah Story. Illus. by author. Bonim, 1977. $7.95.

In this picture-book version for primary school children, Hirsh emphasizes the political background and the ancient battles between the Maccabees and Antiochus, the Greek-Syrian despot. Her colorful and appealing illustrations bring the whole show to life with an authentic reproduction of costume and architecture. Credit is also given to the long-lasting oil, although Hirsh's heart is with the wonder of Judah Maccabee's military victory. A succinct and objective text makes this book recommended for Jewish and non-Jewish collections. Ages 8–10; younger for reading aloud.

Hirsh, Marilyn, adap. One Little Goat: A Passover Song. Illus. by author. Holiday, 1979. $7.95.

A multiracial classroom of happy children is preparing to go on stage. Their performance concerns a very old song sung at the closing of Passover seders, "Had Gadya" ("One Little Goat"). Acting out this story-song about a little goat that father bought for two "zuzim" (old coins), the children tumble on stage in homemade costumes and bring the tune to life with plenty of action and verve. In addition to the play, Hirsh provides the music to the song, an explanation of Passover, and the history of "One Little Goat." Humorously illustrated in red, gray, and black, this charming book will have special appeal for children who will recognize the story from past Passover celebrations. Ages 3–8.

Ish-Kishor, Sulamith. Pathway Through the Jewish Holidays. KTAV, 1967. $5.00.

An attractive and nicely written book about fourteen Jewish holidays. Each commemoration contains a discussion of historic and current customs, a variety of black-and-white photographs, and a glossary of Hebrew terms. Although the book is created in the image of a textbook, the author is a skillful writer (see index for other works), and the photos provide an inviting touch. A good choice for an overall, relatively detailed look at the Jewish calendar, especially for school or wide reference use. Index. Ages 10+.

Klausner, Abraham. A Child's Prayer Book for the Holidays of Rosh Hashana and Yom Kippur. Illus. Shraga Weil and Nachum Gutman. Abrams, 1974. $7.95.

Using Bible stories, legends, prayers, and narrative, Klausner leads the child through two simple and meaningful High Holy Days services. Striking colorful paintings and decorative designs enhance the work. Both parents and teachers will enjoy sharing this title with youngsters. Ages 6–11.

Kripke, Dorothy. Let's Talk About the Jewish Holidays. Illus. Naama Kitov. Jonathan David, 1970. $4.95.
This book about eleven Jewish holidays (excluding the Sabbath) communicates the joy and spiritual meaning of each festival as well as its history and current practices. The writing is warm and inviting; the viewpoint is one of Jew speaking to fellow Jew. The illustrations are functional and the format is attractive. Ages 9–12; younger for reading aloud.

Kustanowitz, Shulamit E., and **Ronnie C. Foont.** A First Haggadah. Illus. Ronnie C. Foont. Bonim, 1979. $5.95.
This lovely guide to the seder service and to the meaning of Passover is strikingly illustrated in vibrant colors and has a very pleasing format. Included are the directions for setting this special table; the prayers, songs, and stories associated with the seder; and informative comments on the role of the adult during the dinner service. The prayers and songs are in English, Hebrew, and a transliteration of the Hebrew. The book is an appealing introduction to the Passover home service for Jewish parents and their young children. Ages 6+.

Orovitz, Norma. Time to Rhyme: Jewish Holiday Book. Illus. Candace Ruskin. Shengold, 1976. $2.50 pb.
Thirteen holidays are introduced to the young child by a simple, brief poem and full-page illustrations. The appealing drawings of celebrating youngsters are just begging for a crayon, and I would recommend this book first as a quality coloring book and second as a read-aloud story title. Unpretentious and homey. Ages 4–9.

Rosen, Anne, and others. A Family Passover. Photos by Laurence Salzmann. Jewish Pubn, 1980. $6.95.
A friendly, informative discussion of the traditions and rituals of the Passover holiday. A ten-year-old girl takes us along as she and her family prepare for and celebrate Passover. We go shopping, attend a model seder at her Hebrew school, and welcome her large family as they gather around the table to thank God for their ancestors' release from Egyptian bondage. The profuse black-and-white photographs (uneven in quality) depict a contemporary observant Jewish family. It would have been even more realistic, perhaps, had we seen a child misbehaving at the seder table or heard our heroine complaining about the hard work that goes into preparing for this holiday. Nonetheless, this is a refreshingly up-to-date look at this spring holiday, one that is valuable for public and school libraries as well as for Jewish collections. Ages 8–10; read aloud to ages 5+.

Saypol, Judyth. My Very Own Haggadah. Illus. Madeline Wikler. Kar-Ben, 1974. $1.95 pb.
Although in soft cover and coloring-book design, this is a joyful, child-oriented Haggadah for the seder service. Including music, recipes, craft ideas, pages to color, the story of Passover, and the preparations (see Daddy cleaning the floor!), Saypol's book will be enjoyed by parent and child alike. Recommended for home use rather than library purchase. Ages 5–10.

Saypol, Judyth, and **Madeline Wikler.** Come, Let Us Welcome Shabbat. Illus. by authors. Kar-Ben, 1978. $1.95 pb.
An attractive oversized paperback that introduces the young family to the joys and customs of the Sabbath. Acting as a guide to the order of the Friday night observance at home, the book describes zedakah (charity), candle-lighting blessings, and prayers. The authors explore the basic Sabbath songs, crafts, and the meaning behind this special weekly holiday. Lovely photographs and an appealing format make this quite a pleasant title. Ages 5–10.

Saypol, Judyth, and **Madeleine Wikler.** My Very Own Rosh Hashanah; My Very Own Yom Kippur. Kar-Ben, 1978. $2.50 pb. each.
Two appealing surveys of Judaism's High Holy Days through child-oriented explanations, legends, prayers, and music. The books have a lovely format, with pretty illustrations and photographs of home services. The bindings are surprisingly sturdy for paperback editions. Tasteful and highly readable, these holiday books offer inexpensive entertainment and information. Ages 9–11; younger for reading aloud.

Simon, Norma. "Festival Series of Picture Story Books" Series. Illus. Harvey Weiss and Ayala Gordon. United Syn Bk, 1959–1961. $2.95 each.
Along with her younger brother, David, and loving parents, Ruth ushers us through ten Jewish holidays. The text is briefer and more poetic than the Cedarbaum books (see review). The emphasis is on how the young children celebrate each holiday. Although the line drawings are more attractive than the Cedarbaum illustrations, a wash of dark colors over the faces greatly reduces the appeal. This is a Conservative Jewish series that is outdated in dress and sex-role portrayals. Separate titles for the following holidays are in print: Hanukkah, Purim, Passover, Sukkot, Rosh ha-Shanah, Yom Kippur, Tu bi-Shevat, Simhat Torah, and the Sabbath. Glossary. Ages 4–7.

Simon, Norma. Hanukkah. Illus. Symeon Shimin. "A Crowell Holiday Book" Series. T Y Crowell, 1966. $6.89.

In this title, published for a wide audience, Simon reveals the story of Judah Maccabee, the legend of the miracle of the oil, and today's Hanukkah customs. More briefly, she explores its celebration in Israel and the history of the Jews in the United States. The text is easy to read and informative. Shimin's gold-washed illustrations are expressive, dignified, and quite lovely. Ages 8–12.

Simon, Norma. Passover. Illus. Symeon Shimin. "A Crowell Holiday Book" Series. T Y Crowell, 1965. $6.89.
Simon retells the biblical story of Passover in this easy-to-read and pleasantly written book designed for a wide audience. She explains the seder in detail as well as touching briefly on the Samaritans in Jordan and the special Israeli seders. Simon compares the Jewish fight for freedom with black history during the Civil War era. Readers searching for a beautifully illustrated Jewish holiday book will be pleased with Shimin's careful and soothing drawings. Ages 8–12.

Sol, Robert. The First Book of Chanukah. Illus. Laszlo Matulay. KTAV, 1956. $2.00 pb.
This brief and simple picture book, illustrated in bright and dramatic colors, portrays a young family's Hanukkah celebration with candle lighting, dreidls, latkes, etc., and reveals the historical basis for the holiday. Appropriate for a wide audience needing a basic introduction to this festival, the book is sufficient (but sex-role stereotyped). Ages 3–6.

Zwerin, Raymond A., and **Audrey Friedman.** Shabbat Can Be. Illus. Yuri Salzman. UAHC, 1979. $4.95.
This large-sized and brightly illustrated picture book explores in simple, brief prose the events and joys associated with the Sabbath (Shabbat). Beginning with the idea that "Shabbat can be many things," the authors picture such customs as singing the blessing called Kiddush, tasting wine, and synagogue services. Children are also shown enjoying hearing a story by the rabbi, singing songs, and reading out loud. Feelings are also expressed: "Shabbat can be like standing on top of a mountain" or like "feeling rich without a penny in your pocket." The book's delightful illustrations, along with the depiction of a large, loving family, will attract young listeners. Ages 3–7.

Supplementary Materials for Jewish Holiday Use

Because of the lack of outstanding nonfiction holiday titles for very young children, parents and teachers might find the following list of high-quality picture books helpful in communicating some of the meanings behind several special Jewish days. These titles are not meant to be substitutes for nonfiction materials. Instead, they might be used to stimulate discussion on one aspect or one emotion associated with the holiday, or they can be included in a program of holiday storytelling. Additional titles can be found in this guide by scanning the chapters on folk tales, fiction, and theology. A few samples have been included here.

DAILY BLESSINGS—
THEMES OF APPRECIATION FOR OUR WORLD

Baylor, Byrd. Guess Who My Favorite Person Is. Illus. Robert Andrew Parker. Scribner, 1977. $7.95.
Resting in an alfalfa field on a sunny afternoon, two friends play a game naming their favorite things; the reader is filled with a sense of gratitude for this beautiful earth. Ages 5–10.

Baylor, Byrd. The Way to Start a Day. Illus. Peter Parnall. Scribner, 1978. $8.95.
A lovely, universal look at how different cultures welcome and honor the new day. Ages 5–9.

Brichto, Mira. The God Around Us. See chapter 11, Theology.

Freeman, Don. A Rainbow of My Own. Illus. by author. Viking Pr, 1966. $6.95; $2.25 pb.
A young boy imagines the fun he can have with a playful rainbow. A delightful story to attach to a retelling of Noah's Ark. Ages 3–7.

LAG BA-OMER—
THEMES OF PICNICS AND SCHOLARLY PURSUITS

Cohen, Miriam. When Will I Read? Illus. Lillian Hoban. Greenwillow, 1977. $7.75.
A small boy is anxious to learn how to read and is delighted when (finally!) he can. Ages 4–6.

Fisher, Aileen. Once We Went on a Picnic. Illus. Tony Chen. T Y Crowell, 1975. $8.95.
Four children go on a joyful picnic in this book with vibrant illustrations. Ages 4–8.

Greenfield, Eloise. Good News. Illus. Pat Cumings. Coward, 1977. O.P.
Another title about a boy who is filled with pride when he begins to read. Ages 5–8.

Lisowski, Gabriel. On the Little Hearth. See chapter 10, Music and Dance.

PASSOVER—THEMES OF FREEDOM FROM BONDAGE;
FREEDOM TO BE WHO YOU ARE; AND SPRINGTIME

Black, Algernon D. The Woman of the Wood: A Tale from Old Russia. Illus. Evaline Ness. HR&W, 1973. O.P.
An entertaining story about a woman carved from wood who values her new freedom above all else. Ages 5–9.

Clifton, Lucille. The Boy Who Didn't Believe in Spring. Illus. Brinton Turkle. Dutton, 1973. $7.95; $1.95 pb.
A touching story about two inner-city boys who are thrilled when they come across the first sign of spring. Ages 4–7.

Lawrence, Jacob. Harriet and the Promised Land. Illus. by author. S&S, 1968. $6.73.
A stunning picture book about Harriet Tubman, the black Moses of the Civil War period who led her people to freedom. This title, like many black spirituals, reveals the identification that black Americans have with the Jews of the Bible. Ages 4+.

Leaf, Munro. The Story of Ferdinand. Illus. Robert Lawson. Viking Pr, 1936. $6.95; $1.95 pb.
Not all bulls relish smashing through china shops or snorting around bull rings; Ferdinand is most himself when he is smelling the flowers. Ages 4–8.

Lionni, Leo. Frederick. Illus. by author. Pantheon, 1967. $6.99; $1.95 pb.
The other field mice ridicule Frederick for not helping them prepare for winter; but Frederick is a poet and his supply of verse eventually brings color to their dismal winter days. Ages 4–9.

Pinkwater, Daniel. The Big Orange Splot. Illus. by author. Hastings, 1977. $6.95; $1.50 pb., Schol Bk Serv.
When a bird drops a can of paint on his house, Mr. Plumbean decides to enlarge the design and paint up a storm. The neighbors are aghast until they realize that being "different" can be fun! Ages 4–10.

ROSH HA-SHANAH AND YOM KIPPUR—
THEMES OF SELF-IMPROVEMENT AND NEW PROMISES

Beim, Jerrold. The Smallest Boy in the Class. Illus. Meg Wohlbert. Morrow, 1949. $6.96.
When Tiny, who is usually a pushy, uncooperative boy, shares his lunch with a hungry schoolmate, the class learns that there is more than one way to be big. Ages 5–8.

Goffstein, M. B. Natural History. See chapter 8, Literature; Fiction: Ages 3 to 8.

Matsuno, Masako. A Pair of Red Clogs. Illus. Kazue Mizmura. Collins Pubs, 1960. O.P.
A small girl repents for the lie she told her mother in order to get a new pair of shoes. Ages 4–7.

Piper, Watty. The Little Engine That Could. Illus. George and Doris Hauman. Schol Bk Serv, 1979. $1.95 pb.
A small blue engine reaches his goal by making a big effort and with a now-classic chant: "I think I can, I think I can." Ages 3–7.

Tobias, Tobi. The Quitting Deal. Illus. Trina Schart Hyman. Viking Pr, 1975. $6.95; $2.25 pb.
Jennifer and her mother help each other overcome some bad habits. Ages 6–9.

Van Woerkom, Dorothy. The Queen Who Couldn't Bake Gingerbread. Illus. Paul Galdone. Knopf, 1975. $5.99.
Instead of complaining about each other's shortcomings, this royal pair finally opts for self-improvement. Ages 5–10.

THE SABBATH—
THEMES OF LOVE AND FAMILY

Adoff, Arnold. Make a Circle Keep Us In: Poems for a Good Day. Illus. Arnold Himler. Delacorte, 1975. $5.95.
A lovable, chubby daddy steals the show in this tribute to a close family. Ages 4–10.

Alexander, Lloyd. The King's Fountain. Illus. Ezra Jack Keats. Dutton, 1971. $7.95.
Written in the tradition of the Hebrew parable is this stunningly told and illustrated tale of personal responsibility and inner strength. When a scholar, a merchant, and a strong man are incapable of telling the king that his plans for a fountain will cut off the city's water supply, a poor, uneducated man is successful because of his concerns for his family's safety. All ages.

Charlip, Remy, and **Lillian Moore.** Hooray for Me! Illus. Vera B. Williams. Parents, 1975. $5.95. Schol Bk Serv, 1980. rev. ed. $8.95.
A joyous look at family relationships, illustrated in vibrant watercolors. Ages 3–7.

Miles, Betty. Around and Around . . . Love. Illus. with photos. Knopf, 1975. $5.99; $2.50 pb.
A simple poem and attractive photographs explore love. Ages 3+.

Zolotow, Charlotte. Do You Know What I'll Do? Illus. Garth Williams. Har-Row, 1958. $8.95
Lovely soft-toned illustrations and a brief text reveal a small girl's love for her baby brother as she imagines all the (nonmaterialistic) things she can do for him, e.g., "Do you know what I'll do at the movie? I'll remember the song and sing it to you." Ages 3–7.

SHAVUOT—THEMES OF THE TEN COMMANDMENTS
AND THE GOLDEN RULE

Keats, Ezra. Louie. Illus. by author. Greenwillow, 1975. $7.75; $1.95 pb., Schol Bk Serv.
Two neighborhood puppeteers offer a puppet to an extremely shy child, because the puppet excited Louie enough to make him speak out for the very first time. Here are two children who care! Ages 4–8.

Reyher, Becky. My Mother Is the Most Beautiful Woman in the World. Illus. Ruth Gannett. Lothrop, 1945. $7.44.
This Russian folk tale reveals a girl's love for her plain mother. Ages 5–9.

Sharmat, Marjorie. A Big Fat Enormous Lie. Illus. David McPhail. Dutton, 1978. $6.95.
Growing more uncomfortable with the lie he told his parents, a small boy keeps up a steady, humorous monologue with a bothersome monster who represents this lie. Ages 4–8.

Zolotow, Charlotte. Mr. Rabbit and the Lovely Present. Illus. Maurice Sendak. Har-Row, 1962. $8.95; $1.95 pb.
A little girl searches for the perfect, natural gift for her mother. Ages 3–7.

SUKKOT—
THEMES OF HARVESTING

Adler, David. The House on the Roof. See chapter 6, Literature: Fiction: Ages 3 to 8.

Krauss, Ruth. The Carrot Seed. Illus. Crockett Johnson. Har-Row, 1945. $5.95; $1.95 pb., Schol Bk Serv.
A small boy carefully plants and tends a carrot seed. His family says it won't come up, but it does, "just as the little boy knew it would." Ages 2–6.

Tresselt, Alvin. Autumn Harvest. Illus. Roger Duvoisin. Lothrop, 1951. $7.44.
A pretty look at the sounds, colors, and crops of the fall season. Ages 4–8.

TISHAH BE-AV—
THEMES OF MOURNING AND TEARS

Hazen, Nancy. Grownups Cry Too. Illus. by author. Lollipop Power, 1973. $1.85 pb.
The saddest day in the Jewish calendar can be shared in part with a book that expresses the adult's need to cry in order to release a variety of strong feelings. Ages 3–8. (Note: Along these lines of letting sadness out, don't forget Carol Hall's "It's All Right to Cry" in *Free to Be . . . You and Me.* Ms. Foundation, 1974.)

TU BI-SHEVAT—
THEMES OF THE PLANTING AND BENEFITS OF TREES

Carrick, Donald. The Tree. Illus. by author. Macmillan, 1971. $4.95.
A boy misses the huge tree that had to be cut down; fortunately, Dad understands and fills the yard with new surprises. Ages 4–8.

Ernst, Kathryn. Mr. Tamarin's Trees. Illus. Diane De Groat. Crown, 1976. $5.95.
Angry about the endless task of raking leaves, the foolish Mr. Tamarin lives to regret the day he chopped down his fine trees. Ages 4–9.

Gershator, Phillis. Honi and His Magic Circle. See chapter 9, Literature: Folk Tales and Anthologies.

Gross, Michael. The Fable of the Fig Tree. See chapter 9, Literature: Folk Tales and Anthologies.

Silverstein, Shel. The Giving Tree. Illus. by author. Har-Row, 1964. $5.95.
From climbing toy to resting stump, an old tree has met the many needs of one man in his lifetime. Ages 4+.

Tresselt, Alvin. The Dead Tree. Illus. by author. Parents 1962. $5.41.
A respectful homage is paid to the life of a forest tree for the way it provided refuge and food for so many creatures. Ages 5–8.

Udry, Janice. A Tree Is Nice. Illus. Marc Simont. Har-Row, 1956. $7.89.
A lovely and simple tribute to the many pleasures and comforts brought to people and animals by trees. Ages 3–6.

Literature: Fiction

The most widely read books reviewed in this chapter enjoy great popularity among Jewish and non-Jewish readers. Judy Blume, an extremely popular author, has written several books for children with Jewish themes. Children are attracted by her humor and by her ability to write uncondescendingly about subjects (sex and puberty) that are on their minds. E. L. Konigsburg is another writer who appeals to both Jewish and non-Jewish readers. In *About the B'nai Bagels,* a Jewish boy has a problem: His mother and his older brother coach and manage his baseball team. This raises issues recognizable by everyone. In another widely read story by Barbara Cohen, *The Carp in the Bathtub,* Leah and Harry's mother is busily preparing a special seder, while the children are frantically trying to save their pet carp from becoming gefilte fish, a favorite holiday dish. All pet fanciers will identify with this twosome.

Most of the novels with Jewish topics belong to the genre of fictionalized history. Several good titles deal with the Middle Ages. The dominant themes in these books are persecution and the stifling nature of the ghetto.

Many fine works describe shtetl life in Russia and Eastern Europe at the turn of the century. The cozy security of a small friendly town is dramatically contrasted with poverty and pogrom. The devastating period of the 1930s and 1940s is also the subject of many juvenile novels. These books deal with people escaping Nazi-occupied lands to become refugees. Some deal with the experience of being a prisoner or a survivor; some deal with situations from which there was no escape.

How successful are these books in reaching young readers? Friendship is a vital theme for youngsters of ages nine to twelve, and books that tell a good friendship story are in great demand. When I recommend *Friedrich* by Hans Richter, I generally receive a personal thank-you the following month. It is the chilling account of a young Jewish boy who is left to die on the streets of Europe when he is denied admission to an air-raid shelter. The book is narrated by a close Christian friend.

The children who read the works reviewed in this chapter will be introduced to the fact that Jews have been fighting for their very existence since ancient times. The books discuss the entire gamut of anti-Semitism from social snubbing to death camps. Youngsters will be exposed to the harsh truths of Jewish history, and in the course of this initiation, they will also learn respect for the values embodied by and transmitted through the Jewish heritage.

The joy inherent in this tradition is best expressed in fiction based on the Jewish holidays. Give a character the opportunity to partake in a traditional celebration and he loses all worldly cares. For example, when Charlotte Herman's protagonist in *The Difference of Ari Stein* describes the peaceful Saturdays he spent with his parents, the reader envies those quiet, loving times. A wedding in a Russian forest between two partisans during World War II puts a temporary end to all anguish; author Yuri Suhl (*Uncle Misha's Partisans*) knows that Jewish weddings are for feasting and merriment.

More books extolling the joys of being Jewish are needed. The materials from Orthodox publishers express the deep satisfaction of living an ethical and spiritual life in books that do not separate Judaism from everyday life. But these books are largely written to teach a lesson or to make a point, and although this is a fine method for writing textbooks, it does not make for good fiction.

Much of the recent fiction about Jews is by authors writing about their American childhood in the past thirty years, during the era of assimilation. Many of these writers toss in a holiday, a bowl of chicken soup, and perhaps an anti-Semitic word to remind the reader and character that this is a book about Jews.

The novels about modern Israel, on the other hand, are full of the joy of helping a nation grow. Israeli fiction differs from its American counterpart in several ways. Contemporary American juvenile fiction is largely introspective, dealing with a child's relationship with her- or himself and other people, while Israeli characters are caught up in the survival of their country. Relationships with other Israelis and Arabs are important, but for political as well as personal reasons. Novels about Israel often include stock characters who represent types or arguments for Israel's importance to Jews. Here you will find the spoiled Westerner, aghast at the lack of privacy on the kibbutz and the lack of first-class accommodations; the tough patriot scornful of any criticism; the unfortunate character killed in an act of terrorism; the friendly Arab who is proud of his heritage yet is attracted to Israel's technical genius. Repetitive and deductive as these books are, they do reach youngsters who might otherwise never be exposed to any of the complexities of Israeli life.

This chapter, unlike others, is subdivided into four age categories. This is done for two reasons: because the number of titles is greatest in this chapter, and because the contents in juvenile novels are often geared to particular age and reading levels. Nonetheless, some small public libraries shelve their adult and children's nonfiction together because juvenile materials are often much appreciated by the adult patron and vice versa.

The four divisions provide only general guidelines. Picture books, for example, found in the youngest juvenile category, are often more appreciated by older children sophisticated enough to appreciate the humor and art work on many levels. Individual reviews will state age range; many times this will overlap with the general subdivisions employed here.

Ages 3 to 8

Adler, David. The House on the Roof: A Sukkot Story. Illus. Marilyn Hirsh. Bonim, 1976. $6.95; $1.95 pb.
"Off my roof!" the landlady shouted. "I rent you an apartment not a roof." So announces an unlikely Elijah as she and her angry broom invade the sukkah built by an elderly man for his grandchildren to enjoy. After carefully gathering, sewing, and hammering his materials together, will this inner-city grandpa have to tear down his holiday retreat? Swept into court, the tenant tells of the sukkah's meaning and that in four more days the Jewish feast will end. Smiling, the judge provides a Solomonian solution by giving the old gentleman ten days to remove the construction. Brief, cheery, and nondidactic, this is a charming story for any audience. Hirsh's lively, colorful drawings are humorous and respectful. Ages 4–10.

Brodsky, Beverly. Secret Places. Illus. by author. Lippincott, 1979. $8.95.
With all the sights and sounds of an old Jewish neighborhood surrounding the young heroine, this introspective and poetic picture book explores the need to find secret places in which to dream and create. Brodsky successfully combines the rare (blooming irises) with the common (booming merchants); the reality (hanging laundry) with the make-believe (hidden treasures); and the noisy streets with the peace of the Sabbath home. From the clink of the penny tossed down to the candy-hungry child to the fear of the basement bogey-

man, Brodsky's beautiful watercolors and brief narrative evoke genuine memories of her own childhood and probably a little of everyone else's. Children will enjoy this. Ages 5–10.

Emberley, Barbara, adap. One Wide River to Cross. Illus. Ed Emberley. P-H, 1966. O.P.
This adapted folk song about Noah's ark is a nonsensical counting rhyme: "The animals came in five by five/The yak in slippers did arrive." Ed Emberley places his humorous black animal woodcuts against an array of vibrantly colored backgrounds; the last page holds a happy surprise when all the colors form a lovely rainbow behind a mountain-borne ark. Music and lyrics are included too. Ed Emberley, famous for his unique how-to-draw books for children, has created another artistic treat. Especially good for a young storytime audience. Ages 3+.

Glasgow, Aline. The Pair of Shoes. Illus. Symeon Shimin. Dial, 1971. $4.95.
Wisdom can be learned from one's own dear family, and even from an old pair of shoes. There lived in Poland many years ago a poor Jewish family and a cow. Together, they owned one pair of shoes. Although the crippled, scholarly father and the selfless mother could do without them, the shoes were desperately longed for by the family children. Sadly, illness makes it necessary to sell the family's only treasure—the samovar. The eldest son, however, who was growing defiant and bitter over his desire to monopolize the shoes, sells the worn boots instead. In return, the father, learning that books are not the only place to go for solace, pawns his tomes in order to provide shoes for all three youngsters. Beautiful paintings in gold and black reflect the anguish and goodness of this family. Ages 6+.

Goffstein, M. B. My Noah's Ark. Illus. by author. Har-Row, 1978. $6.95.
The master of brevity in art and prose portrays an old woman reflecting upon her greatest treasure, a toy Noah's ark made by her father and cherished throughout her long lifetime. "I know he had fun building it," she tells us, "because once I heard his voice behind a closed door, booming like God's. 'Make it three hundred cubits long.'" This is a special, effective picture book which uses the Noah theme to unite a whole lifetime of events. In fact, Father must have been quite an unusual man: Mrs. Noah was carved carrying a saw and Noah holds a hammer in one hand and a mop in the other. (Note: The following picture books also use the story of Noah's ark as a basis for their original tales: Norma Farber's *Where's Gomer?*, Dut-

ton, 1974, $8.50; Norma Farber's *How the Left-Behind Beasts Built Ararat,* Walker & Co., 1978, $7.50; Gail Haley's *Noah's Ark,* Atheneum, 1971, $8.95.) Ages 3+.

Goffstein, M. B. Natural History. Illus. by author. FS&G, $7.95.
You don't have to be Jewish to agree with the author's viewpoint, but one could hardly be a "mensh" (a decent human being) if one didn't. In a brief text and simple, lovely watercolors, Goffstein tells about our responsibility to each other. Materialism pales next to the riches of our natural earth. "Let us be like tiny grains of sand," urges the writer, "and protect all life from fear and suffering!" Legend has it that the great Jewish teacher Hillel was once asked to reveal the Torah's wisdom while standing on one leg. "Do not do to others what is hateful to you," he replied. "That is the heart of the Torah." Little children stand on one foot too (so it seems) while attending to their lessons. Reading this book will take only a few minutes, but an important precept will have been shared. (Note: Two new Goffstein titles are as follows: *An Artist,* Har-Row, 1980. $7.95. A lovely book that depicts an artist (similar to God) creating the universe. Ages 4+. *Laughing Latkes,* FS&G, 1980. $5.95. A story with a flat ending about potato pancakes served at Hanukkah.) Ages 3-10.

Hirsh, Marilyn. Ben Goes into Business. Illus. by author. Holiday, 1973. $4.95.
A satisfying story complete with charming illustrations about a Jewish immigrant's first venture into business as a lollipop seller at fashionable Coney Island. Quite a psychologist at ten, Ben approaches mothers and crying children with his sugary pacifiers. When hunger threatens to eat up his profits, he cleverly creates an exciting pancake-eating job for himself with a high-wire act. The sights and sounds of a younger Coney Island are added attractions. But what about the stereotype of the Jew as foxy merchant? Should we deny the skills of Jewish businesspeople because their success causes envy among anti-Semites? Ages 5-10.

Hirsh, Marilyn. Deborah the Dybbuk: A Ghost Story. Illus. by author. Holiday, 1978. $5.95.
This original story iş based on the old Jewish belief in the dibbuk, the troubled spirit of a dead person who enters a living body and takes control. The troubled soul in this case belongs to Deborah, a mischievous child, who delighted in turning her Hungarian shtetl upside down. After Deborah falls from a tree and dies, she enters the body of timid Hannah, changing her into a naughty child. The village is now faced with an exorcism. All ends well with Deborah going to heaven and Hannah having a more interesting personality. The well-re-

searched illustrations produced in grays and oranges perfectly complement the narrative. Using this tragic folk theme in a light-hearted picture book, however, will not appeal to all parents and educators. The story is enjoyed by children old enough to comprehend the plot and dialogue. Ages 7–11.

Hirsh, Marilyn. Potato Pancakes All Around: A Hanukkah Tale. Illus. by author. Bonim, 1978. $6.95.
A wise peddler stops at a shtetl home for a Hanukkah meal and hears the two grandmothers angrily defending their own potato pancake recipe. In a variation on the folk tale "Stone Soup," the peddler announces that he will make latkes (potato pancakes) out of bread. Grandmas Sophie and Yetta can barely hide their contempt. The peddler cheerfully humors them out of their bad mood and soon the entire family is enjoying a delicious dinner. The book is humorously illustrated in gold and brown to match the crispy pancakes. Yetta and Sophie's joint latkes recipe is printed at the end of this delightful story. (Note: Several picture books by Hirsh are reviewed in chapter 9. Her two out-of-print fictional picture books with Jewish themes are *Where is Yonkela?*, Crown, 1969; and *The Pink Suit*, Crown, 1970.). Ages 3–10.

Muchnik, Michoel. The Cuckoo Clock Castle of Shir. Illus. by author. Bloch, 1980. $7.95.
When the joy of the Sabbath causes a wooden sky-blue cuckoo bird to come to life, Kalman the clockmaker and the small town of Shir are in for some romantic surprises. Muchnik's fantasy, revolving around the sweetness of the Sabbath celebration, is charmingly illustrated in pretty, soft tones (as well as black-and-white drawings) and is fun to read. Ages 5–8.

Muchnik, Michoel. The Double Decker Purple Shul Bus. Illus. by author. Merkos L'Inoyne Chinuch, 1977. $3.25.
In a mythical village where there are several shuls (synagogues), the most intriguing shul of all is closed on the Sabbath. Call it a shulmobile, for it carries workers to and from their jobs, conducting services aboard. The book is published by an Orthodox organization and, not surprisingly, the upper deck of the bus is where the females sit, pray, and sometimes cook breakfast. The illustrations are pleasantly drawn in shades of purple, and young children who love all sorts of transports will be amused by this unorthodox Orthodox bus. The publisher has a number of books for children. They are moral tales which teach Jewish values. *Double Decker* has no moral; it just takes us for a pleasant ride. (Note: See Muchnik's other pleasant, if not so exciting,

titles for young Orthodox children from the same publisher: *David Comes Home,* 1976; *Hershel's Houseboat,* 1977; and *The Scribe Who Lived in a Tree,* 1976.) Ages 4–8.

Rose, Anne K. How Does a Czar Eat Potatoes? Illus. Janosch. Lothrop, 1973. $6.96.
A Yiddish folk song is the basis for this lyrical and memorable picture book, which compares a czar's life to that of a Russian peasant. The czar (pictured in bright colors) enjoys life with much extravagance and waste. For example, how does a czar cry? The people's tears are collected in a bowl and poured over his head. Father (pictured in black and white) lives in a hut with the barest necessities. However, when Father is happy, "when the violins sing and balalaikas weep," his joy is greater than even a czar's. This title is especially effective when read to a group. Ages 5+.

Ruggill, Peter. The Return of the Golem. Illus. by author. HR&W, 1979. $6.95.
When outer-space creatures attack a synagogue during Hanukkah, the shtetl's rabbi re-creates the golem to restore order. The idea of anti-Semitism from aliens is not acceptable. Although Hanukkah picture-book stories are scarce, this book is not worth purchasing. Ages 4–9.

Shulevitz, Uri. The Magician. Illus. by the author. Macmillan, 1973. $7.95; $1.95 pb.
"He pulled ribbons out of his mouth and turkeys out of his boots." Yes, he arrived at the village looking like a beggar, but he provided a poor and pious couple with a complete seder one Passover eve. From a story by the great Yiddish writer I. L. Peretz, Shulevitz has written and illustrated a gem of a book about the lovable prophet Elijah. Disguised as a beggar, with a heart of gold, Elijah brings help to needy people and is portrayed as a jaunty, yet gaunt-looking magician. Expressive black-and-white drawings and a brief, poetic text make this a perfect story for small group tellings. Ages 4+.

Singer, Isaac Bashevis. A Tale of Three Wishes. Illus. Irene Lieblich. FS&G, 1975. $5.95.
Legend promises that on the holy night of Hoshanah Rabba (the seventh day of Sukkot, the Feast of Tabernacles) the sky will open for a moment and wishes will come true. On this night, two boys and a girl decide to wish for things beyond their years: wisdom, wealth, and beauty. Instead, their spur-of-the-moment wishes temporarily turn little Esther into a blintz! Heaven gently warns them to "go home and try to deserve by effort what you wanted to get too easily." The

children do grow up into great people: The boys get their wishes for wealth and brains, the girl becomes wise and, of course, beautiful. While not one of Singer's most effective titles, the wonderful full-color paintings of a small Jewish community make the book worth owning. Ages 8–12.

Singer, Isaac Bashevis. Why Noah Chose the Dove. Trans. Elizabeth Shub. Illus. Eric Carle. FS&G, 1974. $8.95.
Rumors are flying that Noah is to select only the best animals to live with him on the ark. Boldly illustrated animals compete with each other by proclaiming their own importance. Only the dove refrains from boasting: "Each one of us has something the other doesn't have, given us by God who created us all," she coos. Because of her modesty, Noah appoints her to test the readiness of God's new world. Singer and Carle have created an entertaining expansion of the Bible story. This might be the only book in which Singer is upstaged by the illustrator. The humor in the text and drawings enhances the slim plot, making the book unique and effective. (Note: See chapter 9, Literature: Folk Tales and Anthologies, for additional picture books by Singer.) Ages 3–8.

Weinbach, Sheindel. Avi Names His Price. Illus. Bracha Sorotzkin. Feldheim, 1976. $3.50.
A pleasantly illustrated picture book about an Orthodox boy. Forever collecting odds and ends, Avi is dismayed each Passover when Mother urges him to clean out his closet. One year, Father suggests that Avi earn and collect mitzvah (good deed) cards and trade them in at the end of the year for a special toy. At the year's end, however, Avi turns down the offer to trade in his cards for a gift: A toy will cheapen the joy he has felt from doing the good works. Noble, but doubtful. Readers might even feel that the rug has been pulled from under them. The contemporary flavor and nice drawings set this above other Orthodox materials. A glossary would have been helpful to explain non-English words. Ages 4–8.

Ages 7 to 9

Cohen, Barbara. The Carp in the Bathtub. Illus. Joan Halpern. Lothrop, 1972. $6.96; 95¢ pb. Dell.
Not all children enjoy gefilte fish, but Leah and Harry have a compelling excuse: Could you eat a friend? Leah's mother always buys her carp a full week before she cooks it, providing the fish with bathtub privileges. Otherwise petless, Leah and Harry keep each new catch company and hate to see it go. One Passover carp, however, is particularly hard to part with. The children name it Joe (after a de-

ceased neighbor) and try to rescue it from its fate. Here is a funny, ethnic tale with a universal theme for all animal lovers. It is a good read-aloud title, and the many art nouveau–like drawings create an atmosphere of New York City two generations ago. Ages 8–10; younger for reading aloud.

Cohen, Floreva G. Sneakers to Shul. Illus. Zephyr Cooper. Board of Jewish Ed, 1978. $2.75 pb.
Danny watches his family prepare for Yom Kippur in this low-key story set in New York City. Many customs associated with this holiday are touched upon as Danny, a chubby, inquisitive youngster, helps his family prepare dinner and get dressed (in sneakers because of a ban on leather shoes at this time) for the Kol Nidre service. Young readers might enjoy mastering this brief story. Ages 6–7; younger for reading aloud.

Eisenberg, Phyllis Rose. A Mitzvah Is Something Special. Illus. Susan Jeschke. Har-Row, 1978. $7.95.
Lisa performs her own mitzvah (blessed deed) when she brings her two very different grandmothers (one unconventional, one traditional) together for a slumber party at her house. Eisenberg explores Lisa's special relationship with each grandmother through warm and humorous descriptions and comparisons. There is no plot, but the author brings all the love and both the grandmothers together for a satisfying end. Black-and-white line drawings in Jeschke's familiar droll fashion are right and extend the story. Ages 8–10; younger for reading aloud.

Finkelstein, Ruth. Mendel the Mouse. Illus. Anol Amay. Torah Umesorah. Vol. I, 1972; vol. II, 1979. $3.75 pb. each.
These two volumes of forty short stories feature an amiable mouse, Mendel, who represents the concerns and joys of the Orthodox child. Written in rhymed verse, the tales are aids in teaching the keeping of the commandments. The brief stories often reflect the Orthodox Jew's minority (but protected) status in the United States. Mendel frequently reminds himself that being different might cause discomfort, but it is only God he should fear. Another repeated theme is that good deeds bring us good feelings and closer to God. All Jewish children can appreciate Mendel's world. For example, when Mendel asks a saleswoman for a Purim costume, she replies: "You want a pudding ... a pudding what?" Pleasant illustrations and a tolerable verse make Mendel an attractive role-mouse. Glossary. Ages 5–10.

Goffstein, M. B. Family Scrapbook. Illus. by author. FS&G, 1978. $5.95.
Seven brief tales narrated by a curly-haired little girl are written and

illustrated in Goffstein's uniquely succinct style. Easy-to-read stories about her birthday, a visitor, a pickup truck, neighbors, and Yom Kippur reveal a close family and a plucky heroine. Life's sweet, simple times are highlighted, such as walking through the park and picking up colorful autumn leaves after the morning Yom Kippur services. (Note: See Goffstein's *Two Piano Tuners* for a fine story about a Jewish piano tuner and his remarkable granddaughter. FS&G, 1970. $5.95. Ages 5–9.) Ages 5–9.

Jaffe, Leonard. The Pitzel Holiday Book. Illus. Bill Giacalone. KTAV, 1962. $5.00 pb.

The Pitzels are a Jewish family who live in a snug little house under the strawberry bushes and are good friends with the neighboring insects and birds. In this pleasant and mildly amusing collection of stories, the Pitzel children celebrate the Jewish holidays with the help of their insect pals. In one story, Mrs. Spinner (a spider) makes the Queen Esther costume for young Sarah Pitzel while four fireflies provide the stage lights for a Purim play. Young children (who like bugs better than adults do) will enjoy these stories best in a read-aloud session. Ages 5–9.

Kimmel, Eric A. Nicanor's Gate. Illus. Jerry Joyner. Jewish Pubn, 1979. $5.95.

Kimmel retells the Talmudic tale of Nicanor, a wealthy Jew who lived in Alexandria, Egypt, two thousand years ago. Upon hearing that King Solomon's Temple in Jerusalem is to be restored by King Herod of Judea, Nicanor liquidates his business in order to furnish the huge and exquisitely crafted doors for the Temple. On the ship to Jerusalem, one of the doors is lost during a storm, and Nicanor broken-heartedly disembarks at the port of Acre. A sudden billow, however, brings the missing door to his feet, and the dying old man's joy knows no bounds. This low-key, well-told, and dramatic story of strong faith, sacrifice, and pride is illustrated in effective black, white, and blue woodcuts. Because of the small, picture-book format and serious theme, the book might require a gentle push toward the older child who might otherwise pass it by. A fine read-aloud narrative. Ages 7+.

Kleinbard, Gitel. Oh! Zalmy! The Tale of the Porcelain Pony; Oh! Zalmy! Or, the Tale of the Tooth. Illus. Shmuel Kunda. Mah Tov, 1976–1977. $4.50; $2.25 pb.

Two inexpensive and pleasant titles about a young Orthodox boy and how his Jewish values affect his everyday life. Children will like the young hero. Ages 5–8.

Levitin, Sonia. A Sound to Remember. Illus. Gabriel Lisowski. Har-BraceJ, 1979. $6.95.
A pleasant, gentle story about the Jewish New Year that subtly teaches a lesson in the spirit of this solemn holiday. Long ago in a European town, Jacov, a simple-minded boy, is chosen by the rabbi to blow the shofar at the High Holy Days services. Jacov's shofar, however, emits but a weak cry at Rosh ha-Shanah and the disappointed congregation wears an "I told you so!" expression. When Yom Kippur comes, the kindly rabbi uses his wits to prevent further humiliation for the boy, yet ensures the happiness of the congregation. Skillfully illustrated in soft black-and-white sketches, the book reveals the importance of caring for one another—and if not on Yom Kippur, when? Ages 8–10; younger for reading aloud.

Moskin, Marietta. Waiting for Mama. Illus. Richard Lebenson. Coward, 1975. $6.96.
Two years have passed since Becky and her family came to America, leaving Mama and a sick infant behind in Russia. Becky has used that lonely time to learn English and to find her way around the busy streets of turn-of-the-century New York. Although life is still very hard for this poor family, at least no one has to worry about the czar's army; and when Mama and Leah finally arrive, Becky's happiness is complete. In an easy-to-read narrative, the author has written a tender and realistic story. Generously illustrated in lovely detailed watercolors, the book provides a pleasant and personal history of Becky's era. Ages 7–10.

Sharoff, Victor. The Heart of the Wood. Illus. Wallace Tripp. Coward, 1971. O.P.
Isaac is an eleven-year-old woodcutter living in medieval Spain. A dilemma arises when the wealthy Duke Francisco asks Isaac to carve a bowl with deer pictured around the rim. How can Isaac possibly do this when the rabbi has forbidden him to carve animals? Too bad that Isaac has already promised to carve such a bowl for the powerful duke. In the course of the book, Isaac learns that there are many right answers to the same argument. This wisdom later enables the boy to stop a battle between two knights. As for the bowl, the young carver finds a lovely piece of wood with pictures of deer seemingly carved in the heart of the material. This is an unusually philosophical title for beginning readers. Ages 7–8.

Skolsky, Mindy. Carnival and Kopeck and More About Hannah. Illus. Karen Ann Weinhaus. Har-Row, 1979. $7.95.   Whistling Teakettle and Other Stories About Hannah. Illus. Karen Ann Weinhaus. Har-Row, 1977. $5.95.

These two books offer an entertaining collection of short stories about Hannah, a young New Jersey girl of the 1930s and her loving parents and grandparents. The author captures childhood concerns and communicates them in a natural and humorous dialogue. Hannah's special relationship with Grandma is developed in the newer title; and while their loving and arguing are universal, the Yiddish background makes these stories personal and genuine. Adults looking for read-aloud titles will find a delightful choice here. (Note: See Vicky Shiefman's *Mindy* for another easy-to-read story in which a young girl and her Tante Toba (great-aunt) try to understand each other. Macmillan, 1974. $4.95.) Ages 8–10.

Slobodkin, Florence. Sarah Somebody. Illus. Louis Slobodkin. Vanguard, 1969. $5.95.
A gentle story about a nine-year-old girl who begins school in a nineteenth-century Polish shtetl. Both Sarah and her wise old grandmother are overjoyed at this rare opportunity for a poor Jewish girl. The book ends with the grandma's peaceful death, sweetened with the knowledge that Sarah, "a somebody," can write her own name. Sarah's adventures in this primitive school will entertain and surprise young readers. Ages 7–10.

Snyder, Carol. Ike and Mama and the Block Wedding. Illus. Charles Robinson. Coward, 1979. $6.95.
Mama's neighbor, Mrs. Weinstein, is hysterical: Daughter Rosie's big wedding must be canceled because Mr. Weinstein lost his job (it's 1919). So indomitable Mama plans a successful block wedding with the help of son Ikey, his thirteen multi-ethnic pals, and God. There are snags, of course. This warm, amusing, and idealized picture of neighborly love in the South Bronx is reminiscent of Sydney Taylor's All-of-a-Kind Family stories. The soft pencil sketches add a nostalgic touch to this easy-to-read tale. Ages 8–10.

Snyder, Carol. Ike and Mama and the Once-a-Year Suit. Illus. Charles Robinson. Coward, 1978. $5.95.
It's 1918 and a dozen boys on Mrs. Greenberg's Bronx street need that special suit to last from Passover to Yom Kippur, or from Easter to Christmas. With her son, Ike, his cousins, and neighborhood friends trailing behind, Mrs. Greenberg awes the storekeeper with her bargaining skills. As each boy gets the suit of his dreams, the reader learns of the special relationship between Ike and his mother, and about the busy days of East Side shopping. The author and illustrator successfully avoid the stereotype of the bargaining Jew. The slight but genuine story is fun to read aloud. Ages 7–9.

Soyer, Abraham. Adventures of Yemima and Other Stories. Trans. Rebecca Beagle and Rebecca Soyer. Illus. Raphael Soyer. Viking Pr, 1979. $8.95.
Abraham Soyer, a Russian Jew, originally published these stories in Hebrew over forty years ago. Here are six of his original tales, which contain folkloristic themes, gentle humor, and rich imagery. Although Yemima, a kind and clever girl, is the featured heroine, the true protagonists are the villain, Hunger, and the hero, Hope. Poverty afflicts all Soyer's characters, from the pious mothers to the crafty animals. In these stories, righteousness never goes unrewarded, and there is always the desperate hope that tomorrow will bring food for each child and beast. The handsomely published book is expressively illustrated in soft pencil sketches by Soyer's nephew, artist Raphael Soyer. Especially recommended for reading aloud. Ages 8–12; younger for reading aloud.

Spector, Shoshannah. Five Young Heroes of Israel. Illus. Aharon Shevo. Shengold, 1970. $3.95.
Five youngsters secretly leave their kibbutz with the intention of helping the soldiers keep Israel safe. The three boys and two girls are safely returned to their home, after their anxious parents have heard a radio broadcast announcing their admirable, but premature, offer. Upon their return, the children are given a hero's welcome and join the kibbutz in a gala Hanukkah celebration. The book's asset is its introduction to the kibbutz, describing the responsibilities of each child. The text is unexceptional and somewhat sex-role-stereotyped. The illustrations are bright and attractive. (Note: Margalit Banai's *Yael and the Queen of the Goats* is another mediocre book that informs young children about Israel in a fictional form. Bonim reprint, c. 1968. $1.49 pb.) Ages 7–10.

Suhl, Yuri. The Merrymaker. Illus. Thomas di Grazia. Four Winds, 1975. $5.95; $1.95 pb. Collier.
This story takes place several generations ago in a poor Jewish home in Eastern Europe. Ten-year-old Shloimeh becomes enchanted with the family's Sabbath guest, a merrymaker at weddings, who speaks to the boy in rhyme and eventually brings the family good fortune. Illustrations re-create the mood of a poor but dignified household. Readers will enjoy meeting a "badchen" (jester), a traditional figure in shtetl life whose job was to "make the guests gay / The in-laws pay / And the bride weep." The forty-five page story makes for a delightful read-aloud and the handsome format is a pleasure to hold. Ages 8+.

Suhl, Yuri. The Purim Goat. Illus. Kaethe Zemach. Four Winds, 1980. $7.95.

Adults and children will want to share aloud this entertaining story about a boy and his goat. Yossele lives in a small East European town, Betchootch ("a name that sounds like a sneeze"), with his poor mother and a skinny goat. In order to keep his pet, Yossele must pay off the cost of buying her. Unfortunately, it won't be from the sale of her meager milk supply. How the lad manages to reach his goal by teaching his affectionate goat to dance at the Purim celebration makes for a good-natured and humorous tale. It is too bad that only the cover is illustrated in color, for Zemach's appealing drawings are a bit too dark and heavy for the lively text. (Note: Teachers might like to couple this story with Isaac Bashevis Singer's tale about a boy and his goat, "Zlateh the Goat," from his book with the same name. Suhl's boy saves the goat's life; Singer's goat saves the boy.) Ages 8–10; read aloud to ages 6+.

Weilerstein, Sadie Rose. Ten and a Kid. Illus. Janina Domanska. Jewish Pubn., 1961. $3.95.
Young Reizel lives with her parents and numerous siblings in a small cottage in Lithuania many generations ago. When a little white goat mysteriously appears at the Passover seder, he brings good fortune to the family and a special delight to spunky Reizel. As readers follow the rollicking kid through the year, we see this loving family celebrating Jewish holidays and having some dreams come true. Lively Reizel and Gadya, the goat, are shown in many graceful line drawings, which enhance this appealing book. (Note: There are other Weilerstein titles that portray in great detail Jewish beliefs and holidays in fictional form. The books are didactic and predictable, but have a tremendous nostalgic appeal for many parents and do provide a wealth of information. *Adventures of K'tonton.* Bloch, rev. ed., 1964, $4.50, Ages 5–10; *K'tonton in Israel,* Bloch, 1964, $3.50, Ages 5–10; *K'tonton on an Island in the Sea,* Jewish Pubn., 1976, $4.50, Ages 5–10; *What the Moon Brought,* Jewish Pubn., 1942, $4.50, Ages 6–9. In addition, Marilyn Hirsh has a new illustrated edition, *The Best of K'tonton.* Jewish Pubn., 1980. $9.95; $5.95 pb. Ages 6–10.) Ages 8–11; younger for reading aloud.

Weinberg, Yona. "Dov Dov" Series. Illus. Esky Cook and Esther Lefkowitz. Dov Dov, 1975–1979. $2.00 pb. each.
These seven books contain short stories that teach religious values from an Orthodox point of view. In these tales children act upon their own problems, which are always brought to a happy conclusion, thanks to Ha-Shem (God). This series received rave reviews from several Orthodox leaders and a very positive annotation in Judaica Book News (Spring/Summer 1979). Though not great literature, these

stories do reveal the unity of the secular and the religious in the life of the Orthodox Jew. With so much good will in this series, it is astonishing to read the story "Pesach in Japan" (*Ninety-Nine for Dov Dov*) in which a Japanese waiter becomes the laughing stock of a U.S. Army seder. The illustrations by Cook are especially pleasant. Recommended for an Orthodox audience. Ages 7–10; read aloud to ages 4+.

Ages 9 to 12

Aleichem, Sholom. Holiday Tales of Sholom Aleichem. Trans. Aliza Shevrin. Illus. Thomas di Grazia. Scribner, 1979. $8.95.
Shevrin has done a most competent job in translating these seven stories, two of which enjoy their first English translation. The protagonists are boys who live in the fictional Ukrainian Jewish community of Kasrilevka. The youths share their personal tales of woe, e.g., the widow's son who loses his treasured prayer book after gambling with a lad with a "fixed" dreidl. As humorous and entertaining as these holiday stories are, I do not think Sholom Aleichem is a children's writer. He is a leisurely observer of Yiddish culture and personalities. Most children have little patience with descriptive prose or character studies. The book is a fine title, enhanced by expressive black-and-white drawings; but it calls for the special child or for families who share their books aloud. (Note: *Hanukah Money* is another such Sholom Aleichem title published for children. Trans. and adap. Uri Shulevitz and Elizabeth Shub. Greenwillow, 1978. $7.50.) Ages 10+.

Biber, Yehoash. The Treasure of the Turkish Pasha. Trans. Baruch Hochman. Illus. Uri Shulevitz. Blue Star reprint, c. 1968. $1.25 pb.
Yirmi is assigned by the Haganah (Israeli underground defense organization) to recover a treasure pirated from the Jewish community of Jerusalem by a Turkish pasha (ruler) over thirty years before. Yirmi's mission leads him across the Sinai Desert, to the ancient monastery of St. Catherine, and into battle with Bedouin bandits. Biber has an appealing writing style. His words travel at a nice clip down a road paved with humor and action. Glossary. (Note: See Biber's *Adventures in the Galilee* for another rip-roaring adventure in Palestine during the days of the British mandate. Jewish Pubn., 1973. $3.95. Ages 10–14.) Ages 10–14.

Blaine, Marge. Dvora's Journey. Illus. Gabriel Lisowski. HR&W, 1979. $6.95.
This easy-to-read title describes the journey to America attempted by a Jewish Russian family and the pitfalls that await them. The excitement and drama of escaping across the Russian border, and across

chilling waters, are well described. Unfortunately, the journey goes awry and Dvora's family meets up with a host of problems. The unexpected and devastating ending makes up for the somewhat stock characterizations and unexceptional writing. Ages 8–11.

Blue, Rose. Cold Rain on the Water. McGraw, 1979. $7.95.
This contemporary problem novel focuses on seventeen-year-old Alec Steinoff, a Russian emigrant who resides with his family in Brighton Beach (Brooklyn). Trying to adjust to a society in which freedom is plentiful—along with TV and drug addiction, youth crimes, red tape, and unemployment—the Steinoffs' hope for the future diminishes with each chapter. Blue does a good job in describing the plight of the newly arrived Soviet family against the background of a New York Spanish and Jewish neighborhood. It is obvious, however, that the novel serves primarily as a platform from which to air these many concerns. Culminating with the murder of Alec's dad (a former teacher) at a custard stand where he was employed, Blue's story approaches melodrama. Withal, it is a book to ponder. Ages 11–14.

Blume, Judy. Are You There God? It's Me, Margaret. Bradbury, 1970. $6.95; $1.50 pb., Dell.
Margaret Simon is the twelve-year-old daughter of a mixed marriage. Neither her Jewish father nor her Christian mother recognize religion; they expect Margaret to make her own decisions when grown. Margaret, however, talks to God in secret, telling Him her problems and asking for help. Important questions nag her: Should she join the "Y" or the Jewish Community Center? Will she ever get her period? Is she even normal? Touched with genius for this genre, Judy Blume has written an often hilarious novel that will reassure (and highly entertain) preteens. Margaret's story is touching, breezy, and realistic. Boys like it too! Ages 9–12.

Blume, Judy. Starring Sally J. Freedman As Herself. Bradbury, 1977. $8.95; $1.50 pb., Dell.
Sally moves from New Jersey in 1947 for a temporary stay in Florida. Although she must leave her loving father, she lives with her mother, brother, and grandmother. Sally's imagination leads her to believe that a harmless neighbor is really Adolf Hitler in disguise, and her wild fantasies conclude with her capture of the odious creature. Fourth-grade girls adore this book, and their mothers would certainly enjoy its nostalgia. Blume's title is funny and full of Sally's everyday concerns. Jewish culture is sprinkled throughout this novel, which has an autobiographical tone. Ages 9–12.

Brodie, Deborah, ed. Stories My Grandfather Should Have Told Me. Illus. Carmela Tal Baron. Bonim, 1977. $6.95.

A dozen short stories about Jewish life in Europe, Israel, and the United States reveal the customs and dreams of twentieth-century Jews. Ten of the stories are adapted from full-length books; two were written for this edition. Although the stories are not of memorable literary quality, they are very pleasant to read and have a universal appeal. The tales contain a variety of themes, e.g., kibbutz life, American immigration, shtetl days, and holiday times. Appealing pencil sketches and a glossary are added attractions. Ages 8–11.

Burstein, Chaya. Rifka Bangs the Teakettle. Illus. by author. Har-BraceJ, 1970. $4.95; Sequel: Rifka Grows Up. Illus. by author. Bonim, 1976. $6.95.
Meet young Rifka, a Jewish girl growing up in czarist and Revolutionary Russia. The author skillfully integrates Jewish culture, history, and customs into the daily life of an intelligent, loving girl. Burstein's main theme is Rifka's love for learning and her determination to get an education. Unfortunately, poverty, shtetl culture, and anti-Semitism make the achievement of these goals unlikely. America, the answer to so many of the family's other problems, promises to be Rifka's best bet. Based on stories told to the author by her mother, Burstein's novels are pleasant family stories and informal historic fiction. Ages 10–12.

Chaikin, Miriam. I Should Worry, I Should Care. Illus. Richard Egielski. Har-Row, 1979. $7.95.
Here is an entertaining, nicely written, and easy-to-read story about Molly, a ten-year-old Brooklyn girl of the late 1930s. A recent move has made Molly friendless and surly. In addition to local woes, there are those increasingly awful radio broadcasts about European Jewry. However, surrounded by a loving, good-humored family, Molly finds happiness in the busy Brooklyn neighborhood. Jewish customs are woven into this story in which everyday troubles cannot keep those surges of childhood joy down. Sings Molly: "I should worry, I should care/I should marry a millionaire." (Note: The sequel, *Finder's Weepers* (published too late for review), concerns Molly's tough Rosh ha-Shanah decision. Har-Row, 1980. $8.95. Ages 8–11.) Ages 8–11.

Cohen, Barbara. Benny. Lothrop, 1977. $6.96.
This nice piece of writing is about a Brooklyn boy who lives for baseball. Unfortunately, life is not that simple for Benny Rifkind, who resents working in Pa's store and sharing his home with two older and more competent siblings. To make matters worse, young Arnuf enters his life. Who needs this obnoxious foreign boy who hates the United States and whines about going home? Sadly, home for this half-Jewish child is Germany and the year is 1939. Benny matures during the

novel; he learns to care about another's unhappiness and to relate to things in life other than a home run and the 1939 World's Fair. Ages 9–12.

Cone, Molly. A Promise Is a Promise. Illus. John Gretzer. HM, 1964. $8.95.
While Ruthy Morgan prepares for her bat mitzvah, she begins to learn the meaning of Judaism. Not always satisfied with her family, neighbors, religion, or herself, Ruthy comes to see the need for tolerance and for living by one's convictions. She emerges as a kind and thoughtful person who wants others to treat her as she would them. Most memorable and humorous is the chapter in which Ruthy, dressed as Queen Esther, accompanies her friend to a Christian Sunday school costume party (to feel accepted) and is given a cross as a prize. The queen now learns the meaning of guilt. That Judaism touches our daily life is well brought out in this successful novel. Recommended for a wide audience. Ages 9–12.

Eisenberg, Azriel, and **Leah Ain Globe,** ed. and trans. Sabra Children: Stories of Fun and Adventure in Israel. Jonathan David, 1970. O.P.
Twenty-five stories by a variety of Israeli children's writers are translated from the Hebrew for American youngsters. Sabra (Israeli-born) children are the heroes of this pleasant, if not memorable, anthology of life in Israel. The tensions of war, the love of the land, and the variety of surrounding cultures are some of the recurring themes. Perhaps it is the danger of living in a hostile environment that causes the children's writers to adopt a more sentimental tone than American authors do. Unfortunately, the mood of many of the stories is broken by the incongruous cartoon drawings. Ages 8–11.

Eisenberg, Ronald Lee. The Iguana Corps of the Haganah. Bloch, 1977. $5.95.
Three iguanas trained to carry messages and weapons across enemy lines are the Haganah heroes of this nicely paced fantasy. Taking place before the Partition of Palestine in 1947, the Haganah utilizes these animals to help their guerilla warfare against the Arabs and the British. The book's strong points are a clever, suspenseful plot and good physical descriptions of the area. The weak spots are the misuse of dialogue to impart information in long-winded speeches and the strongly one-sided political viewpoint. The title is recommended as an exciting tale for animal and adventure enthusiasts. Ages 10–14.

Ellentuck, Shan. Yankel the Fool. See chapter 9, Literature: Folk Tales and Anthologies.

Feder-Tal, Karah. The Ring. Trans. Adrienne Dixon. Illus. Tsofia Langer. Abelard, 1965. O.P.
A realistic story with interesting characters set in Tamaria, a small southern Israeli town. When a timid Yemenite, Mazal, steals the gold ring intended for her father's fiancée, she enlists the aid of a neighborhood boy, Jair, to help hide it. The ring gets misplaced and Jair goes off in search of it. The author introduces us to a small town where everyone has a different personality and birthplace. The writing is quite agreeable and should appeal to the good reader. Ages 11–13.

Garvey, Robert. What Feast? And Other Tales. Illus. Laszlo Matulay. KTAV, 1974. O.P.
Many of these fourteen original stories, which center around Jewish holidays, first appeared in the magazines *World Over* and *Young Israel.* Although the quality of plot and prose in the collection is uneven, on the whole, it is an entertaining book. Especially fun to read are these stories: "The Slaves" (in which chickens revolt); "The Dragon That Learned"; and "The Better Play" (about Hanukkah). Garvey does best when he is not narrating through the mouths of animated mazzot (unleavened breads), groggers, pine trees, and ark curtains. The illustrations are not subtle: a Nazi guard looks more like King Kong in uniform. Glossary. Ages 8–11.

Geras, Adele. The Girls in the Velvet Frame. Atheneum, 1979. $7.95.
A delightful novel about five sisters, their hard-working mother, and their flamboyant aunt who live in early-twentieth-century Jerusalem. Geras creates individuals out of each Bernstein sister, one old enough to meet her intended at fourteen and one young enough to long for a pet rabbit. Vivacious Aunt Mimi, who wears outrageous clothes and lovingly indulges her nieces, is the novel's heroine. It is she who arranges for the girls to sit for their collective portrait (how modern!), enabling the photograph to travel to America and finally locate Isaac, the darling brother who left for New York never to be heard from again. Without a cause to rally around or a message to relay, the author skillfully weaves an enchanting story and naturally develops her own sharp picture of life in this hot but endearing land. Ages 9–12.

Greene, Bette. Summer of My German Soldier. Dial, 1973. $7.95; $1.95 pb., Bantam.
A rich and powerful novel that enjoys a wide audience and stays with the reader for a long time. It is the story of an abused twelve-year-old Jewish girl who lives in Arkansas near a World War II POW camp and helps a kind German soldier escape. In one ironic scene, Patty is

being beaten by her Jewish father while the German soldier stands nearby, helpless and infuriated. Although the adult reader groans in disbelief, the dust jacket claims that this work is based on Greene's painful experiences. Greene's hurtful childhood is remodeled into a saddening novel with deft characterization. At the book's end, Anton, the soldier, is killed in New York, and Patty, now linked to his escape, is sent to reform school. Although an award-winning book, the novel evokes both positive and negative reactions from adult critics. What is the author really telling us? If she was the abused child of Jewish parents, was this love for a Nazi (albeit an anti-Hitler intellectual) the ultimate revenge? Or is Greene saying that love can come from totally unexpected sources? Or does the author harbor such feelings of self-hate—due perhaps to being a Jew in a small southern town—that she could write the beating scene described above? Is this book irony at its best or anti-Semitism at its worse? (Note: Greene's sequel, *Morning Is a Long Time Coming* (Dial, 1978), relates Patty's first love affair in France and her unsuccessful attempt to meet Anton's mother in Germany. Not as well written as her first book, this uncontrolled narrative is full of rage, parental hatred, and deep unhappiness. A marginal selection that might hold the interest of Patty's older sympathizers. Ages 14+.) Ages 10–16.

Greenspan, Sophie. Masada Will Not Fall Again. Jewish Pubn., 1973. $4.25.
A competent novel about first-century Jews who fought for freedom in the fortress of Massadah in the Judean Desert. Creating fictional characters who were likely to have been there (Eleazar ben Ya'ir actually was), the author writes about their ingenious adaptation to life in this austere environment. The novel, which takes place after the destruction of the Holy Temple, reveals how the Jews kept the Roman army at bay for three years. When the enemy finally entered, they were shocked to discover that the Jews had committed suicide, their treasure houses emptied. The fortress remains today as a powerful symbol of Jewish resistance and freedom. Ages 10–14.

Gutman, Nahum. Path of the Orange Peels: Adventures in the Early Days of Tel Aviv. Trans. Nelly Segal. Dodd, 1979. $7.95.
During World War I when the British and Turks struggled for control of Palestine, a fifteen-year-old Jewish boy, Nahum, becomes involved in a dangerous mission in Tel Aviv while escaping from Turkish army recruiters. Gutman's wise, tongue-in-cheek narrative reveals early life in Tel Aviv. His portraits of a beloved grandmother, British army officers, local townsfolk, hospital nurses, and even the town's animals give the suspenseful story zest and humor. The illustrations and pho-

tographs enhance the story, and the translation is bright and crisp. The hero says about himself: "I always put my shoes on joyfully, happy to welcome a new day." His spirit is catching. First published in Israel in 1958, it is a fine choice for sharing aloud. Ages 10+.

Hamori, Laszlo. Flight to the Promised Land. Trans. Annabelle Macmillan. Illus. Mel Silverman. HarBraceJ, 1963. O.P.
A story based on the early life of Shalom Mizrachi, an El Al pilot from Yemen. Readers will be introduced to the Yemenite Jews, people from a tiny, backward land who came to Israel and found it hard to adjust to its technical and secular society. Watching a fearful boy reacting with wonder to every modern convenience we take for granted, the reader will enjoy Shalom's development into a brave Israeli flier. The book takes place in 1948 and is written with humor and empathy. Ages 11–14.

Herman, Charlotte. The Difference of Ari Stein. Illus. Ben Shecter. Har-Row, 1976. $5.95.
A recent move finds Ari Stein looking for friends in Brooklyn's Coney Island area of the early 1940s. Ari is a religious boy; he wears a yarmulke (skullcap) and enjoys traditional Sabbaths with his parents. But the other boys scorn Ari's ways and urge him to become "all-American." The loosely strung episodes about boys growing up are funny and touching in turns, revealing Ari's warm family life and the growing concerns for European Jewry. At the book's end, Ari feels at ease with his decision to remain a practicing Jew. Ages 9–12.

Herman, Charlotte. Our Snowman Had Olive Eyes. Dutton, 1977. $7.95.
Although a bit hesitant at first, Sheila has no trouble adjusting to Grandma's arrival as a permanent member of the household. Bubbie, however, feels stifled and overprotected in her daughter's home. When she decides to leave, Sheila is heartbroken. How she will miss this lovely, capable woman! The story is a well-written, unpretentious slice of life. (Note: For two other novels in which a Jewish girl has a close relationship with an elderly grandmother, see Rose Blue, *Grandma Didn't Wave Back*, Watts, 1972, $4.90, 95¢ pb., Dell, Ages 9–12; and Doris Orgel, *The Mulberry Music*, Har-Row, 1971, O.P., $1.95 pb., Ages 9–12.) Ages 10–13.

Hoban, Lillian. I Met a Traveller. Har-Row, 1977. $6.95.
Josie is an American girl living in Jerusalem with her divorced artist-mother. She is a lonely child; her mother gads-about and her missionary school offers no friends. When Josie befriends a widowed Russian immigrant, some warmth and love finally enter her life.

Josie's Jewish mother is certainly not a stereotype; rather, she is an unsteady but not always unappealing woman who is raising an embittered child. Both the characters love Jerusalem (although Josie longs for home), and the reader is left with a warm feeling for the city. Parts of this book are good; parts drag. But the unresolved bitterness between the mother and daughter—and between the lines—remains. Ages 10–14.

Hoff, Syd. Irving and Me. Har-Row, 1967. O.P.; $1.25 pb., Dell.
Thirteen-year-old Artie Granick has just moved from Brooklyn to Florida and is undergoing the usual traumas of a teenage uprooting. The author, a humorist and cartoonist, has endowed young Artie with a sharp mind, a kind heart, and a good sense of humor. How Artie relates to Irving (his not-too-bright friend), Arlene (his not-so-devoted girlfriend), and Charlie Wolper (the local gang leader) will keep youngsters chuckling and nodding in understanding. The book is a bit dated. That black people are called "colored" is just one example. Artie's Jewishness is one of the patterns in the book's lively fabric, and the boy often draws from his religious education when facing a moral issue. Judy Blume fans will like Hoff's similar approach to adolescent fiction. Ages 10–14.

Holman, Felice. The Murderer. Scribner, 1978. $7.95.
In a small, poor Pennsylvania mining town of the late 1930s there lives a twelve-year-old named Hershy Marks. Hershy is a fun-loving boy who would like to change the world, or at least his neighborhood. Why can't the Poles and the Jews be friends? When will the many Polish sons of the miners stop beating up the few Jewish sons of the merchants? Do they really think Hershy Marks murdered Christ? Is that why Hitler is mad at his people too? Even his German shepherd dog gets more respect than he does; the Poles admire the pet's genealogy. In a novel both funny and moving (the title is much too somber for the tone), Holman portrays the boyhood antics and quiet concerns of this good-natured child. Affirming his own individuality but longing for community acceptance, Hershy Marks is a protagonist we can all identify with. Ages 10–13.

Hubner, Carol Korb. The Haunted Shul and Other Devora Doresh Mysteries. Illus. Devorah Kramer. Judaica, 1979. $5.95; $4.95 pb.
Devora Doresh uses her natural intelligence and her Yeshiva high school learning to help her solve local crimes and mysteries. The cases are no less plausible than Nancy Drew plots and the writing is no less mundane. The book's concept is very clever, and mystery fans with an avid interest in Judaism will enjoy watching this Orthodox detec-

tive at work. (Note: See also Hubner's sequels, *The Tattered Tallis and Other Devora Doresh Mysteries* and *The Whispering Mezuzah and Other Devora Doresh Mysteries.* Both by Judaica, 1979, $5.95 pb.) Ages 9–12.

Hurwitz, Johanna. Once I Was a Plum Tree. Illus. Ingrid Fetz. Morrow, 1980. $7.50.
Imagine being all dressed up on Easter Sunday and having no place to go. Sitting on her Bronx stoop in 1947, ten-year-old Gerry Flam (the name used to be Pflaumenbaum) ponders her identity. Gerry's parents are assimilated Jews who offer no Judaic heritage, only the sideline experiences of the American-Christian culture, e.g., Christmas trees and Easter baskets. Gerry decides that waiting for her Christian friends to come home from church does not fill her spiritual needs, and she sets out to learn about her religion from a family of Jewish German refugees who live in her apartment building. Although this pleasantly written, easy-to-read story has its poignant and amusing scenes, it tells a single-minded story. It will find more success as a discussion starter than as a widely appealing tale. Ages 8–11.

Ish-Kishor, Sulamith. A Boy of Old Prague. Illus. Ben Shahn. Pantheon, 1963. $5.99; $1.50 pb., Schol Bk Serv.
This haunting and dramatic story takes us into the world of feudal Prague. When a peasant boy is bonded to a Jewish scholar, all his acquired anti-Semitism vanishes. Unfortunately, this wisdom goes unshared, and a tragic pogrom erupts, resulting in a human bonfire of ghetto Jews. The boy, Tomas, vows to find his master and to spread the word of brotherhood. The social setting and descriptions of architecture are fascinating. Shahn's varied drawings add another dimension to the work. Although slandered and imprisoned inside a stinking ghetto, the Jews still managed to value life and kindness. This book is worth the adult introduction needed to get children to read it. Ages 10+.

Ish-Kishor, Sulamith. The Master of Miracle. See chapter 9, Literature: Folk Tales and Anthologies.

Kaplan, Bess. The Empty Chair. Har-Row, 1978. $8.79.
An excellent novel about a poor Jewish-Canadian girl growing up in the 1930s. When ten-year-old Becky Devine's mother and baby sister die in childbirth, the life of this sharp-witted, imaginative child is shattered. Lonely and disturbed by the matchmaking efforts of her aunts, a fearful Becky is certain that Mama is close by, expecting her child to prevent the remarriage of the widower. Papa does marry a lovely woman, and it takes a good while for Becky to accept and finally love her. The humor and pain in everyday Jewish life are skill-

fully blended with fine characterizations and an entertaining style. Ages 10–13.

Karp, Naomi. The Turning Point. HarBraceJ, 1976. $6.95.
When twelve-year-old Hannah Brand moves from the city to a Queens suburb in the late 1930s, she and her older brother encounter anti-Semitism in school officials and neighborhood kids. Hannah is an assertive, bright girl who, with the help of her closely knit family, attempts to understand the ignorance of neighbors, the violent hatred in Germany that drove her new friend Trudy to emigrate, and the Jewish family in town who coped with prejudice by pretending to be Christians. Good characterization and a quick pace make this a satisfying novel. Ages 9–12.

Kay, Mara. In Face of Danger. Crown, 1977. $6.95.
After a car accident, Ann Lindsay is recuperating in a 1930s German household, and she becomes instrumental in saving a Jewish family from Nazi extinction. This slick but exciting novel combines mystery, history, and adventure. (Note: For another satisfying novel about helping people escape Nazi capture, see Hilda Van Stockum's *The Winged Watchman.* FS&G, 1963. $6.95. Ages 9–12.) Ages 11–14.

Kerr, Judith. When Hitler Stole Pink Rabbit. Illus. by author. Coward, 1971. $6.95; $1.25 pb., Dell.
This memorable novel tells the story of young Anna and her family, who are forced to flee their German home and wander in France, Switzerland, and England. Anna's adventure, based on the life of the author, enjoys a wide readership. The characters are well developed and the detailed incidents, reflecting a warm home life, are a tribute to family solidarity. As long as Anna has her parents and older brother, Max, she can find the courage to leave everything behind—including her dear stuffed rabbit. This book makes an excellent introduction to the Holocaust for children. Because Anna escaped early, her family is not threatened with death, and the reader can feel some distance from the horror. The book is informative about the historic events, and the writing is controlled and effective. (Note: For two further stories about Anna, see the next section, for ages 12+.) Ages 10–13.

Konigsburg, E. L. About the B'nai Bagels. Illus. by author. Atheneum, 1969. $8.95; $1.95 pb.
Mark Setzer is used to his mother's habit of talking to God as if He lived in the kitchen light fixture, but could he ever adjust to her new position as manager of his Little League team? In this very funny and popular novel, Konigsburg pitches Mark some tough problems con-

cerning friendship, prejudice, and honesty. It is unusual to read a contemporary novel with Jewish characters in which Judaism is not denied or only casually referred to. Mark (called Moishe at home) gains wisdom from his background and is very proud of his heritage. Written before girls were permitted to play in the Little League, this title might be a bit dated, but its humor is still fresh and delicious. Ages 9–12.

Levoy, Myron. Alan and Naomi. Har-Row, 1977. $7.95; $1.50 pb., Dell.
Alan, a New York City boy, is urged by his parents to befriend Naomi, an emotionally disturbed French refugee who witnessed her father's fatal beating by Nazis. At first, Alan is reluctant to give up baseball practice for such tragedy; but as he and his Charlie McCarthy doll begin to relax Naomi, Alan is thrilled. Tragedy reappears when an anti-Semitic boy strikes Alan before Naomi's horrified eyes. The book is touching, compelling, and entertaining, although the writing is a bit sentimental at times and the plot is not always credible. (Note: See Levoy's *Witch of Fourth Street and Other Stories* for a collection of multi-ethnic tales of New York City. Har-Row, 1972. $1.95 pb.). Ages 10–14.

Little, Jean. Kate. Har-Row, 1971. $8.79; $1.95 pb.
Kate Bloomfield is the daughter of a mixed marriage and the best friend of Emily Blair. Suddenly, religion becomes quite important to this introspective Canadian girl. Kate's parents, who are bookstore owners and individuals in their own right (which is rare in novels for the young), have shut religion out of their lives. Their daughter, however, considers herself Jewish and adores listening to the wonderful stories Father tells about his spirited mother and their Jewish home of long ago. Kate later learns that Father was disowned by his family for marrying a Gentile and has hidden a whole set of relatives from his child. Kate struggles to understand her father's revelation along with her own problems of a declining friendship with Emily. Turning to Judaism and to her father's past for answers, Kate is determined to find out who she really is. An excellent novel. (Note: This is the sequel to Little's *Look Through My Window*, which also features Emily and Kate. Har-Row, 1970. $8.79; $2.95 pb. Ages 9–13.) Ages 10–14.

Madison, Winifred. Becky's Horse. Schol Bk Serv, 1975. O.P.; $1.50 pb.
Becky Golden, a poor American-Jewish girl of the late 1930s, has a passion for horses. When she wins a horse in a breakfast cereal contest, Becky becomes the happiest girl on Hope Street and an instant

celebrity. But here's the rub: Along with dreams of beautiful horses come nightmarish letters from Papa's dying brother in crumbling Vienna. Money is desperately needed to rescue his homeless young son. Becky gives up the horse and uses her prize money for little David's fare. This is an entertaining family-life story with an engaging heroine written in a very pleasant style. (Note: Older readers will enjoy *Max's Wonderful Delicatessen*, Madison's novel about a Jewish boy's passion for sculptoring and his need for independence. Little, 1972. O.P.; $1.25 pb.) Ages 8–12.

Melnikoff, Pamela. The Star and the Sword. Illus. Hans Schwarz. Blue Star, 1965. $1.25 pb.
Orphaned after a medieval pogrom, young Bennedict and his sister, Elvira, have many adventures before reaching relatives in Oxford. This is a fast-moving and unique title. It takes us into Sherwood Forest where the children find temporary refuge with Robin Hood, and on a dangerous political mission with an anti-Semitic Crusader who uses the children as part of his disguise. Melnikoff does not mince words about the not-so-merry condition of Jews in old England, but these lovely children effectively touch the hearts of several Christians who had never really known a Jew. Lively characters, humor, poignancy, excitement, and a commitment to Jewish values travel together in this readable adventure story. Ages 9–12.

Neville, Emily C. Berries Goodman. Har-Row, 1965. $9.89; $1.50 pb.
When Berries Goodman (son of a liberal-minded Mormon) moves from Manhattan to New Jersey, he is surprised to find himself in an anti-Semitic, segregated community. His confusion turns to deep anger when his newly found best friend, Sidney Fine, is almost fatally injured in an accident resulting from prejudice. Forced to give up the friendship by Sidney's parents, Berries still feels hurt as he relates the story six years later. This is an entertaining problem novel written in a popular style and with good intentions, but with some shortcomings. It is interesting to note that Berries' anti-Semitic young neighbor is ridiculed by the author almost as much for her sex as for her prejudice. Ages 10–12.

Ofek, Uriel. Smoke Over Golan: A Novel of the 1973 Yom Kippur War in Israel. Trans. Israel I. Taslitt. Illus. Lloyd Bloom. Har-Row, 1979. $7.95.
Young Eitan lives on a farm in the Golan Heights near the Syrian border. When the book begins, he is the only pupil in the world's smallest school and is busy making friends with Saleem, a Syrian boy.

Eitan is unintentionally left alone when the war breaks out, and it is he who helps rescue an injured Israeli soldier and capture a Syrian spy. Although the Israeli tale has some improbable events and twists of plot, it is a lively, fast-paced novel, condescending toward none. The likable young hero will find many sympathetic and interested ears. Ages 9–12.

Omer, Devorah. The Gideonites: The Story of the "Nili" Spies in the Middle East. Trans. Ruth Reznick. Illustrated. Bonim reprint, c. 1969. $1.49 pb.
A fictionalized account of the life of Sarah Aaronson, a woman who led a Jewish spy ring to help the British drive the Turks out of Palestine during the early twentieth century. Beginning at the time when Sarah was still a girl and ending with her suicide while in the custody of Turkish soldiers, this interesting saga covers many family happenings and historic events. This tragic and exciting novel incorporates history, romance, and memorable heroes to tell its true story. (Note: Omer, an Israeli author, has two other worthy titles for this age level now out of print: *The Path Beneath the Sea*, Sabra, 1969; and *Journey to the Land of the Rain*, Massada, 1969.) Ages 11–16.

Orgel, Doris. The Devil in Vienna. Dial, 1978. $7.95; $1.50 pb., Dell. Rich in detail about everyday life in Vienna during the late 1930s, Orgel's scene is set for the dissolution of a girlhood friendship and the crumbling of a civilized society. A Jewish child and a Nazi's daughter have been best friends since they started school. The novel records the destruction of this friendship by events outside their control (Inge's wrecked home life and Lieselotte's Nazi Youth training). But even the Devil (and his partners) could not trick Lieselotte into giving up her loyalty and love. This is an entertaining and effective novel. (Note: See also Orgel's *A Certain Magic* for a good story about eleven-year-old Jenny, who stumbles upon her aunt's diary of her adolescent years spent as a World War II refugee. Dial, 1976. $7.95; $1.50 pb. Ages 10–13.) Ages 10–14.

Rabin, Gil. False Start. Illus. John Gundelfinger. Har-Row, 1969. O.P.
An unusual portrait of a Jewish family. Richard, living with his mother in a New York City Jewish ghetto of the 1930s, is abused by his unemployed, alcoholic father. Based on the author's life, this highly readable and touching novel portrays a sensitive teenage boy trying to make a life for himself by shutting out the emotional pain inflicted by his cruel father. Richard is a very likable protagonist; his

attempts to understand the adult world will not go unappreciated by young readers. Ages 11–15.

Reboul, Antoine. Thou Shalt Not Kill. Trans. Stephanie Craig. S G Phillips, 1969. $8.95.
Wandering alone on the Sinai Desert during the 1967 Arab-Israeli War, Slimane, a thirteen-year-old Egyptian boy, is confronted by an enemy. After a night of shooting it out from behind the dunes, his adversary is wounded. Slimane, planning to finish the job, is shocked to confront a fourteen-year-old Israeli girl. Friendship blooms between the two, and kindness replaces the blind hatred that first existed. The children survive the brutal desert and, once rescued, teach their elders a surprising lesson. Written by a Frenchman with an objective viewpoint, this adventure-survival novel is both timely and entertaining. Ages 9–12.

Richter, Hans Peter. Friedrich. Trans. Edite Kroll. HR&W, 1970. $5.95; $1.25 pb., Dell.
A young Jewish orphan dies on the streets of Nazi Germany during an air raid because he was refused admission to an underground shelter. Told through the eyes of Friedrich's Gentile friend, the story revolves around their friendship and the change of fortunes for both families. Brief and to the point, not sparing us pain or offering false hope, Richter's novel tells the story of a nonsurvivor. Because *Friedrich* is so well written, the novel is especially effective. Ages 11–16.

Rosten, Norman. The Wineglass: A Passover Story. Illus. Kaethe Zemach. Walker & Co., 1978. $6.95.
A young boy living with an atheist father and a stern, religious grandfather causes a family confrontation when he sees Elijah appear at the seder table. Although the story has an adult appeal, it is told through the eyes of a youngster and will appeal to older children. The question of how religious rituals can coexist with modern man's disbelief in miracles is well dramatized in this title. Although the boy's father is very angry and his grandfather extremely jealous, the mother believes in her son's vision. So will the reader. The illustrations by Kaethe Zemach (daughter of the talented artist Margot Zemach) are pleasant wash drawings that further enhance the use of this title with youngsters. Ages 11+.

Sachs, Marilyn. A Pocket Full of Seeds. Illus. Ben Stahl. Doubleday, 1973. $6.95.
The author has based this novel on the life of a friend, and her title is from a poem by Edna St. Vincent Millay. Like the novel, it is a poem about people's incredible will to proceed with life when their world

lies in ruins around them. Young Nicole Nieman spends World War II hiding in a French boarding school. At the book's end, her family is being deported to German camps while she is left to await their fate. Sachs has written a memorable novel with deft characterization and good detail to the historic era. Nicole's loneliness will arouse deep feelings of empathy and hope in young readers. It is a lively, readable story. Ages 10–13.

Shecter, Ben. Someplace Else. Illus. by author. Har-Row, 1971. $7.89.
Autobiographical and light in tone, but serious in subject, *Someplace Else* relates the events of one year in the life of twelve-year-old Arnie Schiffman. Only after the book has ended does one realize how many traumatic events have occurred: a move, bar mitzvah lessons with a foul-smelling rabbi, Mother's serious operation, the loss of Arnie's dog, and the deaths of his father and grandmother. Humor is provided in the characters of Miss Noonan, his obnoxious teacher, and Gloria Becker, a pesty girl. Shecter has a 1950s mentality when it comes to females and the book falls short in this area. On the whole, however, it is a very good book, quite genuine in setting and feeling; it is also quite funny despite the long list of tragedies. Ages 9–13.

Singer, Isaac Bashevis. See chapter 9, Literature: Folk Tales and Anthologies, for many of his fictional/folkloric titles.

Steinberg, Fannie. Birthday in Kishinev. Illus. Luba Hanuschak. Jewish Pubn, 1978. $5.95.
On April 6, 1903, the day of her twelfth birthday, Sarah spends the morning helping with party preparations; the afternoon and evening as the happy queen of the feast; and the night in a small Russian cemetery hiding from murderous Cossacks. Just your typical day in the life of an early-twentieth-century shtetl Jew, combining the mundane and the morbid, the joy and the horror, the celebrating and the mourning. Based on her own childhood, this touching story has enough historical background to answer the questions children will ask. On April 7, 1903, Sarah's papa decides to leave Russia. With love for each other and a belief in God's protection, the family goes. Ages 9–12.

Suhl, Yuri. Uncle Misha's Partisans. Four Winds, 1973. $6.95.
This fine novel is one of the most effective and meaningful of the books reviewed in this guide. Based on historic events, it is the story of young Motele, a rural Russian Jew, who joins Uncle Misha's resistant fighters after his family is murdered by Nazis. As we are introduced to

these traumatized Jews now taking part in guerrilla warfare, and learn about their deep sadness and extraordinary courage, we are deeply impressed by their fortitude and shocked by their tormentors. Suhl has used great care and talent in creating characters, situations, and language that will appeal to children and be appropriate for them. Youngsters will be drawn to twelve-year-old Motele, a gentle but enraged fiddler, who participates in dangerous missions in the guise of a musician. The author is an authority on Jewish resistance; his dramatic and sensitive novel is a valuable contribution to children's literature. (Note: See also Gertrude Samuel's *Mottele: A Partisan Odyssey* for another competent novel on this subject. Har-Row, 1976. O.P.; $1.50 pb., Signet. Ages 12–adult.) Ages 10–14.

Taylor, Sydney. All-of-a-Kind Family. Illus. Helen John. Follett, 1951. $5.97; $1.50 pb., Dell.
The five titles in this series comprise a rich portrait of a Jewish family in the Lower East Side of New York before World War I. The books are enjoyed by a wide audience of children who identify with the loving family, their deep pleasure with the public library, and the well-incorporated descriptions of Jewish holiday celebrations. When a boy is born to the family of five girls, it is not "all of a kind" any longer, but it is still in its own class. Recommended for reading aloud. (Sequels: *All-of-a-Kind Family Downtown,* Illus. Beth and Joe Krush, Follett, 1972, $4.95, $1.25 pb., Dell; *All-of-a-Kind Family Uptown,* Illus. Mary Stevens, Follett, 1958, $4.95, $1.25 pb., Dell; *Ella of All-of-a-Kind Family,* Illus. Gail Owens, Dutton, 1978, $7.95, $1.50 pb., Dell; *More of All-of-a-Kind Family,* Illus. Mary Stevens, Follett, 1954, $4.95, $1.25 pb., Dell.) Ages 8–12.

Trease, Geoffrey. The Red Towers of Granada. Illus. C. Keeping. Vanguard, 1967. $6.95.
An adventure story about a Christian boy's quest for a secret medicine to cure Queen Eleanor of medieval England. Robin's link to this challenge is Solomon, an elderly Jewish doctor who takes Robin under his wing when the lad is wrongly diagnosed as being a leper. Solomon's friendship introduces Robin to the harsh realities of Jewish ghetto life as well as setting him on an exciting journey to Spain, where time and enemies threaten Robin's mission. Ages 11–15.

Trigoboff, Joseph. Abu. Lothrop, 1975. $6.48.
The War of 1967 has just ended, and Itzhak, a young Israeli soldier, decides to spend some time in Jerusalem. Hatred between Jews and Arabs floods the old streets. Itzhak feels it and approves. Then he meets Abu, a nine-year-old cigar-smoking street urchin with the wis-

dom of a businessman and the bright eyes of a child. The author tells of the strong but difficult friendship that grows between man and boy. In hard-hitting, unsentimental prose Trigoboff shows how two enemies discard their hatred and mistrust. Entertaining and thought-provoking, the novel should appeal to a wide audience; however, the stereotype of the street-wise Arab boy, ragged and needy, may raise some objections. Ages 10–14.

Van Stockum, Hilda. The Borrowed House. FS&G, 1975. $6.95.
An effective blend of history, mystery, and romance, this story takes place in a lovely house in rural Amsterdam during World War II. The Jewish owners were evacuated to accommodate a prominent German theatrical family. During the course of the novel, the new tenant, twelve-year-old Janna, changes from an avid Hitler supporter to an anti-Nazi activist. At the book's end, she burns down the borrowed house in order to save the life and work of a young Jewish resister. (Note: See also the following good novels about young people who took an active role in the underground movements, risking their own lives to save Nazi victims: Nathaniel Benchley, *Bright Candles,* Har-Row, 1974, $8.95, Ages 12+; Christian Bernhardsen, *Fight in the Mountains,* HarBraceJ, 1968, $4.50, Ages 10–14; Claire Bishop, *Twenty and Ten,* Puffin reprint, c. 1952, $1.95 pb., Ages 10–13; and Marie McSwigan, *Snow Treasure,* Dutton, 1942, $9.95, $1.25 pb., Schol Bk Serv, Ages 9–12.) Ages 10–14.

Watson, Sally. Mukhtar's Children. HR&W, c. 1968;   Other Sandals. HR&W, c. 1966;   To Build a Land. HR&W, c. 1957.
Three competent titles about Israel. Although these books are out of print, they should still be available in most public libraries. Containing both good character portrayals and appealing narratives, the books are very informative and effective novels about a struggling country and its diverse people. *Mukhtar's Children:* Following the 1948 War of Liberation, an Arab leader's daughter becomes attracted to kibbutz living. Ages 11–15. *Other Sandals:* a look at tricultural Israel: the city, the kibbutz, an Arab village. Ages 10–13. *To Build a Land:* the story of young people on a kibbutz during Arab–Israeli hostilities. Ages 11–14.

Ages 12+

Banks, Lynne Reid. Sarah and After: Five Women Who Founded a Nation. Doubleday, 1977. $6.95.
A very entertaining novel about six biblical women: Sarah and Hagar, Rebecca, Leah and Rachel, and Dinah. Although divided

into four sections, the stories flow together, for example, Isaac's cold personality, which gave his wife, Rebecca, much grief, was caused by Abraham's treatment. The book is very well written, the dialogue lively, and the characters well developed. Although the author gives the women modern mentalities and broadly interprets their feelings and actions, her novel allows us to relate to these people who are only briefly sketched in the Bible. Future Bible readings are made more meaningful by this novel. Ages 11–16.

Brooks, Jerome. Make Me a Hero. Dutton, 1980. $8.95.
This novel takes place in Chicago during World War II when twelve-year-old Jake Ackerman's three brothers have all left for army life. Jake's struggle against the enemy, however, began when he was seven and witnessed the death of his friend Chris, who was chased up a telephone pole by some neighborhood bullies and subsequently fell to his death. This introspective glimpse into a boy's coming of age describes Jake's desire to grow up fast, get a job, meet a friend (a buddy who would help him lick those local ruffians), have his bar mitzvah, and become a man. Revealing that wars can be fought on many fronts, and that the struggle for survival, self-respect, and identity is a part of growing up, the novel has many thought-provoking scenes that young readers can sympathize with. Ages 11–15.

Cohen, Barbara. Bitter Herbs and Honey. Lothrop, 1976. $6.95.
Becky, an intelligent teenage daughter of Russian-Jewish immigrants, rebels against her Old World parents. The scene is a small New Jersey community in 1916. Becky falls in and out of love with a non-Jewish classmate and scorns her parents' attempts at choosing her husband and limiting her career goals. The author introduces the reader to many traditional Jewish customs, as well as offering a low-key, romantic, and warmly written story. (Note: Cohen's newer novel, *The Innkeeper's Daughter,* concerns the teenage Rachel Gold and her growing-up days in a New Jersey hotel in the late 1940s. Lothrop, 1979. $7.50. Ages 11–15.) Ages 11–15.

Colman, Hila. Rachel's Legacy. Morrow, 1978. $7.50.
Sequel: Ellie's Inheritance. Morrow, 1979. $6.95.
Rachel Ginsberg left Russia in 1908 with her mother and two sisters. Not satisfied with the poverty around her or the roles open to women, Rachel worked hard and long (since childhood) to build a children's dress factory. Matchmaking, courting, mixed marriage (shades of *Fiddler on the Roof*), union problems, tuberculosis, etc., are all here in this dramatic novel. Although Rachel's character is well developed, the writing, which imitates Yiddish syntax and expressions (there is no

glossary), is a bit overdone. The story starts off slowly as Rachel's daughter discovers that she was cheated out of her mother's fortune. Although the book has its problems, it entertainingly reveals the story of a strong Jewish woman not told before in children's literature. Ages 12–16. In the sequel, we get to know Rachel's daughter, Eileen, who must adjust to a new life of poverty and uncertainty during the Depression. In addition to romance (one love dies fighting Franco in Spain), there is a backdrop of social, political, business, and ethnic scenes that gives the reader a clue about life in pre–World War II New York. Although not a memorable work, Ellie's story is a fast-paced, entertaining novel that young teens will enjoy. Ages 12–16.

Cone, Molly. Dance Around the Fire. HM, 1974. $5.95.
Joanne Reuben thinks about Jacob's struggle with an unknown power as she struggles with her own identity as a Jew and as a young person. Dissatisfied with her parents' unobservant ways, she takes off for Israel via Rome. There, she and a friend become the unsuspecting pawns of two male terrorists. This is a dramatic, easy-to-read, and introspective novel. Joanne's need for independence will strike a responsive chord, and its fast pace will attract a wide audience. Ages 11–15.

Fast, Howard. My Glorious Brothers. Bonim reprint, c. 1948. $4.95 pb.
Simon Maccabeus narrates this remarkable story of his ancient family headed by the Jewish priest Mattathias and immortalized by his younger brother, Judas. The tale begins about 150 B.C.E. in Modin, a tiny farming village near Jerusalem. The evil Syrian-Greek king, Antiochus, rules the land, and petty, anti-Semitic tyrants control the villages. Simon describes the increasingly savage treatment of the area's Jews that inspires Judas's small but determined army to fight the eventually defeated Antiochus. The historic novel, reminiscent of Nikos Kazantzakis' work, is passionately narrated in a prose overflowing with poetic imagery, tenderness, and love for justice. Recommended for readers who want something more from Hanukkah than potato pancakes and a spin of the dreidl. (Note: See also Donald Lieberman's *Heroes of Hanukkah* for a fast-paced historical novel that takes us onto the battlefields with Judah Maccabee and his dedicated family. KTAV, 1980. $5.95 pb. Ages 10+.) Ages 13+.

Forman, James. My Enemy, My Brother. Schol Bk Serv, 1972. $1.50 pb.
Daniel Baratz is sixteen when he trudges heavily out of a Hitler death camp. He soon meets up with some Palestine-bound teenagers, and

together they try to find happiness in still another war-torn land. The prize-winning, well-written novel is realistic and thought-provoking. It does not give pat solutions or offer one-sided views on the Middle East. Here is an adventure story woven around the needs and dreams of some very desperate youngsters. Ages 12–16.

Forman, James. The Survivor. FS&G, 1976. $8.95.
A very memorable novel about the Holocaust. The Ullmans, an Amsterdam family, wait too long to leave their beloved home, and only one survives: young David. He narrates this often harrowing tale about hiding and death camps. Forman's characterizations are acute, his details are meticulous, and his writing is forceful and restrained. The survivor leaves the Netherlands when the war ends. Says David: "If any covenant had come out of the fires of the European holocaust, as it had come to Moses from the fires of Mt. Sinai, it would be found in Palestine." (Note: See the following young adult titles by Forman about anti-Nazi bravery: *Ceremony of Innocence,* Hawthorn, 1970, $7.95, $1.25 pb., Dell; *Horses of Anger,* FS&G, 1967, $3.95; and *The Traitors,* FS&G, 1968, $3.95.) Ages 13+.

Goldreich, Gloria. Lori. HR&W, 1979. $6.95.
Lori, a wealthy American teenager, is sent to Israel for a year after being expelled from school for smoking marijuana. Although the writing is shallow and bubbles over with soap-opera conversation, the reader gets a rare glimpse into contemporary Israel through Lori's varied experiences. The fast pace will appeal to readers. Goldreich's previous juvenile novel, *Season of Discovery* (Nelson, 1976), about an American girl gaining insights into her heritage while preparing for her bat mitzvah, is too verbose and would not reach as wide an audience. Ages 12–15.

Heyman, Anita. Exit from Home. Crown, 1977. $7.50.
Samuel lives with an oppressive Orthodox father in a Russian shtetl of the early twentieth century. When a brother dies of smallpox, Samuel feels that God punished his family because of his worldly ideas. In atonement, he decides to study at a yeshivah (Orthodox Jewish school) to become a rabbi. Once there, his contact with the Enlightenment turns him into an early revolutionist. At the book's end, however, Samuel realizes that no Russian government will befriend Jews, and at fifteen he is enroute to America, alone. This is for serious readers who like detailed historical novels with excellent storytelling techniques. Ages 12+.

Ish-Kishor, Sulamith. Our Eddie. Pantheon, 1969. $5.99; 75¢ pb.
This skillful novel, which features the conflicts between an insensitive father and his lively son, begins in London during the early part of

the twentieth century. Mr. Raphael, a schoolmaster, is adored by his students and feared by his children. With great attention to detail, the author sketches the personalities and life style of this poor Jewish family. Life deteriorates for the Raphaels after their move to New York: Mother is an invalid and Eddie has recently died of cancer. When the book ends, the repentant father is gently serving afternoon tea to his remaining family. Ish-Kishor has created a fine slice of life: bitter, poignant, and honest. Ages 12–14.

Kerr, Judith. The Other Way Round. Coward, 1975. $7.95. $1.50 pb., Dell; Sequel: A Small Person Very Far Away. T Y Crowell, 1978. $7.95.
The sequel to *When Hitler Stole Pink Rabbit* (see the previous section, for ages 9–12) finds fifteen-year-old Anna and her parents in London. Brother Max has joined the British air force. Anna has developed a passion for drawing, a talent that allows her to find her place in this war-torn country. Kerr introduces another timeless theme: Anna's parents are now dependent on their children for comfort and security. The same fine attention to detail and sensitive characterizations make this a popular title among older children. In the sequel, Anna, now happily married in London, is distressed to get a call from Mama's lover in Berlin that she has attempted suicide because of his infidelity. Kerr's writing is as excellent as ever, but the reader of *When Hitler Stole Pink Rabbit* must grow up a bit before enjoying this set's third volume. Ages 12–15; sequel, 15+.

Kerr, M. E. Gentlehands. Har-Row, 1978. $8.95; $1.95 pb., Bantam.
Middle-class Buddy uses his rich and genteel grandfather to impress a wealthy girlfriend. Later, he is aghast to discover that a Jewish Nazi hunter has unveiled Grandpa Frank Trenker for what he was: Gentlehands, an Auschwitz murderer. The book strives to create an individual out of this mass murderer and to air opinions as to whether he should be forgiven or imprisoned. The themes of class differences and family responsibilities are developed too. Kerr's books are unique, witty, and urbane. Established review sources liked this one: the Council on Interracial Books for Children did not. I have to agree with the latter. Although Kerr's book is a grabber and youngsters will find it entertaining, I was offended by her stereotyped characters and felt that her writing was too slick and superficial for this subject. This book is included here because of Kerr's popularity and should be examined before ordered. Ages 12–16.

Lange, Suzanne. The Year. S G Phillips, 1970. $8.95.
Eighteen-year-old Ann Sanger, an American, spends a year on an Israeli kibbutz, falls in love, and vows to return with her new husband

to continue their pioneering life. The book is especially recommended for readers who want to know what kibbutz life is like but do not like to read nonfiction. As a novel, the book is unexceptional; it delivers more information than literary style. Ages 13–16.

Lustig, Arnost. Dita Saxova. Trans. Jeanne Nemcova. Har-Row, 1979. $9.95.

Lustig's title is included here because it was awarded the 1979 Charles and Bertie G. Schwartz Juvenile Award by the Jewish Book Council. Although this is a fine novel about a young woman's attempt to continue a meaningful existence after the Holocaust, it is strictly an adult work in language, content, and appeal. Ages 17+.

Mark, Jan. The Ennead. Crowell, 1978. $7.89.

"Isaac danced in the dust and the dust danced with him." So begins this stunning and memorable science fiction tale, which takes place on a sterile, unfriendly planet (Earth is dead) where creativity is punished and only the dust is free to explore. Isaac is a young servant, unhappy but adjusting to his mean environment, when Eleanor (a sculptor) and Moshe (a gardener) enter his life and unleash passions in Isaac long suppressed on this planet. Little by little the author introduces the elements of a residual Judaism alive in Moshe. When the gardener finally wears his little black hat to a mock church, the townspeople do not recall its purpose but they recognize its power. The two lovers of life and of each other, Moshe and Eleanor, are destroyed at the book's end, but their impact on Isaac is great. Don't be a golem (robot) for these wicked masters, Moshe warns him. Isaac won't. This is a powerful and beautifully written book. Ages 12+.

Mazer, Harry. The Last Mission. Delacorte, 1979. $7.95; $1.75 pb., Dell.

Jack Raab is a fifteen-year-old New York City Jew who has nightmares about the Nazis coming to murder his family. Fantasizing about killing Hitler and becoming a hero, Jack steals his brother's birth certificate and joins the air force to become a bomber in 1945. In the course of the story, Jack develops friendships with his (doomed) crew, meets his first love, and is shot down and imprisoned by the Nazis. Fortunately, the war is over and he is freed by American liberators. Jack's urgent, personal need to stop Hitler is steadily felt throughout the book, although the story reveals his growing disgust for war. His fantasies are over, and all he visualizes now are his dead buddies. Young Sergeant Raab is a heroic and credible protagonist whose action-packed story (complete with barrack profanity) will appeal to a wide audience. Ages 12–14.

Moskin, Marietta. I Am Rosemarie. John Day, 1972. $8.95; $1.50 pb., Schol Bk Serv.

Rosemarie Brenner of Amsterdam spends her adolescence in Hitler's concentration camps and survives. The book is adequately written, and although it informs the reader about real events (down to the Nazi guards' names), the book weaves a personal, touching tale. Not so explicit as James Forman's *The Survivor,* it is nonetheless a painful and important novel. Ages 12–15.

Murray, Michele. The Crystal Nights. Seabury, 1973. $7.95; $1.25 pb., Dell.
A remarkable novel, rich in characterization and evoking deep feelings. It is the story of Elly, a half-Jewish adolescent who lives on a Connecticut farm and dreams of a life in the theater. Her parents' love for the simple life is disrupted when relatives fleeing from Nazi Germany move in. The two families struggle to understand each other's ways and to sacrifice for each other's sake. Girls will appreciate Elly's own battle to make her dreams come true and to cope with frustration when overwhelming forces threaten to destroy them. Ages 12–15.

Nurenberg, Thelma. My Cousin, the Arab. Abelard, 1965. O.P.
The engrossing story of Emmi, a seventeen-year-old cultured German Jew who reluctantly comes to a kibbutz on the eve of Israeli independence. Despondent about the primitive and violent surroundings, she sees her future as a pianist vanishing like a desert mirage. Eventually, with the help of a nurturing kibbutz and a hard-earned awareness of her people's needs and dreams, Emmi becomes a dedicated Israeli. Containing romance, adventure, violence, history, and strong emotions, this novel will both inform and entertain a wide audience. (Note: Nurenberg's *Time of Anger,* Abelard, 1975, also set in Israel, suffers from having too many characters.) Ages 12–15.

Schwartz, Sheila. Growing Up Guilty. Pantheon, 1978. $6.95.
Smooth writing and genuine sentiments distinguish this story about a lonely Jewish girl growing up in the late 1930s. Burdened with an angry mother, a weak father, limited finances, and an unattractive body, Susan Green uses her intelligence and love for books to escape her hurts and isolation. Her mother relates horrendous tales of her Russian childhood, and Grandmother cries out in dreams of satanic cossacks. The author is brutally honest about this Jewish family. One fat uncle, who hates blacks, tries to seduce Susan. The only independent female who displays affection for her is her boyfriend's mother, a Communist. Susan's family shows the strains of past persecutions and present anxieties. This is the introspective work of an honest, intelligent writer. Ages 13+.

Suhl, Yuri. On the Other Side of the Gate. Watts, 1975. $5.90; $1.25 pb., Avon.

When pregnancy becomes forbidden in the Warsaw Ghetto, a young couple is determined to fight against Nazi tyranny and save their unborn baby's life. The novel succeeds as a dramatic and touching story; the gradual withdrawal of human rights (jobs, food, and eventually life itself) from Warsaw Jewry is met with courage and dignity by this young couple and their fellow victims. The book is gentle and romantic, yet it does not shirk from describing historic realities. Ages 12–16.

Reference Aids

Blatt, Gloria T. "The Jewish-American Experience: The View from Children's Fiction." *Top of the News.* Summer 1979, pp. 391–397. Blatt refutes the theories of the Sadkers (*Now Upon a Time*) and Eric Kimmel (*Horn Book Magazine,* April 1973) that the American Jew in children's fiction is not handled with sensitivity or with a variety of religious expressions.

Daniels, Leona. "The 34th Man: How Well Is Jewish Minority Culture Represented in Children's Fiction?" *School Library Journal,* February 1970, pp. 38–43. The ups and downs of this field; contains a lengthy bibliography.

Kimmel, Eric A. "Confronting the Ovens: The Holocaust and Juvenile Fiction." *Horn Book Magazine.* February 1977, pp. 84–91. Kimmel discusses the new trends in writing about the Holocaust in children's novels.

Kimmel, Eric A. "Jewish Identity in Juvenile Fiction: A Look at Three Recommended Books." *Horn Book Magazine.* April 1973. Gloria T. Blatt refers to Kimmel's disappointment in novels with Jewish themes in her article in *Top of the News* (see above).

Nodelman, Perry M. "The Case of the Disappearing Jew." *Children's Literature in Education.* Vol. 10, no. 1, pp. 44–48.

Nodelman discusses a fairy tale by the brothers Grimm, "The Jew in the Bush," and considers whether literature should be censored if it contains racism. Nodelman thinks not.

Sadker, Myra Pollack, and **David Miller Sadker.** "Jewish-Americans in Children's Books." *Now Upon a Time; A Contemporary View of Children's Literature.* Har-Row, 1977, pp. 191–209. Discussion and bibliography. The Sadkers are unhappy with the selection of American Judaica for children: ". . . few children's books portray the Jewish American experience with depth, sensitivity, sophistication, or even seriousness."

Literature: Folk
Tales and Anthologies

The three major sources for Jewish folklore and legend are the Bible, the Talmud, and medieval rabbinical writings. While retellings of Old Testament stories are plentiful and well represented in children's books, there are fewer titles from the other two sources.

Recent trends in writing for children, however, mark a change in this area of juvenile literature. For example, the growing number of children's titles with Jewish themes winning national recognition for literary quality and universal appeal have encouraged more authors to write about their Jewishness. In addition, two authors relatively new to the field of juvenile literature have made invaluable contributions to folklore collections: Isaac Bashevis Singer and Marilyn Hirsh. In addition to the fine books created by author-illustrator Hirsh, many new folk tales have been gloriously illustrated by such artists as Beverly Brodsky, Margot Zemach, and Uri Shulevitz.

Many of the tales included in this section are of a religious nature, while some are purely secular. The writings of I. L. Peretz and Sholom Aleichem, the fathers of nineteenth-century East European Yiddish literature, are inspired by more recent folk sources. Whether the stories are original Talmudic folklore, Hebraized versions of medieval tales collected throughout the Diaspora, or reminiscences of nineteenth-century yarns spun around the shtetl (small town) stove, they all share common features: They are marked by good humor and strong wit. The need to laugh at oneself and.at one's troubles is an obvious characteristic of a folk heritage with a long and difficult history.

It should be noted that folklore is not the place to find alternative female role models. Women fill traditional roles in these tales. They are expected to be lovely, demure, and pious. Males also fill stereotypical roles, but whereas in the Bible they flex their muscles, in these folk legends the models are Elijah, Hillel, Solomon, wonder-working rabbis, and rich men who are charitable and pious. The antiheroes are here too: the schlemiels (simpletons), the schlimazels (losers), and the fools of Chelm. Their suffering, however, is often depicted as being exacerbated by nagging, bossy wives who undermine their masculinity.

Very few stories have female protagonists, although there are exceptions like Sara Bath Tuvim, a strong legendary figure. A few tales about clever young peasant women also exist. However, the nagging shtetl wife is still the norm, without whom the daydreaming husband would probably forget to eat and so would starve to death.

The books reviewed in this chapter are a vital part of the Jewish heritage, and children everywhere can be enriched by these tales of justice, peace, and happiness. For every wolf that comes to blow down the house, there is an Elijah to offer aid. For all the times that children feel stupid and powerless, there is the fool of Chelm, infinitely more stupid and even less powerful. And for all the wrongs that children feel are done to them, here is a body of literature that shares their troubles and sweetens their medicine.

Many college English majors take a course called "The Bible as Literature." The Old Testament's poetry and prose are discussed, and its great themes analyzed: sibling rivalry, passion, and war. Three thousand years have passed since the Jews delivered the original bestseller to the world, and people are still writing about sibling rivalry, passion, and war.

There is, however, a dearth of new titles in poetry, drama, and literary anthologies. Only one title on Hebrew poetry for older children is in print. The plays that were reviewed for this guide were rejected because of their poor literary quality. Madeleine L'Engle's *Journey with Jonah* and J. L. Klink's anthology, *Bible for Children with Plays and Songs,* are the two good titles reviewed here. A handful of good essays are included; they deal with the darker side of Jewish history: the Holocaust and religious persecution. Even the poetry that is written by children is concerned with war and death.

Any adult working with children who has searched for an entertaining poem about Hanukkah or a poignant verse about Yom Kippur knows that nothing of this sort exists. What is needed is a Jewish version of an anthology like Shel Silverstein's *Where the Sidewalk Ends* (Har-Row, 1974), which does contain several poems that can be used on Jewish storytelling occasions. Perhaps someone will soon do for children's Jewish poetry what Isaac Bashevis Singer and Marilyn Hirsh have done for folklore.

Folk Tales

Adler, David A. The Children of Chelm. Illus. Arthur Friedman. Bonim, 1979. $5.95; $1.95 pb.
Adler bases his three nicely retold stories on Chelm folklore. He cleverly centers the brief tales of foolish folks around their children: How to prevent screaming at bath time? How will the children leave school without stepping on the freshly fallen snow? And what is the most efficient (i.e., idiotic) way to build a new schoolhouse? By slightly altering the original plots, Adler is able to retain the spirit and humor of the stories while making them accessible to children too young for Isaac Bashevis Singer and Solomon Simon. The lively and humorous line drawings on cream-colored paper burst forth with all the energy of a busy shtetl. Ages 5–10.

Aronin, Ben. The Secret of the Sabbath Fish. Illus. Shay Reiger. Jewish Pubn. 1978. $5.95.
The tale of old Tante (Aunt) Mashe, who makes the first gefilte fish as a gift to the poor after a Russian pogrom. A disguised Elijah sells her the carp, instructing her to prepare it while thinking about "what has been happening to the Jewish people." Sharing the fate of the Jews throughout history, the fish gets pounded, stripped, crushed, and has salt rubbed in its wounds. However, she also adds eggs to represent the long life of Judaism. The divinely inspired recipe is a big success, and Tante Mashe is pleased with her contribution to the Jewish people. This handsomely made picture book is produced in soft green and cream and is gracefully illustrated by a talented artist. Ages 6+.

Barash, Asher, ed. A Golden Treasury of Jewish Tales. Trans. Murray Roston. Illus. Henry Hechtkopf. Dodd, 1966. O.P.
Forty stories from rabbinical writings promise victory for the oppressed and the pious. Tales of mysticism, miracles, and holy men teach that faith conquers evil and frees Jews from the enemy's grasp. This storybook is not light entertainment; its purpose is to instruct, and it does so with drama and dignity. The stories are not for all youngsters, but a good retelling could bring out the wisdom and power inherent in many of the legends. Ages 10–16.

Bialik, Hayyim. Knight of Onions and Knight of Garlic. Trans. Herbert Danby. Illus. Emanuel Romano. Hebrew Pub, 1939. $2.50.
Bialik based this narrative poem on an anecdote told by East European Jews. It is the highly ethical and amusing story of a wise prince who introduces the art of cooking with onions to an isolated nation.

As a reward, he is dubbed "Knight of Onions" and is showered with gold coins. Another, less worthy prince tries his luck. His gift of garlic is also well received, earning him the title "Knight of Garlic." Unfortunately, his reward is a basket of onions. The poem is unrhymed with irregular four-beat lines. The translation is flowing and colorful; its mock grandeur creates genuine entertainment. The line drawings, on the other hand, are grotesque and detract from the book. Ages 10+.

Buber, Martin. Tales of the Hasidim: Early Masters. Schocken, 1947. $5.95 pb.
Tales of the Hasidim: Later Masters. Schocken, 1948. $4.95 pb.
These legends of the zaddikim, the righteous masters of Hasidim, will introduce adults and older teenagers to the rich literary heritage of this unique branch of Judaism. Although the collections will not interest children, folklorists working with youngsters will be able to adapt many tales to share with them. Ages 15+.

Cone, Molly. The Shema Story Books. See chapter 11, Theology.

Cone, Molly. Who Knows Ten? Children's Tales of the Ten Commandments. Illus. Uri Shulevitz. UAHC, 1965. $5.00.
Cone gives a brief introduction to each commandment and then illustrates its meaning with an entertaining story from Jewish folklore. Children will enjoy these nondidactic, airy tales about a spoiled princess who insists upon seeing God; a husband who orders his wife to spit in the rabbi's eye; a king who once wore chicken feathers in his hair; and seven others. Storytellers will find good, easily retellable material here. This nicely illustrated book is also available on cassette and record from UAHC. Ages 8–11.

Einhorn, David. The Seventh Candle and Other Folk Tales of Eastern Europe. Trans. Gertrude Pashin. Illus. Ezekiel Schloss. KTAV, 1968. $5.00.
These twenty-seven stories reflect a world in which faith and backs had to be strong to ensure survival. Highly ethical and lacking subtlety, the tales invite biblical heroes, supernatural powers, and ingenious animals to help the needy protagonists. While humor is not a high priority, several stories are amusing. For example, "The Tailor and the Sprite" has a universal flavor and a playful lilt. The animal tales also have a unique appeal and would be fun to tell. Unfortunately, the stories also feature weeping synagogues, talking siddurs (prayer books), and trees that fall on their hands and knees. A mixed blessing. Ages 9–14.

Elkin, Benjamin. The Wisest Man in the World. Illus. Anita Lobel.
Parents, 1968. O.P.
This ancient Israeli legend concerns the wise King Solomon, whose
past kindness to a bee rescued him from great humiliation. When the
jealous Queen of Sheba comes to test Solomon's wisdom, she finds
herself surprised and annoyed by his powers. She cannot succeed in
perplexing him until he is asked to select the real flower from among
one hundred artificial blossoms. But look! Here comes the little bee,
who, unseen by others, leads the monarch to the only real flower. The
king is humbled, the queen is impressed, and the reader is entertained. The smooth text is accompanied by detailed and brilliantly
colored illustrations. Ages 5–10.

Ellentuck, Shan. Yankel the Fool. Illus. by author. Doubleday, 1973.
$4.95.
Follow the adventures of Yankel Schlimazel, a poor noodleheaded
orphan who cannot support himself and his old grandmother. The
book's eight chapters lead Yankel from one bad experience to another, until he is reduced to a life of crime. Ellentuck promises us a
happy ending, however, and she sends in a wonder-working rabbi
who creates the image of a wise and successful Yankel. The author's
writing is friendly, fast-paced, and reminiscent of Sholom Aleichem.
She carries on a running dialogue with the reader and with the
angels. Yankel is a shtetl stereotype; his mentality is similar to other
schlimazels who are blessed with more ignorance than bliss. His story
is fun to share aloud. Ages 9–12.

Freehof, Lillian S. Stories of King Solomon. Illus. Seymour Kaplan.
Jewish Pubn. 1955. $3.95.
These twenty-six stories of the wise King Solomon are Midrashic-
Talmudic legends. Talking animals, mischievous demons, magical
events, and wise decisions abound. The tales are presented in a large
format and are nicely illustrated. This is a good source for Solomon
legends, but the stories are wordier than necessary. The text could be
abridged by the reader-aloud or storyteller. (Note: Freehof's *Stories of
King David,* Jewish Pubn, 1952, is not as interesting.) Ages 10–12.

Gershator, Phillis. Honi and His Magic Circle. Illus. Shay Reiger.
Jewish Pubn, 1979. $6.95.
All American school children know about Johnny Appleseed, and
now Jewish youngsters can meet Honi Ha-Me'aggel, Honi the Circle
Maker, a legendary folk prophet who planted carob trees throughout
the Holy Land. Gershator's pleasant retelling of this first-century
B.C.E. miracle worker, whose deeds are recorded in the Talmud, is ac-
companied by graceful, cheerful illustrations in gold and gray by the

talented Reiger. Readers will admire old Honi, who had but to draw a circle and step inside in order to obtain God's attention and support. Honi's devotion to planting trees to nourish humans and animals alike earned him the reputation of being a saintly, magical man. This is a handsomely produced book. Ages 5–10.

Goitein, S. D. From the Land of Sheba: Tales of the Jews of Yemen. Schocken, 1973 (rev. ed.). O.P.; $3.45 pb.
The adult working with children and folklore might be interested in knowing about this adult collection of Jewish legends from an area not covered in juvenile collections. These entertaining tales blend the religious and ethical beliefs of Judaism with the cultural attitudes of the Oriental people. Ages 15+.

Goldin, Hyman. The Magic Ring and Other Medieval Jewish Tales. Illus. Ernest E. Rook. Hebrew Pub, 1946. O.P.
A strange but haunting collection of stories told by an intelligent Jewish mother to her young son. Their impoverished lives in France under an anti-Semitic king are contrasted with the brilliance and glory in the supernatural tales she unfolds. Although the writing is lucid and appealing, many of the stories are long and difficult. The book is recommended for older children who like detailed narrative fantasy. Ages 12–16.

Gross, Michael. The Fable of the Fig Tree. Illus. Mila Lazarevich. Walck, 1975. O.P.
In the ancient kingdom now known as Turkey, old Elisha was found planting a fig tree by the wise king. Impressed by Elisha's generosity (after all, his death might precede the appearance of figs), the monarch asks the old man to bring the figs to the castle when they finally grow. Happily, Elisha lives to fulfill his promise and returns to his village with his basket heaped with gold coins. A local opportunist assumes that the king rewards all such fig bearers, and he makes haste to the castle. His reward is a public humiliation. This has a similar theme to Bialik's *Knight of Onions and Knight of Garlic* (reviewed in this chapter). The soft gray, yellow, and green illustrations depict old Turkish dress and attractively complement the old Hebrew folk tale. Ages 5–10.

Hirsh, Marilyn. Captain Jiri and Rabbi Jacob. Illus. by author. Holiday, 1976. $6.95.
Due to a mixup by their guardian angels, a rabbi and a soldier accidentally meet and learn from each other. The rabbi can now teach the art of self-defense to his students, while the captain offers reading and refinement to his unruly men. Colorful and good-humored illus-

trations enhance the smooth, understated text. This is a satisfying European folk tale with universal appeal. Ages 5–10.

Hirsh, Marilyn. Could Anything Be Worse? Illus. by author. Holiday, 1974. $7.95.
Hirsh retells a Yiddish folk tale about a discontented man who learns a lesson from a wise rabbi. Complaining that his house is too crowded and his family too bothersome, the protagonist is instructed to invite a succession of noisy animals and relatives into his hut to live with him. When the distraught fellow finally lets his intruders go, he comes to appreciate his given lot. The story is very well retold with a familiar Yiddish intonation: " 'Could things be worse?' he asked himself. 'No, they couldn't,' he answered himself. 'I'll go to the rabbi.' " The humorous double-spread illustrations are both in color and black and white. (Note: Two other versions of this story without a specifically Jewish content are also available: Rose Dobbs, *No Room,* McKay, 1944; Ann McGovern, *Too Much Noise,* HM, 1967. Margot Zemach's Jewish version is reviewed in this chapter.) Ages 4+.

Hirsh, Marilyn. The Rabbi and the Twenty-nine Witches. Illus. by author. Holiday, 1976. $7.95; $1.25 pb. Schol Bk Serv.
Here is a Talmudic legend just perfect for a late October telling. It is the story of a rabbi's victory in ridding his village of the "meanest, scariest, ugliest, wickedest witches that ever were." The great triumph takes place at a witches' dance; the town's bravest men twirl their ill-tempered partners into the rain, and the witches melt. Cinderella's ball never knew such excitement. The picture book's humorous illustrations in black, gray, and blue complete this entertaining package: "Dooo come in." Ages 5–10.

Ish-kishor, Sulamith. The Carpet of Solomon. Illus. Uri Shulevitz. Pantheon, 1966. $4.99.
Share an adventure with the great king Solomon, who often receives a humbling lesson. In this Hebrew legend, Solomon soars above the heavens on a diabolical magic carpet. After being locked in an isolated castle, being faced with nightmarish visions, and learning an unhappy truth about a trusted servant, Solomon floats down to earth a repentant man. The subject matter is sensitively handled for a young audience. The large print and graceful pen-and-ink sketches move the story along at a fast pace. Solomon's pre-spaceship adventure will keep science fiction fans on the edge of their seats. Ages 10–14.

Ish-Kishor, Sulamith. The Master of Miracle: A New Novel of the Golem. Illus. Arnold Lobel. Har-Row, 1971. $7.89.

The golem (medieval Hebrew for "shapeless mass") is popular material for literary and artistic interpretation. As the legend goes, the golem was formed from clay and given life by a great medieval rabbi of Prague. Created to protect the Jews from yearly pogroms during Passover, the golem was eventually destroyed by its maker and returned to a shapeless heap after performing its duties. Told through the eyes of the orphan boy, Gideon, the legend is expanded into an exciting novel by Ish-Kishor. Gideon has watched the birth of this clay creature with great fascination; and together they succeed in finding a missing village girl accused of being stolen by the Jews. Later, the boy's unwillingness to destroy his helpmate causes dire consequences. Here is a satisfying substitute for less memorable "monster" tales. Ages 9–13.

Kushner, Lawrence. The Book of Letters: A Mystical Alef-bait. See chapter 2, The Hebrew Alphabet.

McDermott, Beverly Brodsky. The Golem: A Jewish Legend. Illus. by author. Lippincott, 1975. $8.95.
A stunning and emotional picture book for older children and adults. Painted with brilliant colors and dramatic black outlines and shadows, it looks as if angry stained-glass windows are exploding in sorrow and frustration. The golem in McDermott's version reacts with tremendous anger when the Christians storm the Jewish ghetto. Growing into a giant, he all but demolishes his surroundings with his supernatural strength. Here is a work to study and discuss. Brief and powerful, it could be read during a seder or presented by a thoughtful guest as a memorable gift. Ages 10+.

Nahmad, H. M., trans. A Portion in Paradise and Other Jewish Folktales. Schocken, 1974. $2.95 pb.
Here is an excellent source of Jewish folklore for older children with an interest in the subject. Beginning with a preface, "The Nature of Jewish Legend and Folklore," Nahmad further introduces each of six sections with an informative discussion. The stories, concerning Elijah, Solomon, women, piety, wit, and the golem, are drawn from biblical, Talmudic, and medieval sources. These forty-one tales are varied in mood and subject; they should entertain both teenagers and adults. Storytellers working with children will find this a valuable resource. Ages 13+.

Noy, Dov, ed. Folktales of Israel. Trans. Gene Baharav. "Folktales of the World" Series. U of Chicago Pr, 1963. O.P.; $4.25 pb.
An impressive and informative book for the young adult folklorist. Seventy-one stories from seventeen nations are presented with grace

and lucidity. Including both secular and religious tales, the stories are introduced by a detailed account of their origins, relationships to other stories, and various themes. The book also contains an informative foreword, an introduction, a glossary, a bibliography, four subject indexes, and a general index. Although written for adults, this is a valuable resource and reference guide for the Jewish storyteller working with children. Ages 14+.

Peretz, I. L. The Case Against the Wind and Other Stories. Trans. and adap. Esther Hautzig. Illus. Leon Shtainmets. Macmillan, 1975. $6.95.
I. L. Peretz, the father of Yiddish literature, wove his tales from the stuff miracles are made of in order to comfort the deeply suffering Polish Jews of eighty years ago. These ten stories are entertaining, dramatic, and varied in tone and approach. If not genuine folklore, they are very folkloristic. "The Obsession with Clothes" is about a woman who cannot stop shopping, putting Andersen's emperor to shame. "The Match" is reminiscent of "Cinderella." In this story, the fairy godmother, the legendary Jewish heroine Sara Bath Tuvim, gives the groom a pair of pretty slippers and sends him off to find the right Jewish girl. Peretz's tales are well-developed literary pieces. He is equal to such storytellers as Andersen, Jacobs, and Lang. The delicate, glimmering illustrations promise to vanish when the story concludes. Ages 9–15.

Rand, Baruch, and **Barbara Rush.** Around the World with Jewish Folktales: Jews of Kurdistan. Illus. Pete Hoffman. Toledo Board of Jewish Ed, 1978. $3.95 pb.
An introduction to the folklore of the Jews of Kurdistan, a portion of land where Iran, Iraq, and Turkey are today. The book begins with a fictionalized introduction to Kurdish life. About a dozen folk tales follow which combine ancient Hebrew legends with local Kurdish customs. The stories emphasize that charity and repentance will earn material and spiritual returns. Evil spirits called shedim can be conquered by piety. The writing is pleasant, if not outstanding, but the tales lack levity. The format is well done and the illustrations (and some photographs) give us a good idea of the Kurdish culture. Glossary. Ages 11–14.

Rose, Anne. The Triumphs of Fuzzy Fogtop. Illus. Tomie de Paola. Dial, 1979. $8.95.
Three stories loosely based on Chelm folklore. The mildly amusing misadventures of a simpleton named Fuzzy Fogtop include misplacing himself, traveling for three hours on a stationary train, and recog-

nizing an old friend he had never met before. The humor here is a bit too sophisticated for preschoolers, and the watered-down folklore may not hold the attention of older children. On the other hand, de Paola's perky and colorful illustrations give the book enough zest to help compensate for the textual weaknesses. Ages 4–9.

Serwer, Blanche. Let's Steal the Moon: Jewish Tales, Ancient and Recent. Illus. Trina Schart Hyman. Little, 1970. $5.95.
A solid children's introduction to the various legends in Jewish folklore. The eleven stories come from two main sources: the medieval Middle East and nineteenth-century Eastern Europe. The five older tales are about witches, demons, the value of knowledge, King Solomon, and the beloved Hillel. The six newer tales include a golem legend, some Chelm stories, and even an amusing encounter with Napoleon. The stories contain lively dialogue and amusing plots. Hyman's black, gray, and yellow illustrations are a delightful, integral part of the book's character. While many other collections contain abstract or cartoonlike drawings, Hyman's world is populated by genuinely human and easily recognizable people. Ages 9–14.

Shahn, Ben. The Alphabet of Creation. See chapter 2, The Hebrew Alphabet.

Shulevitz, Uri. The Treasure. Illus. by author. FS&G, 1978. $7.95.
A poor old man named Isaac repeatedly dreams about a treasure buried under the bridge near the royal palace. After several days of traveling and exploring the area, Isaac is approached by the captain of the guards. When the captain hears the old man's story, he laughs and says, "Listen, if I believed a dream I had once, I would go right now to the city you came from, and I'd look for a treasure in the house of a fellow named Isaac." When Isaac goes home, he unburies a fortune. The brief and poetic text can open doors to interesting discussions, and the breathtaking scenes in iridescent colors of Eastern Europe's majestic landscapes make this book a treasure in itself. Ages 5–10.

Simon, Solomon. The Wandering Beggar. Illus. Lillian Fischel. Behrman, 1942. $4.95.
Enjoy a touching and funny story about Simple Shmerel, a wandering beggar, who brings luck to everyone but himself. Sent into the world to rub off his simplicity by rubbing elbows, Shmerel develops from a bungling fool to a genuine hero. In the last chapter, Shmerel rescues imprisoned Jews by standing up to a prince. The prince will free the Jews if Shmerel can live through a close encounter with his ferocious dogs. The overanxious canines have only recently been

trained to leave the garden scarecrows alone. The beggar agrees to face them. The dogs take one look at Shmerel, mistake him for a scarecrow, and ignore him completely. The prince frees the Jews. This fine example of classical narrative folklore will entertain families for hours. Ages 9+.

Simon, Solomon. The Wise Men of Helm and Their Merry Tales. Illus. Lillian Fischel. Behrman, 1942. $3.95 pb.
More Wise Men of Helm and Their Merry Tales. Illus. Stephen Kraft. Behrman, 1965. $3.95 pb.
If you have trouble keeping up with the Joneses, be grateful that you do not reside in Helm (Chelm), whose inhabitants' circular logic is hard to top. Simon's two volumes of Helm tales are also difficult to surpass. Well written and charmingly illustrated, these titles offer twenty-eight of the funniest folk tales available from any nationality. It is interesting to compare Solomon Simon's Helm to Isaac Bashevis Singer's Chelm. Simon is genuinely interested in the legendary town as a source for classic folklore. Singer, on the other hand, is a great writer; he uses the legends of Chelm as a framework for his own story as much as for Chelm's. Singer's characters, more fully developed than traditional folklore figures, make us feel their poverty and suffering. Fortunately, readers can purchase tickets to travel to both memorable towns. Ages 9+.

Singer, Isaac Bashevis. Alone in the Wild Forest. Trans. by author and Elizabeth Shub. Illus. Margot Zemach. FS&G, 1971. $8.95.
This Jewish fairy tale is composed of Kabbalistic magic, Talmudic wisdom, and a creative narrative. Young Joseph wins a princess with the aid of an angel, while a wicked prime minister is sent on a repenter's journey for trying to drown Joseph. While Piety attains a beautiful princess (with blue eyes and golden locks), Evilness acquires a monstrous spouse with head of pig, body of ape, and feet of frog. Singer's forest is inhabited by talking animals, angels, and horned creatures. A narrow view of women is also evident, along with the main theme of repentance. Zemach's black-and-white drawings are a fine addition to the powerful, dizzying tale. Ages 10+.

Singer, Isaac Bashevis. Elijah the Slave. Illus. Antonio Frasconi. FS&G, 1970. $6.95.
In Jewish folklore, the biblical prophet Elijah is fond of walking the earth in search of people to aid. Tobias, a holy scribe, has become ill and is unemployed. Upon his wife's urging to meet a miracle halfway, Tobias sets out to look for work and encounters Elijah. Elijah asks to be sold as a slave so that Tobias can earn some money. The prophet

then earns his freedom by magically erecting a handsome castle for his new master, making the angels laugh and God smile. Singer's brief, graceful text and Frasconi's vivid and entrancing woodcuts make this an appealing work to read aloud. Ages 6–10.

Singer, Isaac Bashevis. The Fearsome Inn. Trans. by author and Elizabeth Shub. Illus. Nonny Hogrogian. Scribner, 1967. O.P.
Leibel rescues five young people from the two devils who own a fearsome inn. By drawing a magic circle around this evil couple and their abode, the student of the Kabbalah destroys the demons and ensures a happy conclusion to the romances brewing among the young men and women held captive in the terrifying tavern. Flawless writing fashioned with magic, wintery imagery, and tender romance creates a memorable tale. The artist's watercolor illustrations are large, bright, and integrally woven into this handsome work. Ages 9+.

Singer, Isaac Bashevis. The Fools of Chelm and Their History. Trans. by author and Elizabeth Shub. Illus. Uri Shulevitz. FS&G, 1973. $4.95.
Using the characters from his other adaptations of Chelm folklore, Singer creates a satire on government and human nature. When the ruling sages are overthrown by their failure to win a war, a revolutionist takes over and creates chaos. The book ends with the women in power, holding up banners proclaiming: "Chelm Yentes Unite" (*Yente* is Yiddish for a gossipy woman). Although the writing is clever and fluent, the book distorts the folkloric character of the inhabitants of Chelm. Would a poor schlemiel (fool) ever attempt to murder and enslave a neighboring people? The story brings to mind a version of "Little Red Riding Hood" by Tomi Ungerer in which the heroine marries the wolf and hates her evil grandmother (*A Storybook*, Watts, 1974). Shulevitz's illustrations, which make the Chelmites look like hoodlums, fit the story perfectly. Ages 12+.

Singer, Isaac Bashevis. Mazel and Shlimazel, or the Milk of a Lioness. Trans. by author and Elizabeth Shub. Illus. Margot Zemach. FS&G, 1967. $8.95.
A lengthy picture book based on a Talmudic legend about two spirits: Mazel, who embodies luck, and Shlimazel, the very essence of misfortune. The spirits decide to see who is more powerful and select the simple peasant Tam for their subject. Tam's rise to king's adviser and son-in-law is told with a glib tongue and charming illustrations. Ages 9+; younger for reading aloud.

Singer, Isaac Bashevis. Naftali the Storyteller and His Horse, Sus, and Other Stories. Illus. Margot Zemach. FS&G, 1976. $6.95; $1.25 pb. Dell.

Here is a handsome example of bookmaking: quality paper, fine pencil drawings, and wide margins make the book a joy to read. Among the eight stories Singer tells are tales of Chelm (in which people drown a carp to punish it), a Hanukkah eve spent in a snowstorm, an autobiographical piece, and a moving story about the friendship between a storyteller and his old horse. Naftali is a fine mixture of folklore, original fiction, and nonfiction. It is Singer in a playful, happy mood. Ages 10+.

Singer, Isaac Bashevis. When Shlemiel Went to Warsaw and Other Stories. Trans. by author and Elizabeth Shub. Illus. Margot Zemach. FS&G, 1968. $8.95; $1.25 pb., Dell.
This enchanting collection of eight stories includes three Singer originals. The remaining five are retellings of East European tales passed down by his mother. Singer's original tales feature saintly folk and demonic creatures battling it out in supernatural warfare. The folklore takes place in Chelm, where the poor struggle for survival in an illogical and deceitful world. (Well, is it logical for God to send the snow in the winter? Let Him send some in the summer when it is hot and we can use a little refreshment!) Jewish humor is at its finest in this excellent source for storytelling and drama. Singer uses irony with such precision that you split your sides laughing—without realizing that your fist is clenched. The soft pencil sketches of shtetl life are tender and amusing. Ages 9+.

Singer, Isaac Bashevis. Zlateh the Goat and Other Stories. Illus. Maurice Sendak. Har-Row, 1966. $10.00.
The seven stories in this collection originate from middle-European folklore and legend. Most of the stories take place in Chelm and many center around the Hanukkah celebration. "Grandmother's Tale" and "The Devil's Trick" are short dramatic pieces containing demons and magic. The title story is a gentle tale about a goat who saves her young master's life in a snowstorm. "The First Shlemiel" deals with a man who tries to poison himself with delicious jam and is beginning to enjoy dying. (It is my favorite story in the whole wide world.) The tales are enhanced by the seventeen pen-and-ink drawings by Maurice Sendak. This work is already a classic in its field. Ages 9–14. (Note: Miller-Brody Productions has created some fine filmstrips and cassettes based on many of Singer's Chelm stories. For more Hanukkah tales ranging in themes from two blind children to his own childhood, see Singer's *Eight Stories: The Power of Lights,* a less light-hearted, more contemplative collection than *Zlateh.* FS&G, 1980, $10.95. Ages 12+.)

Suhl, Yuri. The Man Who Made Everyone Late. Illus. Lawrence Di Fiore. Schol Bk Serv, 1974. O.P.

How the town neighbors deal with a man who is both verbose and conceited makes for a very funny East European folk tale. The humorous illustrations capture the man's boastful personality and the exasperation of the townspeople. Ages 5–10.

Suhl, Yuri. Simon Boom Gets a Letter. Illus. Fernando Krahn. Schol Bk Serv, 1976. O.P.
Simon Boom is a man blessed with Chelm logic: nothing but the best, no matter at what cost or usefulness. Simon goes to great effort and expense to build the perfect letter opener. Urgings from his wife to just rip open the envelope fall on deaf ears. Gadget lovers of all ages will respond to Suhl's East European folk tale and to Krahn's comical illustrations. Ages 5+.

Suhl, Yuri. Simon Boom Gives a Wedding. Illus. Margot Zemach. Schol Bk Serv, 1972. $6.95.
Simon sets out to purchase only the best for his daughter's wedding feast and ends up serving only sparkling spring water. Planning a wedding has never been so much fun, although Zemach's famished and dejected wedding guests are not smiling. The illustrations in soft but festive colors enhance this funny story. Especially effective are the marvelous facial expressions on the elegantly clad guests. Ages 4+.

Zemach, Margot. It Could Always Be Worse: A Yiddish Folk Tale. Illus. by author. FS&G, 1976. $7.95; $1.95 pb., Schol Bk Serv.
The moral revealed in this story is that misfortune is relative. The tale concerns a poor man who cannot stand the crowded conditions of his one-room hut. (For plot detail see the review of *Could Anything Be Worse?* by Marilyn Hirsh in this chapter.) Zemach's wonderful illustrations distinguish this title from similar retellings. The artist first creates her drawings of the shtetl from constructed models: the home and inhabitants are made of cardboard, paint, and an assortment of fabrics and accessories. The final result is a picture book in which man and beast, pot and pan, and roof and window actively struggle to make a place for themselves in this crowded hovel. The narrative is certainly adequate and complementary to the drawings. Ages 4+.

Reference Aids

Ginzberg, Louis. The Legends of the Jews. Trans. Henrietta Szold. Jewish Pubn, 1909. 7 vols. $7.00 each.
"In ... *The Legends of the Jews,* I have made the first attempt to gather from the original sources all Jewish legends, in so far as they refer to Biblical personalities and events, and reproduce them with the greatest attainable completeness and accuracy" (preface). With lovely

prose and a dramatic style, Ginzberg offers a wealth of storytelling and story-writing sources for the adult working with children. Volumes 1–4 cover the legends from Creation to Esther; volumes 5 and 6 are notes; and volume 7 is the index.

Ireland, Norma O. Index to Fairy Tales, 1949–1972. Faxon, 1973. $18.00.

This excellent source for locating individual folk tales in collections lists more than seventy Jewish stories found in over twenty different anthologies. Although many of the books indexed by Ireland are reviewed in this chapter, a fair number of additional stories can also be found in popular fairy tale collections in the public library.

Anthologies: Poetry and Essays

Eisenberg, Azriel, and **Leah Ain Globe,** eds. The Bas Mitzvah Treasury. Twayne, 1965. $5.95.

This anthology draws upon biblical, folkloric, classical and modern Jewish writings to introduce the young Jewish woman to her great cultural heritage. Emphasis is put on stories about ancient and modern Jewish womanhood: heroes, poets, wives, and mothers. Far from a feminist viewpoint (we are told right off that God made Eve from the rib to ensure her modest nature), the anthology nonetheless pays homage to woman's mind and soul in addition to her beauty, virtue, and reproductive role. A lively and readable work wrapped in a dull cover. Ages 12–15.

Eisenberg, Azriel, ed. Modern Jewish Life in Literature. United Syn Bk, 1952–1968. Vol. 1, $3.95; vol. 2, $4.50.

A fine collection of essays, stories, and poetry by an impressive body of authors writing about the Jewish experience. Volume 1 includes writings about old-European Jewry, American immigrants, the rise of Hitler, and the young Israel. Volume 2 deals with the Holocaust and the Resistance, modern Israel, America, and Russia. Each volume contains biographical portraits and extensive bibliographies. Although the work is printed in textbook format, the quality and variety of the writing can (with a little push) transcend its dull packaging. Ages 12+.

Friedlander, Albert H., ed. Out of the Whirlwind: A Reader of Holocaust Literature. Illus. Jacob Landau. UAHC, 1968; $7.95 pb., Schocken.

Poetry, music, essays, dialogues, memoirs, book excerpts, and even some children's art work bring some of the best minds on the Holocaust period together in one volume. Considering the subject, such a collection can be disturbing, so I recommend that teenagers dip into this title from time to time. The writing covers this tragic era from the time of the gathering clouds to the ark's second landing in Israel. Ages 12+.

Goodman, Philip, ed. "Jewish Holidays" Series. See chapter 7, The Jewish Holidays.

Henry, Sondra, and **Emily Taitz.** Written out of History: A Hidden Legacy of Jewish Women Revealed Through Their Writings. See chapter 4, Biographies: Collective Biographies.

Klink, J. L., ed. The Bible for Children with Plays and Songs. See chapter 3, The Bible: Bible Stories.

L'Engle, Madeleine. The Journey with Jonah. (A play.) See chapter 3, The Bible: Bible Stories.

Mezey, Robert, ed. Poems from the Hebrew. Illus. Moishe Smith. "Poems of the World" Series. T Y Crowell, 1973. $6.95.
Poems from the Bible comprise Mezey's first section. The sixteen short poems in the second section are from medieval Spanish poetry. The third part offers over fifty poems written in Israel's modern period. Chaim Bialik, Rachel, and Nathan Alterman are only a few of the poets who offer verses in a wide variety of moods and lengths. These poems, which span many thousands of years, have several common themes. Feelings of deep love and bitterness, emotions of profound sorrow and rage over religious persecution, and great exuberance and impatience with God are often repeated. The playful quality characteristic of Yiddish prose is absent in the Hebrew poetry represented here. Mezey includes a fine introduction and indexes, but no biographical notes. (Note: The only other title containing Hebrew poetry for youngsters that I came across was Gems of Hebrew Verse: Poems for Young People edited by Harry Fein. Bruce Humphries, 1940, O.P.) Ages 12+.

Volavkova, Hana, ed. I Never Saw Another Butterfly: Children's Drawings and Poems from Terezin Concentration Camp, 1942–1944. Trans. Jeanne Nemcova. Schocken, 1978. $4.95 pb.
Terezin was a way station to Auschwitz. A total of 15,000 children stopped there; about 100 survived the war. This book is a monument to these youngsters, who have no other headstone. It is also a tribute to the universal optimism of children, for the poetry and paintings not only reveal hatred for the Nazi and despair over their situation, but hope, longing, and love for nature and home. Many of the poems show talent; all touch the reader. Children of all creeds should study

this work. Empathizing with young war victims through their private suffering and dreams is an affecting experience. Ages 10+.

Zim, Jacob, ed. My Shalom, My Peace: Paintings and Poems by Jewish and Arab Children. McGraw, 1975. O.P.
Writing and art work by children usually attract adults rather than youngsters, but this collection of poetry and paintings has enough style and imagination to recommend it to young readers. Jewish and Arab children describe their longing for peace, for an end to violence, and for a daddy who comes home to stay. The brightly colored drawings of suns, birds, flowers, and old foes embracing portray the hopes of these children—and their practical nature as well: "Tomorrow, when peace comes, we won't waste any money on arms / We'll buy more cows for our farms" (from "Tomorrow"). Share these poems out loud. Ages 9+.

Reference Aids

Brewton, John E., and others. Index to Poetry for Children and Young People, 1970–1975. Wilson, 1978. $20.00.

Smith, Dorothy B. Frizzell, and **Eva L. Andrews.** Subject Index to Poetry for Children and Young People, 1957–1975. ALA, 1977. $40.00.
These two indexes will locate individual poems that are included in a large variety of anthologies and collections. The Smith and Andrews index has a more extensive Jewish listing, but both titles will help locate poems with Jewish themes for children. I would not recommend buying either of these titles for their Jewish entries alone, but a good public library should stock these aids in the reference collection.

10

Music and Dance

Music and dance have always been part of the Jewish tradition, and although it is unusual to find musical instruments outside of the Reform movement, Hebrew song plays an important part in the religious services of all Judaic sects. Indeed, the Hasidic branch of Judaism, whose music evolved from the Jewish ghetto, has contributed a remarkable and exuberant style of music to Jewish culture.

Many fine Jewish composers, conductors, and musicians have achieved prominence in the twentieth century, and several children's biographies have been written about Jewish musicians. The life stories of Jerome Kern, Felix Mendelssohn, Leonard Bernstein, George Gershwin, and Artur Rubinstein can still be found on library shelves, although many of these titles are no longer in print. The popular singer Barbra Streisand is also the subject of a juvenile biography.

The materials for children that best reflect the broad spectrum of Jewish music are song books and records. A look through the catalog of Tara Publications, a music distributor, reveals that Jewish music encompasses a great variety of styles, nationalities, and historic eras. Lyrics are sung in Hebrew, Yiddish, Ladino (the Spanish dialect of the Sephardic Jews), and English. The forms include traditional cantorial recitatives, Hasidic melodies, East European lullabies, popular Israeli songs, and children's choruses and holiday stories.

Chapter 12, Multi-Media Resources, contains a listing of record and cassette distributors. Many of these organizations offer inexpensive song books (with music instruction) in paperback and pamphlet form in addition to recordings. See the Reference Aids section for a list of such companies.

Although the hora, the traditional Jewish dance, has entered the mainstream of folk dance, there are very few books for children on Jewish dance. Several instruction guides exist that can be used to teach children Jewish folk dances. Fred Berk and Dvora Lapson, two highly respected people in this field, have written various books and instructional pamphlets on Yemenite, East European, Hasidic, pioneering Israeli, and contemporary American Jewish dancing. In addition to the books reviewed in this chapter, the Reference Aids section highlights multi-media dance resources.

Music and Dance Books

Berk, Fred, ed. The Chasidic Dance. UAHC, 1975. $3.00 pb.
Six brief essays on Hasidism and its dance styles precede the instructions for ten Hasidic dances, Israeli style. Both sexes can participate. Included also are black-and-white photographs depicting the dancers at weddings, on stage, and at the Western Wall. This is an easily understood introduction to the exotic world of Hasidic dance. (Note: See also Berk's *Ha-Rikud: The Jewish Dance,* UAHC, 1972, $3.50, a history and instruction manual.) Ages 12+.

Chochem, Corinne, and **Muriel Roth.** Palestine Dances: Folk Dances of Palestine. Illus. Moses Soyer; photos by John Mills, Jr. Greenwood, 1978. Repr. of 1941 ed. $13.25.
Fourteen dances including the steps, music, and Hebrew and English lyrics are provided in this oversized book complete with large black-and-white photographs of exuberant kibbutz dancers. Two versions of the hora are included as well as other dances that derive from it and yet reflect the influences of various folk dances from Europe and Asia. Several of the dances are recommended for young children. This attractive title would appeal to a wide audience and be useful with many age levels. Ages 8+ with adult supervision.

Coopersmith, Harry, ed. The Songs We Sing. Illus. K. Oechsli. United Syn Commission on Jewish Ed, 1951. $6.95;   Sequel: More of the Songs We Sing. United Syn Commission on Jewish Ed, 1971. $6.95.
Each book contains over four hundred pages of words and music (with piano accompaniment) to a host of Hebrew songs that concern many aspects of Jewish life, e.g., holidays, the Bible and prayer, Israel, and youthful themes. The words are transliterated and translated into English. Many of the songs can be sung in English and Yiddish as well as Hebrew. Storytellers will enjoy adapting several of the songs into poetry, as in the case of the ballad of "Elimeleh," in which a man drinks so much on Purim that his head feels like a whirling grogger. These oversized, attractively illustrated books are a wonderful resource for the religious and secular library. (Note: For a small but diverse collection of Jewish songs for children, see Coopersmith's *New Jewish Song Book,* Behrman, 1965, $4.95.) All ages.

Eisenstein, Judith, and **Frieda Prensky.** Songs of Childhood. Illus. Ayala Gordon. United Syn Commission on Jewish Ed, 1955. $15.00. This large and diverse collection of songs for children ages three to seven contains music and lyrics to over two hundred tunes about the Sabbath, holidays, religious customs, Israel, and the everyday joys of childhood. The songs are gathered from various sources: Yiddish, Hasidic, Israeli, Oriental, and American. The songs are presented in transliterated Hebrew with an English translation and in the Hebrew alphabet. Suggestions for percussion instruments, singing games, folk dances, and activity songs are also given. This big and joyful collection, presented in an attractive format, will bring much pleasure to children learning Hebrew and about their heritage. (Note: Eisenstein has a second large collection of Jewish music with background information written for an older audience. See *Heritage of Music: The Music of the Jewish People,* UAHC, 1972, $15.00.) Ages 3–7.

Englander, Lois, and others. The Jewish Holiday Do-Book. See chapter 5, Fine Arts and Domestic Arts.

Hirsh, Marilyn, adap. and illus. One Little Goat: A Passover Song. See chapter 7, The Jewish Holidays.

Lapson, Dvora. The Bible in Dance. Illus. Cecila Grobla. Board of Jewish Ed, 1970. $4.00 pb. These twenty-three dances that interpret Bible stories represent some of the best creations from the Annual Dance Festivals for Jewish Schools sponsored by the Jewish Education Committee of New York. Clear instructions, costume and prop ideas, and recommended age levels are given for each dance. It looks like great school or camp fun. (Note: Lapson has three additional titles, from the same publisher, that provide full instructions on modern and traditional Jewish dances: *Folk Dances for Jewish Festivals; Jewish Dances the Year Round;* and *Dances of the Jewish People,* $3.50 each.) Ages 5+ with adult supervision.

Lisowski, Gabriel, illus. On the Little Hearth: Words and Music for the Popular Yiddish Classic, Oif'n Pripitchik. Trans. Miriam Chaiken. Words and Music, Mark Warshawski (1848–1907). HR&W, 1978. $5.95. An illustrated picture book with words and music to a favorite Yiddish lullaby in which a kindly rebbe (teacher) encourages young children to learn their alef-bet (Hebrew alphabet). Created and sung during a time of great distress for East European Jews, the song expresses a deep sense of urgency. The appealing black-and-white line sketches with bright blue frames lovingly portray scenes from a small Jewish town. A warm and cozy title with some pathos. Ages 5+.

Rose, Anne K. How Does a Czar Eat Potatoes? See chapter 8, Literature: Fiction: Ages 3–8.

Rubin, Ruth. A Treasury of Jewish Folksong. Illus. T. Herzl. Schocken, 1950. $12.50; $6.95 pb.
A collection of Yiddish and Hebrew folksongs with simple piano settings. Songs about infants, childhood, love, work, resistance, and Israel are presented in transliterated Yiddish or Hebrew with English translations. Often Rubin's introductions to the songs make the tunes very poignant. For example, we learn that the old love song "Tsvey Taybelech" was popularized by a Polish singer who sang the lyrics as she marched naked to her own execution by the Nazis. Many of these songs can be used with children and young teenagers. Ages 12+.

Reference Aids

The American Zionist Youth Foundation (same address as the World Zionist Organization) sponsors the Israeli Folk Dance Institute, headed by Fred Berk. It publishes the *Israel Folk Dance Catalog* (a long list of dance records available for purchase from the foundation) and a dance newsletter, *Hora*.

Berk, Fred, and **Dona Rosenblatt.** "Dance." *The Second Jewish Catalog.* Jewish Pubn, 1976, pp. 337–351. A lengthy article that explores the background and resources concerned with Jewish dance.

The Board of Jewish Education of Greater New York publishes two song books for the young school child, *Hebrew Songster* and *Holidays in Song,* as well as several Israeli song books for all ages.

Nulman, Macy. Concise Encyclopedia of Jewish Music. McGraw, 1975. $14.95. A scholarly dictionary with over 500 entries concerning musical works, terms, instruments, biographies, organizations, and published collections. Ages 18+.

Tara Publications provides various folk dance records with instruction booklets. They also publish anthologies of Hasidic music in paperback and hardcover; Jochsberger's *Favorite Hassidic Melodies for the Young Pianist* is available for $3.25.

The World Zionist Organization offers inexpensive instruction pamphlets on Jewish and Israeli folk dances written by Fred Berk and Tzafrah Tatcher. This group also distributes a wide selection of inexpensive song books for youth activities.

For addresses, see chapter 12, Multi-Media Resources.

11
Theology

There is a saying that goes: "If you put three Jews together, you will get four opinions." Nowhere is this truer than in the area of theology. One of Judaism's distinguishing features is its enormous capacity for multiple interpretation. Of the several religious divisions of Judaism, the Orthodox adhere most closely to a strict traditional theology. Believing in the literal doctrine of revelation, they strive in their everyday life and deeds to live by the Torah, as given to Moses by God.

Hasidism, an offshoot of Orthodox Judaism, became a popular religious movement in Europe in the second half of the eighteenth century. Under the guidance of a charismatic leader, Hasidism channels energy and joy into religious experience seeking a mystical and personal relationship to God.

The Reform movement began in early nineteenth-century Germany and has had its greatest impact in the United States. Putting more emphasis on the ethical aspects of Judaism than on the ritualistic, the Reform synagogues do not demand the use of the skullcap or the prayer shawl and do not require the observance of the Sabbath or Jewish dietary laws. Its strongly liberal orientation has allowed a few women to become rabbis.

The Conservative movement developed in the 1890s as a reaction against both the strictly Orthodox and the nontraditional Reform philosophy. Observing many of the rituals, such as the Sabbath and the requirements of kashrut (dietary law), the Conservatives combine flexibility in their beliefs with a reluctance to give up the qualities that make Judaism a religion with old, sacred customs as well as a distinct culture with a strong ethical philosophy.

Reconstructionism, yet another strand of Judaism, developed in America as a part of Conservative Judaism, emphasizes the joy of the total Jewish experience. Its adherents conceive of Judaism as being a "religious civilization," and encourage the exploration of Jewish art, history, language, music, and a strong Jewish community. Tradition is valuable, but more as a total experience than as a strict, unbending code of behavior. Reconstructionists are flexible in reconstructing Judaism to fit modern times and needs. Women rabbis have also been ordained in this branch of Judaism.

The children's books in this chapter are simple introductions to complicated subject matter. Of varying depths, the books span all age levels, from picture books that enumerate God's blessings upon the world to a bat/bar mitzvah guide to principal laws and customs.

Theology Books

Brichto, Mira. The God Around Us: A Child's Garden of Prayer. Illus. Clare Romano Ross and John Ross. UAHC, 1966. $2.75.
Pleasant illustrations and simple rhymes express gratitude to God for food, love, natural wonders, and joy. Twelve basic prayers are introduced in English and Hebrew, and Brichto bases each of her poems on them. Thus, the prayer "Blessed art Thou—Lord God our King for flowers delighting the heart of man" introduces Brichto's "Frozen grounds begin to break / Sleeping roots push up and wake. / Weeping willow, apple, pear / Tender blossoms everywhere." Ages 4–8.

Chiel, Arthur. Pathways Through the Torah. KTAV, 1975. 3 vols. $2.25 pb. each.
The Torah (the first five books of the Bible) is fully explored for the student in this three-volume work. For each chapter, Chiel provides a translation of selected biblical passages into contemporary English; commentaries on the more difficult sections; a selection on interpretations; and a comment about relevant archeological facts. The books are interesting to read and will not overwhelm the student. The appealing format includes photographs, prints, and maps. Used either as a classroom text or for independent reading, the set offers a manageable guide to the meaning of the Torah. Ages 11+.

Cone, Molly. The Shema Story Books. UAHC, 1973. $5.00 pb. each. Book I: First I Say the Shema. Illus. William L. Steinel. Book II: About Learning. Illus. Iris Schweitzer. Book III: About Belonging. Illus. Susan Perl. Book IV: About God. Illus. Clare and John Ross. In books II–IV Cone uses biblical stories and folkloric legends to illustrate some of the basic principles of Judaism. The simple but effective writing and the colorful drawings by various artists make these titles enjoyable to share aloud. Book I is an introduction to the meaning and usage of the Shema, the Hebrew pledge that begins: "Hear, O Israel: the Lord our God, the Lord is One." Ages 4–9.

Ehrman, Yocheved. My First Siddur: An Illustrated Introduction to the Siddur for Pre-readers and Beginners. Illus. by author. Bloch, 1978. $6.95.

A colorfully illustrated and upbeat introduction on how to sit quietly in the synagogue (a miracle in itself) and daven (pray). What we are thankful for and how we can express gratitude to God are the areas under discussion. The drawings portray an Orthodox way of life, but this does not greatly restrict the audience because of Ehrman's basic approach and general concepts. The text is printed in both English and Hebrew. Ages 4–7.

Fassler, Joan. My Grandpa Died Today. Illus. Stewart Kranz. Human Sci Pr, 1971. $8.95.

A sensitive (but poorly illustrated) story about a young boy's love for his elderly grandfather and the emotional impact of his death on the child. Part of a series designed around psychological concepts to help youngsters cope with difficult issues, this title uses the death of a Jewish man (along with Jewish customs) to show how the child's life should continue without guilt and without hesitation. Valuable for all collections. Ages 5–10.

Fitch, Florence Mary. A Book About God. Illus. Leonard Weisgard. Lothrop, 1953. $7.92.

This lovely picture book illustrated in appealing soft hues and accompanied by a brief poetic text explores how one can feel the presence of an invisible God. Bright as the sky, shiny like the sun, and surrounding us like the air, God is likened to phenomena that the young child can understand. This warm and comforting book touches the heart of many religions with its universal expressions. Ages 4–9.

Freeman, Grace R., and **Joan G. Sugarman.** Inside the Synagogue. Illus. Judith Oren; Photos by Justin Kerr and others. UAHC, 1963. $3.75.

This oversized book with large black-and-white photographs and decorative illustrations reveals the mystery of the synagogue to young people. The authors discuss the sacred objects in the temple, the historical aspects of the synagogue (art, architecture, landmarks), the prayer book, songs, and the spiritual leadership of the rabbi. Each religious object is fully and individually discussed and accompanied by attractive photographs. The book is very useful for introducing children (and adults) to the objects and practices associated with Jewish worship. Ages 9+.

Goodman, Hannah. The Story of Prophecy. See chapter 3, The Bible, Exploration of Biblical Themes.

Greene, Laura. I Am an Orthodox Jew. Illus. Lisa C. Wesson. HR&W, 1979. $5.95.
This is a pleasant, informal look into the life of an Orthodox boy and his family. Young Aaron Katz tells of the dietary laws (keeping kosher), ritual garments (yarmulke and zizit), Hebrew Day School, and the Sabbath celebration in his home. Aaron realizes his minority status, and although he voices some wishful thinking about restaurants and eating at a friend's house, he is comfortable and happy in his Orthodox home. His sister, Rachel, however, voices greater objections concerning her lower status in the religious services. The book will be most useful to non-Orthodox Jews and Gentiles. Its introduction to Orthodox Judaism has a credible tone. The cartoonlike drawings are adequate. Ages 7–10; younger for reading aloud.

Klausner, Abraham. A Child's Prayer Book for the Holidays of Rosh Hashana and Yom Kippur. See chapter 7, The Jewish Holidays.

Kripke, Dorothy. Let's Talk About Judaism. Illus. Bobri. Behrman, 1957. $3.50.
A discussion of the basic tenets of Judaism. How religion and love for God helps people to lead a holy life is revealed in a direct but not a dry style. Kripke touches upon the Sabbath, holidays, good deeds (mitzvot), study, the Bible, Hebrew, the family, and the link with fellow Jews. Parents might enjoy reading this title aloud with their youngsters as a springboard for additional discussions. Ages 9–12; younger for reading aloud.

Kripke, Dorothy. Let's Talk About Right and Wrong. Illus. Bobri. Behrman, 1955. $3.95.
Kripke discusses an ethical code of behavior centering on the belief in God and the desire to live up to the little spark of God in each of us. She touches upon a variety of goals such as honesty, self-respect, and kindness, urging children to obtain them in order to feel good about themselves, to make the world a better place, and to be God's partner in life. Recommended for a general audience and as a tool for furthering discussion of ethics and theology. Ages 9–12; younger for reading aloud.

Moskin, Marietta D. In Search of God: The Story of Religion. Atheneum, 1979. $10.95.
This lucid introduction to comparative religion will give youngsters a basic understanding of why and how the various faiths came to be and still are. Moskin says that religions change and influence one another and that a people's relationship with their God is influenced greatly by their particular society. She treats religion as a human in-

stitution, not as divine revelation. Moskin arranges her chapters by topic, such as death, good and evil, sin and sinners, rather than by religion. Photographs and prints enable the reader to sample the different flavors of many religions. Bibliography, index. Ages 11+.

Rittner, Stephen. Rabbi Simon and His Friends. Rittner, 1978. $5.95 pb.
A storytelling rabbi and a whole cast of puppets teach the child ethical values in a lively, nondidactic style. Whenever Sue and Jeff have a controversy to settle, their friend Rabbi Simon leads them to the right moral judgment by relating a tale from the Bible or Midrash (scriptural commentaries). Some of the topics covered are honesty, charity, the Sabbath, Hillel, Deborah, and Beruriah (an ancient female scholar). The small colorful photographs of the puppets printed on shiny white paper add appeal and intrigue to Rittner's morality puppet plays. His simple, if not remarkable, prose allows young children to understand the philosophy behind the tales. (Note: Rittner is the author of two other books on theological topics for children: *All That You Want to Know About the Bar / Bat Mitzvah.* Arbit, 1978, $3.75 pb; *Jewish Ethics of the 21st Century,* Arbit, 1978, $6.75, Ages 11–14.) Ages 6–10.

Rosenbaum, Samuel. To Live As a Jew. KTAV, 1969. $3.95 pb.
A clear and succinct introduction to Jewish belief and law (concerning food, marriage, death, etc.), prayer and music, the Jewish home, and the holidays. The book is a result of the author's experience teaching bar and bat mitzvah students how to live a Jewish life after the big event. This handbook will enable the young Jew to understand the elementary principles behind his or her faith. Index. (Note: See also Morris Golomb's *Know Jewish Living and Enjoy It* for a similar discussion on the life cycle of the Jew. Shengold, 1978. $7.95. Ages 9–13.) Ages 11+.

Rossel, Seymour. Judaism. "A First Book" Series. Watts, 1976. $4.90. This succinct and informative introduction covers Judaism's history, basic beliefs, holidays, special occasions, and religious movements. Abundant and diverse photographs and prints enhance this survey, which will satisfy young Jews and non-Jews alike. Index. (Note: Rossel is the author of these other theological titles for children: *When a Jew Prays,* Behrman, 1973, $5.95 pb., Ages 10–12; *When a Jew Seeks Wisdom: The Sayings of the Fathers,* Behrman, 1975, $6.50 pb., Ages 13+.) Ages 10–12.

Schwartzman, Sylvan. The Living Bible; A Topical Approach to the Jewish Scriptures. See chapter 3, The Bible: Exploration of Biblical Themes.

Smith, Betsy Covington. Breakthrough: Women in Religion. See chapter 4, Biographies: Collective Biographies.

Stern, Chaim. Gates of Heaven: Services for Children and Their Parents on the Days of Awe. KTAV, 1979 (new ed.). $2.50 pb; Gates of Joy: Services for Children and Their Parents for Sukkot, Simchat Torah, Shabbat, Chanukah, and Purim. KTAV, 1979. $2.50 pb.
Rabbi Stern of New York has developed these family services to meet the needs of parents and children. He includes a brief introduction to the holidays as well as the songs, prayers, and directions for conducting services. The new format of *Gates of Heaven,* concerning Yom Kippur and Rosh ha-Shanah, has been brought into closer accord with the new liturgy of the Central Conference of American Rabbis and is nonsexist in its language. These lovely services should appeal to families who want to share the holidays with children on a level comprehensible to all.

12

Multi-Media Resources

There is an abundance of children's multi-media resources with Jewish themes: striking posters (Ya-El Imports); nonsexist coloring books (Sterling Publications); biblical puppets (Jewish Museum Shop); informative filmstrips (Torah Umesorah); entertaining cassettes, Eli Wallach reading Isaac Bashevis Singer's Chelm stories (Miller-Brody); and organizations that encourage and coordinate programs in Jewish art, music, cinema, and education.

Included in this survey are producers and distributors of children's records and cassettes, toys and activity books, films and filmstrips, and visual works, such as posters, charts, and maps.

Record and film titles are not reviewed individually. Each organization listed answered my inquiry promptly with a free catalogue describing its services or products. These catalogues describe in detail the materials available for rent or purchase.

The last section of this chapter contains a bibliography of up-to-date information on Jewish periodicals for children.

Films and Filmstrips

Resources

The following organizations publish information and evaluations on films and filmstrips available for purchase or rental from various sources:

American Association for Jewish Education, 114 Fifth Ave., New York, NY 10011

Jewish Media Service (National Jewish Welfare Board), 15 E. 26th St., New York, NY 10010

Options Publishing Company, P.O. Box 311, Wayne, NJ 07470

Producers and Distributors

Alden Films, 7820 20th Ave., Brooklyn, NY 11214
Distributes short 16mm films for rental concerning Israel and a variety of Jewish subjects.
Alternatives in Religious Education, 3945 South Oneida St., Denver, CO 80237
Offers a small variety of filmstrips and cassette sets for purchase.
Audio Brandon Films, Inc., 34 MacQuesten Pkway So., Mt. Vernon, NY 10550
Provides a catalogue of Jewish 16mm films for rental for audiences of many ages.
Board of Jewish Education of Greater New York, 426 W. 58th St., New York, NY 10019
Offers a variety of children's filmstrips and films for purchase.
JWB Lecture Bureau, 15 E. 26th St., New York, NY 10010.
Offers a large selection of 16mm films for rental.
Miller-Brody Productions, Div. of Random House, Inc., 201 E. 50th St., New York, NY 10022
Producers of quality filmstrips and cassette sets based on children's books by such authors as Isaac Bashevis Singer and Johanna Reiss.
Shimbal Studios, P.O. Box 313, Flushing, NY 11367
Producer of a favorably reviewed filmstrip on an artist's recollection of the Holocaust.
Torah Umesorah, 229 Park Ave. S., New York, NY 10003
Sells a variety of filmstrips about Jewish law, customs, and holidays.
Union of American Hebrew Congregations, 838 Fifth Ave., New York, NY 10021
Offers a large selection of educational filmstrips on all aspects of Judaica.
University of Michigan Media Resources Center, 416 Fourth St., Ann Arbor, MI 48109
Provides a huge catalogue of educational 16mm films for rental, several directly concerned with Jewish life.
World Zionist Organization, Publications Dept., 515 Park Ave., New York, NY 10022
Lists a great many filmstrips and guides concerning Israel and Jewish life for older children.

Records and Cassettes

Resource

The following organization provides catalogues and information on the field of Jewish music:

Jewish Music Council (National Jewish Welfare Board), 15 E. 26th St., New York, NY 10010

Producers and Distributors

The following companies sell a variety of children's records and cassettes concerning Hebrew songs, hymns, melodies, holiday music and stories, folk songs, dances, educational materials, and stories based on children's books.

Alternatives in Religious Education, 3945 S. Oneida St., Denver, CO 80237
Sing-along songs and song books for the primary grades.

Board of Jewish Education of Greater New York, 426 W. 58th St., New York, NY 10019
Holiday melodies, Israeli music, and song books.

Behrman House, 1261 Broadway, New York, NY 10001
Distributes albums by singer Debbie Friedman.

Caedmon, 1995 Broadway, New York, NY 10023
Biblical readings by well-known actors.

Folkways Records and Service Corporation, 43 W. 61st St., New York, NY 10023
Yiddish and Hebrew holiday tunes, folk songs, and games for children.

Isradisc, Israeli Record Co., P.O. Box 230, 5 Smolenskin St., Tel Aviv, Israel
Children's holiday and Song Festival songs and Bible stories in Hebrew.

J.E.P. Records, 425 E. 9th St., Brooklyn, NY 11218
Uncle Moishy sings about Torah and mitzvos.

KTAV Publishing House, 75 Varick St., New York, NY 10013
Holiday songs and instructional recordings.

Miller-Brody Productions, 201 E. 50th St., New York, NY 10022
Recordings from award-winning children's books with Jewish themes.

Tara Publications, 29 Derby Ave., Cedarhurst, NY 11516
A wide selection of adult recordings as well as storytelling, Mother Goose tunes, and Yiddish and Hebrew songs for children.

Torah Umesorah Publications, 229 Park Ave. S., New York, NY
10003
Religious and holiday instructional cassettes.
Vanguard Recording Society, Inc., 71 W. 23rd St., New York, NY
10010
Features music by the Karmon Israeli singers and Jan Peerce.
World Tone Music, Inc., 230 Seventh Ave., New York, NY 10011
Israeli folk dances, instructional dance books, and Yiddish and He-
brew folk songs.
World Zionist Organization, Publications Dept., 515 Park Ave., New
York, NY 10002
Hebrew songs, Hebrew language instruction, and political discus-
sions.
Zemeron Trading Inc., 114 E. 25th St., New York, NY
A large selection of Israeli music for adults and some holiday stories
and songs in English and Hebrew for children.

Toys

Producers and Distributors

The following firms offer a variety of games, puzzles, puppets, novelty
and holiday items, coloring books, pop-up books, and activity books
(cut, paste, draw):

Alternatives in Religious Education, 3945 South Oneida St., Denver,
CO 80237
Variety of toys.
B. Arbit Books, 8050 N. Port Washington Rd., Milwaukee, WI, 53127
Activity books.
Behrman House, 1261 Broadway, New York, NY 10010
Games.
Bellerophon Books, 153 Steuart St., San Francisco, CA 94105
Coloring books.
Bonim (Hebrew Publication Co.), 80 Fifth Ave., New York, NY
10011
Coloring and activity books.
Contemporary Jewish Learning Materials, Inc., 1414 Glendale,
Ames, IA 50010
Games and puzzles.
David C. Cook Publishing Co., 850 N. Grove Ave., Elgin, IL 60120
Pop-up Bible stories.
The Dreidel Factory, 2445 Prince St., Berkeley, CA 94705
Jewish Museum Shop, 1109 Fifth Ave., New York, NY 10028
Variety of gift items.

KTAV Publishing House, 75 Varick St., New York, NY 10013
Large selection of toys and decorations.
LL Company, 1647 Manning Ave., Los Angeles, CA 90024
Puzzles.
Selchow and Righter Co., 200 Fifth Ave., New York, NY 10010
Play the game of Scrabble with Hebrew letters.
Shulsinger Brothers, Inc., 50 Washington St., Brooklyn, NY 11201
Extensive catalogue of toys and decorations.
Standard Publishing Co., 8121 Hamilton Ave., Cincinnati, OH 45231
Pop-up Bible stories.
Sterling Publications, P.O. Box 17633, Tucson, AZ 85731
Coloring books.
Tahgin Ltd., Etzel St., Apt. 21, French Hill, Jerusalem, Israel
Variety of educational toys and designs.

Pictorial Products

Resource

The following organization has pamphlets and informative fliers about Jewish art and artists:

National Council on Art in Jewish Life, 15 E. 84th St., New York, NY 10028

Producers and Distributors

These firms and organizations distribute visual materials: posters, maps, wall charts, cards and stationery, and reprints of fine art work.

American Jewish Archives, 3101 Clifton Ave., Cincinnati, OH 45220
Beautiful posters on a variety of subjects.
American Library Color Slide Co., P.O. Box 5810, Grand Central Station, New York, NY 10017
Slides of ancient Israel and paintings by and about Jews for purchase.
B. Arbit Books, 8050 N. Port Washington Rd., Milwaukee, WI 53217
Extensive collection of maps and wall charts.
Board of Jewish Education of Greater New York, 426 W. 58th St., New York, NY 10019
Educational wall charts.
Jewish Museum Shop, 1109 Fifth Ave., New York, NY 10028
Art prints and posters.
KTAV Publishing House, 75 Varick St., New York, NY 10013
Variety of maps, wall charts, and language aids.

Torah Umesorah Publications, 229 Park Ave. S., New York, NY
10003
Educational wall charts in Hebrew.
Ya-El Imports, Inc., 137 Main St., Danbury, CT, 06810
Brightly illustrated and strikingly designed posters with biblical,
holiday, and Israeli themes.

Children's Periodicals

Achshav (155 Fifth Ave., New York, NY 10010). Published quarterly
by the United Synagogue Youth. Subscriptions through membership in United Synagogue Youth.
Information on the organization's purpose and activities is given as
well as literary and editorial contributions by teenagers and articles
on Israel and American Jewry. Ages 13+.
Keeping Posted (838 Fifth Ave., New York, NY 10021). Published
eleven times a year by the Union of American Hebrew Congregations. Subscription: $4.00. Rates vary for group and foreign orders.
This periodical discusses an important social issue in each publication and explores its many facets in articles, photographs, and illustrations. Ages 12–14.
Noah's Ark: A Magazine for Jewish Children (5514 Rutherglen, Houston,
TX 77096). Published monthly as an independent periodical and
as a supplement to a variety of American Jewish newspapers. Subscription: $5.00. Rates vary for group orders.
In newspaper form, *Noah's Ark* offers puzzles, riddles, book reviews,
recipes, poetry, and brief articles about Noah, a Jewish theme, and
contemporary American life. Lots of fun. Ages 7–11.
Olomeinu/Our World (229 Park Ave. S., New York, NY 10003). Published eight times a year by Torah Umesorah—National Society
for Hebrew Day Schools. Subscription: $4.00. Rates vary for group
and foreign orders.
Features serious articles, craft projects, puzzles, a story in Hebrew,
an excerpt of "Mendel the Mouse" by Ruth Finkelstein, and a comic
strip, "Jewish Heroes," in each issue. Ages 10–14.
Talks and Tales (770 Eastern Parkway, Brooklyn, NY 11213). Published monthly by Merkos L'Inyonei Chinuch, Inc. Subscription:
$2.50.
In a small newsprint pamphlet, *Talks and Tales* discusses a theme,
e.g., the New Year for Trees (Tu bi-Shevat) from its many aspects
and with an Orthodox viewpoint and serious tone. Ages 12–15.
Tom Thumb: The Israeli Children's Magazine (P.O. Box 28110, Tel Aviv,

Israel). Published ten times a year by *Etzboni Magazine*. Subscription: $7.50.

A pleasant collection of stories, articles, a Hebrew lesson, comic strips, puzzles, games, and riddles based on Jewish holidays and themes. Ages 6–10.

World Over (426 West 58th St., New York, NY 10019). Published ten times a year by the Board of Jewish Education of Greater New York. Subscription: $5.00. Rates vary for group and foreign orders.

An upbeat collection of articles, book excerpts and reviews, recipes, puzzles, riddles, stories, etc., about Jewish holidays, current events, and recreational/educational pursuits. A lively format and contents. Ages 7–12.

Young Judean (817 Broadway, New York, NY 10003). Published eight times a year by National Young Judaea under the auspices of Hadassah Zionist Youth Commission. Subscription: $3.50.

This periodical is an Israeli connection for the American child, with articles, stories, photographs, and games concerning ancient and contemporary Israel. Pleasant and informative. Ages 9–13.

appendix A

BUILDING YOUR LIBRARY: BUYING
AND SELECTING METHODS

Ordering Books

There are several ways to acquire the books reviewed here. Unfortunately, the great majority of them will not be waiting for you on bookstore shelves, as shops carry only a small percentage of children's literature in print. Chances are it will take some time to obtain a book from this bibliography.

Bookstore Ordering

Many bookstores will be happy to order most books in print for you at no extra charge. Some stores charge a small service fee for paperback or inexpensive orders. Books ordered this way can take from two to six weeks to arrive.

Synagogue Gift Shops

Many synagogue gift shops stock children's books and would be pleased to order any book in print or available from their book distributor.

Direct from Publisher

It is possible to order your books directly from the publisher. This can be very time consuming, however, if you are ordering a variety of titles from different firms. Publishers do give discounts of varying degrees to schools and libraries. They will charge for mailing in addition to the price of the book, and ordering from the firm will take several weeks. For minimal purchasing, I would recommend dealing with a reliable bookstore rather than going directly to the publisher. In the case of large or repeated orders, I suggest using a book distributor.

Book Distributors

Institutions regularly purchasing books for a library or school will best be served by using a reliable book distributor. In addition to general book wholesalers who serve the general library market, there are a number of Jewish bookstores throughout the country that service schools and libraries. They are willing to obtain any book in print

(Judaica or not) and sometimes have in stock Jewish titles that are out of print with the publisher. The *American Book Trade Directory* (Bowker) is a source of information on retail and wholesale book dealers in the United States.

Price and Availability Information

Price information was obtained from the 1980/81 edition of *Books in Print* (Bowker). As a rule of thumb, hardcover prices tend to increase about $1.00 a year.

Information about a book's availability from a publisher was obtained from the same reference book. Although *Books in Print* is an invaluable tool, errors occur. Several books still in print from small Jewish publishing firms are not listed. Mistakes are also made about the availability of major trade titles. In short, if you are really eager to obtain a title not listed in *Books in Print,* contact the publisher directly and ask about its availability. A stamped, self-addressed envelope will help obtain a quick response.

Keeping Up with the New Titles

Now that you are hooked on children's Jewish literature, how can you keep informed on the new books released each season? Unfortunately, there is no one source to go to that lists all the new titles along with a critical description of their contents. However, by using a combination of various periodicals, annuals, and catalogues, you can keep up to date in this field. Among the many sources, I have found the following most useful for information on children's Jewish literature.

Booklist: American Library Association, 50 East Huron St., Chicago, IL 60611. Published twice monthly from September to July, and once in August. Subscription: $32.00.

This is an excellent reviewing source for the public library. Because of its generous reviews of children's and young adult titles (including some media), in addition to adult book reviews, it is also very helpful to school librarians. *Booklist* reviews many Jewish titles that would appeal to a wide audience. Although it rarely discusses books from small Jewish publishers, it is nonetheless a worthy source of critical information concerning new Jewish titles for all ages.

The Horn Book Magazine: Park Square Bldg., 31 St. James Avenue, Boston, MA 02116. Published bimonthly.

Each issue contains reviews of books for children and young adults, articles about children's and young adult literature, and lists of recommended paperbacks.

Jewish Book Annual: JWB Jewish Book Council, 15 East 26th St., New York, NY 10010. $12.00; back volumes: $6.00–$10.00.

Each volume contains timely articles and bibliographies concerning the Jewish publishing world. There is a section on new juvenile books that contains brief annotations and critical comments. This is a worthwhile reference tool. Its advantage is the generous children's booklist (noting trade and Jewish publishers' books) and its critical evaluations. Its drawback, of course, is the infrequency of publication.

Jewish publishers' catalogues: See Appendix B: Directory of Book Publishers and Distributors for names and addresses. Writing for these free catalogues will ensure your awareness of new publications that are rarely reviewed elsewhere.

Judaica Book News: Book News, Inc., 303 West 10th St., New York, NY 10014. Published biannually. $2.50 per issue.

Articles, book reviews, and bibliographies concerning new Jewish publications are offered in this attractive, glossy periodical. "New and Forthcoming Judaica: Books for Young Readers" is a noncritical, annotated listing of books scheduled for publication within a six-month period. The advantage of this advertisement-filled magazine is its broad overview of newly released material. The noncritical descriptions, however, prevent it from being an all-inclusive tool for book selection.

Library Journal: R. R. Bowker, Subscription Service Dept., P.O. Box 13731, Philadelphia, PA 19101. Published twice a month, September through June, monthly in July and August.

A collection of articles, bibliographies, news items, and book reviews that would interest public librarians looking for new adult and young adult titles. Most books that would be of interest to school and children's public librarians would be reviewed in *School Library Journal* (see below).

Moment: Moment Magazine, Subscription Dept., P.O. Box 922, Farmingdale, NY 11737. Published monthly except January/February and July/August, when bimonthly. Subscription: $18.00. Rates vary for foreign orders.

Moment, an upbeat periodical concerning contemporary Jewish life, is published by Jewish Educational Ventures, Inc., in Boston, Massachusetts. It contains occasional articles with bibliographies about juvenile Jewish literature. Traditionally, it has published a review of children's books with Jewish themes in the November or December issues. While *Moment* does not serve as an ordering tool, its subscribers will appreciate the book news bonus.

School Library Journal: R. R. Bowker, Subscription Service Dept., P.O. Box 13760, Philadelphia, PA 19101. Published monthly from

September to May. Subscription: $17.00. Rates vary for foreign orders.

A collection of articles, bibliographies, news items, and book reviews that would interest school and children's public librarians. The critical reviews often touch upon new juvenile Jewish literature from major trade publishers that would reach a wide audience.

Connecting with Other Educators and Librarians

The following resource groups will keep you up to date through publications or conferences on new developments in Jewish education and library service.

American Association for Jewish Education, 114 Fifth Ave., New York, NY 10011

American Library Association, Jewish Librarians Caucus, 50 E. Huron St., Chicago, IL 60611

Association of Jewish Libraries, 122 East 42nd St., New York, NY 10017.

Coalition for Alternatives in Jewish Education, 8512 Whitworth Dr., Suite 1, Los Angeles, CA 90035

Jewish Book Council, 15 East 26th St., New York, NY 10010

Summary

Parents wanting to keep up in this field of writing should invest some money in *Judaica Book News* and some time in picking the brain of the school, public, or temple librarian. Many of these reviewing sources are available for examination in the public or synagogue library.

Temple libraries need to consult all the above sources in order to avoid the costly error of purchasing dull or inappropriate books. *Booklist* is preferable to *School Library Journal* in this case.

Day school librarians should also rely on all the above tools, although they might prefer *School Library Journal* to *Booklist*.

appendix B

Directory of Book Publishers and Distributors

A-W (Addison-Wesley Publishing Co., Inc.), Jacob Way, Reading, MA 01867

Abelard (Abelard-Schuman Ltd.), 10 E. 53rd St., New York, NY 10022

Abingdon (Abingdon Press): Orders to 201 Eighth Ave. S., Nashville, TN 37202

Abrams (Harry N. Abrams, Inc.), 110 E. 59th St., New York, NY 10022

ALA (American Library Association), 50 E. Huron St., Chicago, IL 60611

American-Israel (American-Israel Publishing Co.), 15 Carlebach St., P.O. Box 20181, Tel Aviv, Israel

Arbit (B. Arbit Books), 8050 N. Port Washington Rd., Milwaukee, WI 53217

Atheneum (Atheneum Publishers): Orders to Shipping & Service Ctr., Vreeland Ave., Boro of Totowa, Paterson, NJ 07512

Atlantic-Little (Little, Brown & Co.), 34 Beacon St., Boston, MA 02106

Avon (Avon Books), 959 Eighth Ave., New York, NY 10019

Bantam (Bantam Books, Inc.): Orders to 414 E. Golf Rd., Des Plaines, IL 60016

Behrman (Behrman House, Inc.), 1261 Broadway, New York, NY 10001

Bloch (Bloch Publishing Co.), 915 Broadway, New York, NY 10010

Blue Star (Blue Star Book Club), P.O. Box 410, Oceanside, NY 11572

Board of Jewish Ed (Board of Jewish Education—New York, Jewish Education Press), 426 W. 58th St., New York, NY 10019

Bobbs (Bobbs-Merrill Co., Inc.), 4300 W. 62nd St., Indianapolis, IN 46206

Bonim: Imprint of Hebrew Pub

Bowker (R. R. Bowker Co.): Orders to P.O. Box 1807, Ann Arbor, MI 48106

Bradbury Pr (Bradbury Press), dist. by Dutton

Childrens (Childrens Press, Inc.), 1224 W. Van Buren St., Chicago, IL 60607

Collier: Imprint of Macmillan

Collins Pubs (William Collins, Publisher, Inc.), 200 Madison Ave., New York, NY 10016

Cook (David C. Cook Publishing Co.), 850 N. Grove Ave., Elgin, IL 60120

Coward (Coward, McCann & Geoghegan, Inc.), 200 Madison Ave., New York, NY 10016

Creative Ed (Creative Educational Society, Inc.), 123 S. Broad St., Mankato, MN 56001

Crown (Crown Publishers, Inc.), 1 Park Ave., New York, NY 10016

Davey (Davey, Daniel, & Co., Inc.), P.O. Box 6088, Hartford, CT 06106

Delacorte (Delacorte Press), c/o Dell

Dell (Dell Publishing Co., Inc.), 1 Dag Hammarskjold Plaza, 245 E. 47th St., New York, NY 10017

Dial (Dial Press), 1 Dag Hammarskjold Plaza, 245 E. 47th St., New York, NY 10017

Doubleday (Doubleday & Co., Inc.): Orders to 501 Franklin Ave., Garden City, NY 11530

Dov Dov (Dov Dov Publications), 6203 Baltimore Ave., Baltimore, MD 21215

Dutton (E. P. Dutton & Co., Inc.), 2 Park Ave., New York, NY 10016

Faxon (F. W. Faxon Co., Inc.), 15 Southwest Park, Westwood, MA 02090

Feldheim (Philip Feldheim, Inc.), 96 East Broadway, New York, NY 10002

Fleet (Fleet Press Corp.), 160 Fifth Ave., New York, NY 10010

Follett (Follett Publishing Co.), 1010 W. Washington Blvd., Chicago, IL 60607

Four Winds: Imprint of Schol Bk Serv

FS&G (Farrar, Straus & Giroux, Inc.), 19 Union Square West, New York, NY 10003

Gale (Gale Research Co.), Book Tower, Detroit, MI 48226

Garrard (Garrard Publishing Co.): Orders to 1607 N. Market St., Champaign, IL 61820

Golden Pr (Golden Press, imprint of Western Publishing Co., Inc.): Orders to Dept. M, 1220 Mount Ave., Racine, WI 53404

Greenwillow: Imprint of Morrow

Greenwood (Greenwood Press, Inc.), 51 Riverside Ave., Westport, CT 06880

HarBraceJ (Harcourt Brace Jovanovich, Inc.), 757 Third Ave., New York, NY 10017

Har-Row (Harper & Row Publishers, Inc.). Orders to Keystone Industrial Park, Scranton, PA 18512

Harvey (Harvey House, Inc.: Orders to 128 W. River St., Chippewa Falls, WI 54729

Hebrew Pub (Hebrew Publication Co.), 80 Fifth Ave., New York, NY 10011

HM (Houghton Mifflin Co.), 2 Park St., Boston, MA 02107

Holiday (Holiday House, Inc.), 18 E. 53rd St., New York, NY 10022

HR&W (Holt, Rinehart, & Winston, Inc.), 383 Madison Ave., New York, NY 10017

Human Sci Pr (Human Sciences Press, Inc.), 72 Fifth Ave., New York, NY 10011

Jewish Pubn (Jewish Publication Society of America), 117 S. 17th St., Philadelphia, PA 19103

John Day (John Day Co., Inc.), c/o Har-Row

Jonathan David (Jonathan David Publishers, Inc.), 68–22 Eliot Ave., Middle Village, NY 11379

Judaica Pr (Judaica Press), 521 Fifth Ave., New York, NY 10017

Kar Ben (Kar-Ben Copies, Inc.), 11713 Auth Lane, Silver Spring, MD 20902

Knopf (Alfred A. Knopf, Inc.): Orders to 400 Hahn Rd., Westminster, MD 21157

Koren (Koren Publishers Jerusalem), 33 Herzog St., P.O. Box 404, Jerusalem, Israel 60188

KTAV (KTAV Publishing House, Inc.), 75 Varick St., New York, NY 10013

Lerner (Lerner Publications Co.), 241 First Ave. N., Minneapolis, MN 55401

Lippincott: Imprint of Har-Row.

Little (Little, Brown & Co.), 34 Beacon St., Boston, MA 02106

Lollipop Power Inc, P.O. Box 1171, Chapel Hill, NC 27514

Lothrop (Lothrop, Lee & Shepard Co.), div. of Morrow

McGraw (McGraw-Hill Book Co.), 1221 Ave. of the Americas, New York, NY 10020

Macmillan (Macmillan Publishing Co., Inc.): Orders to Front and Brown Sts., Riverside, NJ 08370

Macrae (Macrae Smith Co.), Rtes. 54 and Old 147, Turbotville, PA 17772

Mah Tov (Mah Tov Publications), 1680 45th St., Brooklyn, NY 11204

Massada (Massada Publishing Co., Ltd.), 21 Jabotinsky Rd., P.O. Box 3120, Ramat Gan, Israel

Merkos L'Inoyne Chinuch, Inc., 770 Eastern Pkway., Brooklyn, NY 11213

Messner (Julian Messner, Inc.), 1230 Ave. of the Americas, New York, NY 10020

Morrow (William Morrow & Co., Inc.): Orders to Wilmor Warehouse, 6 Henderson Dr., West Caldwell, NJ 07006

NAL (New American Library), 1633 Broadway, New York, NY 10019

P-H (Prentice-Hall, Inc.), Englewood Cliffs, NJ 07632

Pantheon (Pantheon Books), div. of Random

Parents (Parents Magazine Press), 685 Third Ave., New York, NY 10017

Penguin (Penguin Books, Inc.), 625 Madison Ave., New York, NY 10022

P'Nye Pr (P'Nye Press), The Printers Shop, 4047 Transport, Palo Alto, CA 94303

Putnam (G. P. Putnam Sons): Orders to 1050 Wall St., W. Lyndhurst, NJ 07071

Random (Random House, Inc.): Orders to 400 Hahn Rd., Westminster, MD 21157

Ricwalt (Ricwalt Publishing Co.), C-3 Bldg. Rm 110, Fishermen's Terminal, Seattle, WA 98119

Rittners (Rittners Publishers), 345 Marlborough St., Boston MA 02115

SBS (SBS Publishing, Inc.), 14 W. Forest Ave., Englewood, NJ 07631

S G Philips (S. G. Philips, Inc.), 305 W. 86th St., New York, NY 10024

S&S (Simon & Schuster, Inc.), 1230 Avenue of the Americas, New York, NY 10020

Scarf (Scarf Press), 58 E. 83 St., New York, NY 10028

Schocken (Schocken Books, Inc.), 200 Madison Ave., New York, NY 10016

Schol Bk Serv (Scholastic Book Services): Orders to 906 Sylvan Ave., Englewood Cliffs, NJ 07632

Scribner (Charles Scribner's Sons): Orders to Shipping & Service Ctr., Vreeland Ave., Boro of Totowa, Paterson, NJ 07512

Seabury (Seabury Press, Inc.): Orders to Seabury Service Ctr., Somers, CT 06071

Shengold (Shengold Publishers, Inc.), 45 W. 45th St., New York, NY 10036

Shulsinger Bros (Shulsinger Brothers, Inc.), 50 Washington St., Brooklyn, NY 11201

Signet (Signet Books): Imprint of NAL

Soncino (Soncino Press Ltd.), Audley House, N. Audley St., London, England W2

Stein & Day, Scarborough House, Briarcliff Manor, NY 10510

T Y Crowell (Thomas Y. Crowell Co.), dist. by Har-Row

Taplinger (Taplinger Publishing Co., Inc.), 200 Park Ave. South, New York, NY 10003

Toledo Bd of Jewish Ed (Toledo Board of Jewish Education), 2727 Kenwood Blvd., Toledo, OH 43606

Torah Umesorah, 229 Park Ave. South, New York, NY 10003

Twayne (Twayne Publishers), dist. by G. K. Hall & Co., 70 Lincoln St., Boston, MA 02111

U of Chicago Pr (University of Chicago Press): Orders to 11030 S. Langley Ave., Chicago, IL 60628

UAHC (Union of American Hebrew Congregations), 838 Fifth Ave., New York, NY 10021

United Syn Bk (United Synagogue Book Service), 155 Fifth Ave., New York, NY 10010

United Syn Commission on Jewish Ed (United Synagogue Commission on Jewish Education): Orders to United Synagogue of America, 155 Fifth Ave., New York, NY 10010

Vanguard (Vanguard Press, Inc.), 424 Madison Ave., New York, NY 10017

Viking Pr (Viking Press, Inc.), 625 Madison Ave., New York, NY 10022

Walck (Henry Z. Walck, Inc.): Orders to Promotion Dept., 2 Park Ave., New York, NY 10016

Walker & Co., 720 Fifth Ave., New York, NY 10019

Watts (Franklin Watts, Inc.), 730 Fifth Ave., New York, NY 10019

Westminster (Westminster Press): Orders to Order Dept., P.O. Box 718, Wm Penn Annex, Philadelphia, PA 19105

Wilson (H. W. Wilson), 950 University Ave., Bronx, NY 10452

WSP (Washington Square Press, Inc.), div. of S & S

Ya-El (Ya-El Imports, Inc.), 137 Main Street, Danbury, CT 06810

Zenith: Imprint of Doubleday

Indexes

What is indexed: Each book review and reference aid is included in the author, title, and subject indexes. Works that are noted within the longer reviews are also indexed.

What is not indexed: The Preface and the introductions to the chapters are not indexed. Only the periodicals discussed in Chapter 12 and Appendix A are indexed. See the table of contents for page numbers to the topics covered.

Important reminders: (1) It is important that the reader carefully skim each indexed page in order to find multiple references to authors and subjects. For example, two books by Marilyn Hirsh might appear on one page; two titles about kibbutz life might appear on one page. In addition, extra care must be given to locate an author, title, or subject appearing within a longer review. (2) The subject index serves as a mini-bibliography on many topics. This will help the reader create book exhibits, book talks, or story-telling sessions on a specific subject. It is worthwhile to become familiar with the subject index.

Author Index

Title Index

Subject Index